"Professor Rosenberg provides exceptionally thorough analyses of the legal and moral distinctions between acts and omissions. This book is a must-read by anyone reflecting on this topic and its policy implications in drawing sensible lines between our criminal laws and our moral judgments."

—**Joshua Dressler**, Distinguished University Professor Emeritus, Michael E. Moritz College of Law, The Ohio State University

"Roni Rosenberg has produced a comprehensive treatment of how the philosophical and legal complexity of the contrast between acts and omissions applies to substantive controversies, especially the permissibility of euthanasia. But his book is so much more. It also contains a sophisticated examination of several of the most foundational issues in all of moral and legal philosophy."

—**Douglas Husak**, Distinguished Professor (Emeritus), Rutgers University

"This book provides an enlightening, thorough, and original analysis of one of the challenging issues in moral and legal philosophy—the distinction between acts and omissions. Through a fascinating exploration of various rationales for this prevailing distinction, Roni Rosenberg sharply unpacks fundamental theoretical issues in substantive criminal law and demonstrates the practical implications of his analysis."

—**Hadar Dancig-Rosenberg (no relation to the author)**, Professor of Law, Bar-Ilan University; Visiting Professor of Law, Northwestern Pritzker School of Law (2023–2024)

Act and Omission in Criminal Law

This book offers an innovative perspective on the critical distinction between acts and omissions in criminal law, a distinction that runs like a defining thread through all types of criminal offenses.

While any act that positively causes a prohibited harm is sufficient for a conviction, an omission that causes the very same harm warrants a conviction only when there is a legal duty to act. This fundamental distinction between acts and omissions is not just relevant to criminal law, but it is also deeply rooted in our moral thinking. Thus, it is commonly argued that the difference between acts and omissions is also applicable to the intuitive moral distinction between active euthanasia, forbidden in most countries, and passive euthanasia, permitted in many countries under certain circumstances. Hence, the significance of this book is threefold: First, it offers a comprehensive, coherent, and systematic discussion of the intersections between the philosophical-moral and the legal-criminal aspects of this fundamental topic. Second, it offers a novel rationale for the distinction between acts and omissions, based on the principle of autonomy. Finally, it demonstrates the influences of the theoretical discussion, on the most significant practical questions.

This book will be of interest to researchers, academics and policy-makers working in the areas of criminal law, moral philosophy, and bioethics.

Roni Rosenberg is Senior Lecturer at the Law Faculty of Ono Academic College, Israel. His field of research is the philosophy of substantive criminal law and the relationship between ethics and criminal jurisprudence.

Routledge Research in Legal Philosophy

Constitutional Imaginaries
A Theory of European Societal Constitutionalism
Jiří Přibáň

Human Dignity and the Law
A Personalist Theory
Michał Rupniewski

Legal Ethics for Lawyers
A New Model
Barbara Mescher

Moral Pluralism and the Complexity of Punishment
The Penal Philosophy of H.L.A. Hart
Nicolas Nayfeld

Sport, Law and Philosophy
The Jurisprudence of Sport
Miroslav Imbrisevic

Cosmopolitanism, State Sovereignty and International Law and Politics
A Theory
Jorge E. Núñez

Human Dignity, Judicial Reasoning, and the Law
Comparative Perspectives on a Key Constitutional Concept
Edited by Brett G. Scharffs, Andrea Pin, and Dmytro Vovk

Act and Omission in Criminal Law
Autonomy, Morality and Applications to Euthanasia
Roni Rosenberg

For more information about this series, please visit: www.routledge.com/Routledge-Research-in-Legal-Philosophy/book-series/RRLP

Act and Omission in Criminal Law

Autonomy, Morality and Applications to Euthanasia

Roni Rosenberg

Routledge
Taylor & Francis Group
LONDON AND NEW YORK

First published 2025
by Routledge
4 Park Square, Milton Park, Abingdon, Oxon OX14 4RN

and by Routledge
605 Third Avenue, New York, NY 10158

Routledge is an imprint of the Taylor & Francis Group, an informa business

British Library Cataloguing-in-Publication Data
A catalogue record for this book is available from the British Library

Library of Congress Cataloging-in-Publication Data
Names: Rosenberg, Roni, 1972– author.
Title: Act and omission in criminal law : autonomy, morality, and applications to euthanasia / Roni Rosenberg.
Description: Abingdon, Oxon [UK] ; New York, NY : Routledge, 2024. | Series: Routledge research in legal philosophy | Includes bibliographical references and index.
Identifiers: LCCN 2024018450 | ISBN 9781032461731 (hardback) | ISBN 9781032461748 (paperback) | ISBN 9781003380405 (ebook)
Subjects: LCSH: Euthanasia—Law and legislation. | Euthanasia—Moral and ethical aspects. | Criminal act. | Omission, Criminal. | Criminal liability. | Punishment.
Classification: LCC K3611.E95 R67 2024 | DDC 345/.0252—dc23/eng/20240511
LC record available at https://lccn.loc.gov/2024018450

ISBN: 978-1-032-46173-1 (hbk)
ISBN: 978-1-032-46174-8 (pbk)
ISBN: 978-1-003-38040-5 (ebk)

DOI: 10.4324/9781003380405

Typeset in Galliard
by Apex CoVantage, LLC

Contents

Introduction

The distinction between acts and omissions is deeply rooted in our legal thinking. According to criminal jurisprudence, there is a significant difference between an act that causes harm and an omission that results in similar harm and, accordingly, between killing and letting die. Thus, any act that caused a person's death (strangulation, shooting, etc.) is sufficient for conviction if the other elements of the offense, such as causation and mens rea, are fulfilled. By contrast, when dealing with an omission that resulted in a person's death, conviction is possible only if the accused had a legal duty to act and the violation of that duty led to the victim's death. This position is reflected in the Model Penal Code, which states in section 2.01(3)(b) that an offense can be committed by omission only if there is a duty to act, emphasizing that the duty is not a moral but a legal one.[1]

The distinction between act and omission is also deeply embedded in our "ordinary morality,"[2] which ascribes significance to both the consequential aspects of our behavior and the manner in which it occurs.[3] This distinction is reflected in many contexts that extend to our day-to-day moral judgments. For example, according to ordinary morality, there is a significant moral difference between drowning a man and failing to save him from drowning. More broadly, a moral distinction is made between withholding aid to third-world

1 Joshua Dressler, Understanding Criminal Law 100 (2022); Wayne R. LaFave, Criminal Law 409–10 (2017); Paul H. Robinson, Criminal Law 193 (1997); United States v. Sabhnani, 599 F3d. 215 (2d Cir. 2010).

2 This concept is taken from Shelley Kagan's book: Shelley Kagan, The Limits of Morality 2 (1991).

3 Some have argued that the distinction between act and omission or between doing and allowing is significant because it differentiates between consequentialist and deontological moral theories. According to consequentialist moral theory, if the outcome is the same whether it is an act or an omission, there should be no moral difference between them. By contrast, deontological approaches assign moral weight not only to the outcome but also to how it occurs, whether through an act or an omission. See Philippa Foot, *Morality, Action and Outcome,* in Morality and Objectivity 23 (Ted Honderich ed., 1985); see also Kagan, *supra* note 2, at 1–27.

DOI: 10.4324/9781003380405-1

countries and actively killing individuals in those regions.[4] In medical contexts, there is a moral distinction between passive euthanasia, which is allowed in certain situations, and active euthanasia, which is categorically forbidden in most countries.[5]

Despite this prevailing moral intuition, since the 1960s, the moral distinction between these two types of behavior has faced significant criticism.[6] The central question has been whether there is such a distinction between an act and an omission and, if so, what is the moral rationale behind it. Critics of the moral distinction have been aware that it is one of the most deeply rooted distinctions in moral thinking, which may have provided the main impetus for writing about it. These critics contended that, all other conditions being equal, including intentions, efforts to prevent harm, and outcomes, there is no

4 Three significant points are in order regarding the distinction between killing and letting die. First, even if we argue that a moral distinction exists between the cases, it does not mean that every case of killing is morally worse than any case of letting die. There may be situations where killing is morally permissible while letting die is prohibited. For example, self-defense against an aggressor is morally and legally permissible but a physician not providing medication to a patient constitutes letting die, which is morally and legally prohibited. See James Rachels, *Killing and Starving to Death*, 54 PHIL. 159, 164 (1979) (hereinafter, Rachels 1979). Second, a practical significance of the moral distinction can manifest in one of two ways: (1) if killing is morally worse than letting die, the efforts required from the agent to refrain from killing are greater than those required to refrain from letting die so that we cannot demand the agent to harm himself to save a life but may require him to harm himself to avoid killing; (2) the moral justifications needed to permit killing should be more substantial than that needed to permit letting die. For example, religious or ethical considerations may justify allowing someone to die, but those same considerations may not justify killing. See Bruce Russell, *On the Relative Strictness of Negative and Positive Duties,* 14 AM. PHIL. Q. 87, 88 (1977). Third, to ensure the moral relevance of this distinction, we must detach the definition of killing and letting die from any moral judgment. If we defined these terms based on moral judgment, we could not use this moral distinction effectively. For example, if we define a case that is morally wrong under killing and morally permissible under letting die, we cannot use this distinction to evaluate cases involving moral dilemmas. Hence, these term definitions should be morally neutral. See F. M. KAMM, MORALITY, MORTALITY: RIGHTS, DUTIES, AND STATUS (VOLUME 2) 28–29 (1996); Jeff McMahan, *On Harming and Killing: Replies to Hanser, Person and Savulescu, and Wasserman,* 46 PHIL. BOOKS 34–44 (2005).

5 For an elaboration of the distinction between active and passive euthanasia and its connection to the distinction between acts and omissions in criminal law, see Chapter 9.

6 See Jonathan Bennett, *Whatever the Consequences*, in KILLING AND LETTING DIE 167 (Bonnie Steinbock & Alastair Norcross eds., 1994); Russell, *supra* note 4, at 87–96; Bruce Russell, *Presumption, Intrinsic Relevance, and Equivalence*, J. MED. & PHIL. 263 (1979); James Rachels, *Active and Passive Euthanasia*, in KILLING AND LETTING DIE 112 (Bonnie Steinbock & Alastair Norcross eds., 1994) (hereinafter, Rachels 1975); Rachels 1979, *supra* note 4, 159; John Harris, *The Marxist Conception of Violence*, PHIL. & PUB. AFFS. 192 (1974); Kagan, *supra* note 2, at 83–127; Michael Tooley, *An Irrelevant Consideration: Killing Versus Letting Die*, in KILLING AND LETTING DIE 103 (Bonnie Steinbock & Alastair Norcross eds., 1994); Tracy L. Isaacs, *Moral Theory, Action Theory, Killing and Letting Die*, AM. PHIL. Q. 355 (1995). See also Andrew Stumpf & Dominic Rogalski, *Getting Real about Killing and Allowing to Die: A Critical Discussion of the Literature*, 4 CAN. J. BIOETHICS 8 (2021).

valid justification for a moral distinction between an act and an omission.[7] If a moral distinction is made nevertheless in certain cases, it is due to a moral consideration unrelated to the distinction between act and omission. Occasionally, the intention of the agents differs, and that is the moral foundation for the distinction between the cases rather than the mere categorization of one as an act and the other as an omission.

This revolutionary position challenges our moral intuition and is likely to influence our legal thinking as well. If the moral distinction between an act and an omission is flawed, the legal distinction should also be questioned. Indeed, many attempts have been made, both in moral philosophy and criminal law, to establish a moral and logical foundation for the prevailing intuition that a moral distinction exists between an act and an omission.[8] Yet the task has proved to be complex and challenging.

The purpose of this book is to address several interrelated key questions:

1. What is the rationale that distinguishes between an act and an omission in criminal law? Why does the conviction of a person for an omission require identifying a duty to act, as opposed to an offense committed by an act? In this context, it is essential to clarify why the distinction diminishes when a duty to act has been identified.[9]
2. What is the definition of an act and an omission that derives from the relevant rationale? It warrants examination whether the definitions of an act and an omission are subject to the bodily movement test, where an act is a bodily movement, and an omission denotes its absence.
3. Which duties to act can serve as a basis for conviction in cases of omission? Can every legal duty to act serve as a basis for conviction or only specified ones? For example, can the duty to act imposed by the Good Samaritan law lead to a conviction for manslaughter, or do only certain duties arising from the defendant's relationship with the victim, the source of danger, or the defendant's role meet the duty requirement?
4. Should there be a difference in the level of punishment between an act and an omission that caused the same harm, even when a legal duty to act has been violated?
5. Should the distinction between an act and an omission in criminal law apply also to conduct or only to result offenses?
6. Is the distinction between an act and an omission in criminal law relevant to the distinction made in most countries between active and passive euthanasia?

7 See Rachels 1975, *supra* note 6, at 115–16.
8 See the discussion in Chapter 2.
9 According to some theories, the distinction does not entirely disappear when a duty to act is identified. See the discussion in Chapter 7.

Within this framework, we must differentiate the inquiry regarding the rationale that distinguishes between act and omission in criminal law from the question whether it is appropriate to obligate a citizen to rescue another, even a stranger. This question, discussed extensively in relation to the Good Samaritan law,[10] already stems from the initial premise that there is a significant moral difference between A killing B and A not saving B. In this case, the only remaining inquiry concerns the severity of the offense and punishment. The rationale question is more radical because it aims to clarify whether there should be any difference between an act and an omission in criminal law. Why not convict someone of manslaughter whenever he could have prevented another person's death, just as we do in cases of causing death by an action? This question is more fundamental because it does not stem from a clear premise that there is a moral distinction between an act and an omission, but rather seeks to clarify this premise.

Moreover, it is important to differentiate between the rationale question and another discussion concerning the definition of acts and omissions. On the one hand, we cannot address directly the question of definition because, in my opinion, the definition stems from the rationale that distinguishes between an act and an omission. It is impossible to logically define an act and an omission without addressing the more fundamental question: What is the rationale that sets them apart?[11] On the other hand, relying solely on the rationale is insufficient because one cannot derive a clear definition from a given rationale despite the logical connection between them. Therefore, an additional process is needed to bridge the gap between the rationale on which the distinction is based and the definition. The questions of rationale and definition are therefore different but related. Both form the basis of comprehensive thinking that

10 For example, see Andrew Ashworth, *The Scope of Criminal Liability for Omissions*, 105 Law. Q. Rev. 424 (1989); Andrew Ashworth, Positive Obligations in Criminal Law, Ch 2 (2013). Glanville Williams, *Criminal Omissions: The Conventional View*, 107 Law. Q. Rev. 86 (1991); Joel Feinberg, Harm to Others: The Moral Limits of the Criminal Law 126–28 (1984); John Kleinig, *Good Samaritanism*, 5 Phil. & Pub. Affs. 382 (1976); John Kleinig, *Criminal Liability for Failure to Act*, 49 Law & Contemp. Probs. 161 (1986); Steven J. Heyman, *Foundations of the Duty to Rescue*, 47 Vand. L. Rev. 673 (1994); Paul M. Hughes, *Bad Samaritans, Morality, and the Law*, 7 Int'l J. Applied Phil. 9 (1992); Joshua Dressler, *Some Brief Thoughts (Mostly Negative) About "Bad Samaritan" Laws*, 40 Santa Clara L. Rev. 971 (2000); Ken Levy, *Killing, Letting Die, and the Case for Mildly Punishing Bad Samaritanism*, 44 Ga. L. Rev. 610 (2010); Andreas Von Hirsch, *Criminalizing Failure to Rescue: A Matter of 'Solidarity' or Altruism?* in Crime, Punishment, and Responsibility 241 (Rowan Cruft, Matthew H. Kramer & Mark R. Reiff eds., 2011).

11 It can be questioned; how can we think about the rationale that distinguishes between acts and omissions without having a definition of what is an act and what is an omission? I think that it is more appropriate to consider this question by examining two classic cases where the distinction is clear, then proceed to the moral rationale that distinguishes between the two cases. Next, we should proceed to more complex scenarios and examine whether the original rationale correctly applies to these intricate cases.

embraces all aspects related to the moral and legal distinction between acts and omissions.

Another distinction we must make in this context is between two types of omission offenses: direct[12] and indirect.[13] In direct omission offenses, the behavior element is manifest in a failure to act and the duty to act is embedded in the offense. For example, an offense that requires an individual to submit a report to the tax authorities illustrates a direct omission offense, as the duty to submit the report is part of the offense. An offense that requires a driver involved in an accident to stop and provide assistance also falls within this category, as it is committed by inaction and the duty to act is embedded in the offense itself.

By contrast, indirect omission offenses can generally be committed either by an act or an omission. When seeking a conviction based on an omission, however, it is necessary to identify a legal duty to act that is external to the offense in question. Manslaughter is a pertinent example.[14] A death may be caused by an act or an omission. Yet, in cases of omission, we need to identify a duty to act that exists outside the manslaughter offense. This duty can stem from both civil and criminal law, such as parental duty to care for a child, an employer's responsibility toward an employee, a physician's obligation to provide medical care to a patient, and so on.[15]

Direct omission offenses pose fewer legal challenges because the criminal offense imposes the duty to act, and breaching it is a crime.[16] The main focus of this book is on indirect omission offenses, which raise complex legal and philosophical questions.[17]

Analysis of the literature on this subject suggests that it is appropriate to divide the rationales that differentiate between acts and omissions in criminal law into two main types: moral and legal. Moral rationales base the distinction between acts and omissions in criminal jurisprudence on moral rationality. An

12 Some refer to these failures to act as "pure omissions." See Jacobo Dopico Gomez-Aller, *Criminal Omissions: A European Perspective,* 11 New Crim. L. Rev. 419, 421 (2008).

13 Regarding the distinction between two types of omission offenses, see also Richard Card, Card, Cross & Jones: criminal law 36–38 (2012); A. P. Simester, J. R. Spencer, F. stark, G. R. Sullivan & G. J. Virgo, Simester and sullivan's Criminal Law – Theory and Doctrine 77 (2019); LaFave, *supra* note 1, at 408–09.

14 Some refer to these types of cases as "commission by omission" or "improper omissions." Gomez-Aller, *supra* note 12, at 420.

15 For an extensive discussion of the various disputes regarding the sources of the duty to act, see Chapter 6.

16 Recently, the number of direct criminal omissions has been increasing. For discussion, see Andrew Ashworth, *A New Generation of Omissions Offences?* 5 Crim. L. Rev. 354 (2018).

17 Indirect omission offenses can exist in both result and conduct crimes. The legal literature, however, focuses primarily on result crimes, where there is typically no interpretative challenge in including an omission within the provisions of the offense, unlike in conduct crimes. Chapter 8 discusses the distinction between result and conduct crimes in relation to the duty to act in cases of omission.

act that causes harm morally differs from an omission that leads to the same harm, a moral difference that serves as the foundation for the legal distinction between acts and omissions. Legal rationales base that distinction on legal rationality. According to these rationales, the distinction is not based on a substantial difference in the agent's moral guilt or on other moral value but rather on pragmatic legal considerations.

The division into different rationales and the consideration of moral and legal aspects in each theory have been overlooked by the legal and philosophical literature. The rationale question that distinguishes between acts and omissions, however, has broad consequences that extend beyond the issue of definition. It directly influences the types of duties that can serve as the basis for criminal liability in offenses committed by omission and determines whether the level of punishment for acts and omissions should differ. By exposing these rationales, analyzing them, and identifying the differences between them, a more original and comprehensive understanding can be reached of the distinction between acts and omissions in criminal jurisprudence.

As part of moral rationales, I analyze some of the main ones showing how they each focus on a different vertex of the relevant triangle: the agent, the causal connection between the agent's behavior and the harm, and the severity of the harm inflicted on the victim.

The first moral rationale concerns the agent vertex and involves several perspectives. One approach considers the effect on the agent's choices, suggesting that prohibiting an act is less infringing on the agent's liberty than compelling the agent to perform a given act. Another rationale sees an omission offense as a violation of the agent's autonomy because it treats the agent as a means for saving another person, unlike a prohibition of an act.

The second moral rationale focuses on the causal link between the agent's behavior and the harm suffered by the victim. According to this rationale, a direct causal link may exist between an act and the harm, while there is no direct causal link or, at most, an indirect one between an omission and the harm.

The third moral rationale concerns the severity of the harm to the third vertex of the triangle—namely, the victim. According to this rationale, an act worsens the victim's situation whereas an omission merely fails to improve it. Another approach argues that in acts causing harm, the victim loses life or property that could have been preserved independently from the agent, whereas in omissions causing a similar harm, preserving life or property is contingent on the agent's assistance.

In contrast to moral rationales, legal ones do not base the legislator's distinction between an act and an omission on a substantial difference in the culpability of the agent or on other moral considerations but rather on external pragmatic factors.

The first legal rationale focuses on the problem of legality. According to this rationale, the duty requirement in omissions stems from the need to inform the citizen about the causal link in relevant cases. The second legal rationale argues that the duty to act is derived from the principle of lenity, which favors interpretations of criminal laws that are more favorable to defendants. The duty requirement leads to a natural understanding that omissions are included within the scope of the offense.

Another legal rationale addresses the need for coordination between citizens. Failing to differentiate between an act and an omission would result in a challenging coordination problem, leading to a substantial waste of resources. Requiring every citizen to save others whenever possible would create inefficiencies. To overcome this coordination problem and its associated inefficiencies, legislators establish concrete duties to act, applying only to certain individuals. The final legal rationale states that the duty requirement in omissions is intended to limit the number of individuals who can be convicted for omission cases, promoting social efficiency in all systems of governance.[18]

After presenting the possible criticism of the moral and legal rationales, I propose an innovative autonomy-based rationale for distinguishing between an act and an omission, focusing on the distinction between killing and letting die. I argue that the distinction between the prohibition against killing and that against letting die should be examined in light of the interests underlying the two prohibitions. Contrary to the assumption of all other rationales suggesting these interests are identical, I contend that they are different: the interests underlying the prohibition against killing are broader and more substantial than those underlying the prohibition against letting die.

I demonstrate the compatibility of the autonomy-based rationale with rule utilitarianism and social contract theories, and I point out the areas of convergence and essential distinctions between the proposed rationale and the moral and legal rationales put forth in the legal and philosophical literature.

The critique of various rationales and the influence of the autonomy-based rationale shows that the intuitive bodily movement test, which defines an act as a bodily movement and an omission as a lack thereof, is inadequate for properly categorizing certain cases that lead to harm. I also point out that the American judiciary has not been united concerning the bodily movement test, as there is no consensus regarding the rationale for distinguishing between acts and omissions.

The structure of the book

The book is composed of two interrelated parts: one theoretical, the other practical. One of my research goals was to demonstrate that practical questions rely heavily on the various theoretical rationales that distinguish between acts and omissions in criminal law. Based on these considerations, the book is divided into the following chapters:

18 The liberty rationale can be interpreted as either a moral or a legal rationale. I consider both possibilities in the analysis of this rationale.

In Chapter 1, I analyze skeptical theories that challenge the distinction between acts and omissions and examine the various methods and critiques related to these viewpoints. Examining these approaches and analyzing their underlying arguments provides a comprehensive and nuanced understanding of the moral and legal distinction between acts and omissions.

Chapter 2 examines the arguments for a distinction between acts and omissions based on a moral rationale. Given the interconnectedness between the questions of rationale and definition, I also outline how acts and omissions are defined under each perspective.

Chapter 3 analyzes the perspectives arguing that the distinction between acts and omissions is based on a legal rationale.

In Chapter 4, I propose a novel, autonomy-based rationale for distinguishing between acts and omissions in criminal law, focusing on the distinction between killing and letting die. I offer a different definition for killing and letting die based on this rationale.

The second part of the book starts with Chapter 5, where I examine the stance of American courts regarding the definition of acts and omissions in criminal law. I show that the position of the courts is not uniform, and whereas some decisions adhered to the bodily movement test, others did not. I argue that the lack of uniformity stems from different approaches to the rationale distinguishing between acts and omissions in criminal law.

Chapter 6 explores which duties may serve as a basis for conviction in conduct and result offenses when the agent's behavior involves an omission. In addition, I investigate the connection between the various rationales and the resolution of this inquiry.

In Chapter 7, I address the question of whether there should be a difference in the severity of punishment between acts and omissions that caused the same harm, even if a legal duty to act was violated.

Chapter 8 considers the possibility of distinguishing between conduct and result offenses based on the rationales that distinguish between acts and omissions in criminal law.

In Chapter 9, I distinguish between active euthanasia, which is strictly prohibited in most countries, and passive euthanasia, which is allowed under certain conditions. I examine whether the rationales for distinguishing between acts and omissions in criminal law are relevant to the distinction between these two types of mercy killing or whether they should be separated.

In the conclusion to the book, I address the legal and ethical challenges related to the distinction between acts and omissions based on the technological, cultural, and societal developments that affect our lives.

Part I

The distinction between act and omission

Rationales and classifications

1 The skeptical theory

1. Introduction

In this chapter, I analyze the skeptical theory that posits that, when all conditions are equal—intentions, motives, outcomes, and the cost of preventing harm—there is no difference between causing harm by act or by omission. This is not a peripheral theory but rather a central one that has been widely debated in moral philosophy.[1] Accepting the skeptical theory would require a radical change in our moral thinking and way of life.

Skeptical theory maintains that the duty to aid a person in life-threatening danger is equivalent to the duty not to kill him. This seems to suggest that it is forbidden for a person to spend a sum of money on personal pleasures if that same amount could have been used to save people in danger. Presumably, accepting this theory would also lead to a change in the approach to mercy killing. Many believe that it is permissible for a physician to allow a terminally ill patient to die and not administer drugs that would only prolong his suffering. At the same time, physicians are forbidden to actively kill a patient by injecting a poison, even if the terminally ill patient requests it. But if there is no moral distinction between an act and an omission, there should be no distinction between active and passive euthanasia.

The skeptical positions that challenge the moral distinction are not without difficulties. In this chapter, I analyze the different positions and the methodology they use to undermine the moral distinction between acts and omissions in general and between killing and letting die in particular.

1 For example, Trammell, who disagrees with the skeptical approach, notes: "It seems to be widely doubted by philosophers today whether any intrinsically relevant moral distinction can be drawn between taking a life and failing to save a life." Richard L. Trammell, *The Presumption Against Taking Life*, 3 J. MED. & PHIL. 53 (1978). See also: Andrew Stumpf & Dominic Rogalski, *Getting Real about Killing and Allowing to Die: A Critical Discussion of the Literature*, 4 CAN. J. BIOETHICS 8 (2021). The writers stated: "Over the last four decades at least, the debate has raged on with few signs of consensus emerging."

DOI: 10.4324/9781003380405-3

2. The comparable cases argument

One position that denies a moral distinction between acts and omissions presents two cases that are identical in all conditions except for the fact that one case is classified as an act and the other as an omission.[2] In an article discussing mercy killings, James Rachels used this method to argue that there is no moral distinction between killing and letting die. Here are the two cases he presented.[3]

Inheritance 1: Smith is supposed to inherit a large fortune if his nephew dies. After planning it, Smith enters his nephew's bathroom and drowns him.
Inheritance 2: Jones is supposed to inherit a large fortune if his nephew dies. Jones notices his nephew slipping in the bathtub but chooses not to save him. As a result, the nephew dies.

In Inheritance 1, Smith kills his nephew by an act, while in Inheritance 2, Jones merely lets his nephew die. All other conditions are identical—the motives of Smith and Jones are identical, the effort required to prevent death is similar, and the outcome is the same because the nephew dies. Rachels argues that despite Inheritance 1 involving an act of killing and Inheritance 2 involving a passive letting die, there is no moral difference between the cases.[4] According to Rachels, these cases demonstrate that when all other conditions are equal, and the only difference is one case involving killing and the other letting die, there is no moral distinction between the two.

Rachels' claim that there is no moral distinction between killing and letting die is not limited to cases involving the intention to kill, as there is no moral distinction even when we are indifferent to another person's death. Therefore, there is no moral distinction between sending poison to third-world countries and not saving these countries from starvation.[5] Similarly, there is no differ-

2 James Rachels, *Active and Passive Euthanasia*, in KILLING AND LETTING DIE 112 (Bonnie Steinbock & Alastair Norcross eds., 1994) (hereinafter, Rachels 1975); James Rachels, *Killing and Starving to Death*, 54 PHIL. 159 (1979) (hereinafter, Rachels 1979); James Rachels, *Reasoning About Killing and Letting Die,* 19 S. J. PHIL. 465 (1981); Roy W. Perrett, *Killing, Letting Die and the Bare Difference Argument*, 10 BIOETHICS 131 (1996); Michael Tooley, *An Irrelevant Consideration: Killing Versus Letting Die*, in KILLING AND LETTING DIE 103 (Bonnie Steinbock & Alastair Norcross eds., 1994); Michael Tooley, *Abortion and Infanticide*, 2 PHIL. & PUB. AFFS. 58 (1972); Judith Lichtenberg, *The Moral Equivalence of Action and Omission*, in KILLING AND LETTING DIE 210 (Bonnie Steinbock & Alastair Norcross eds., 1994).

3 Rachels 1975, *supra* note 2, at 115.

4 *Id.* at 116.

5 Rachels 1979, *supra* note 2, at 159. About failing to give aid to the hungry, Rachels contends: "I shall argue that we are wrong to take comfort in the fact that we 'only' let these people die, because our duty not to let them die is equally as strong as our duty not to kill them, which, of course, is very strong indeed."

ence between a case where A kills B to keep a sum of money and one where A does not save B to keep the same sum of money.[6]

2.1 *The underlying reasoning of Rachels*

Rachels argues that most people find it difficult to accept the position that denies the moral distinction between killing and letting die because they do not make a sharp distinction between the question of whether killing in itself is worse than letting die and the question of whether, empirically, most cases categorized as killing are more severe than most cases categorized as letting die. In most cases of killing, the agent's intention is evil, the effort to prevent death is negligible, and the motive is malicious. By contrast, in the majority of cases categorized as letting die, the expense required to save the victim is significant and the agent's intention is not malicious but rather indifferent to the outcome.[7]

Nevertheless, according to Rachels, these differences do not indicate that killing is intrinsically worse than letting die but rather that other elements influence the severity of the behavior, such as the agent's intentions or motives. Therefore, when the motives, intentions, and outcomes are equal, there should be no moral difference between the cases.[8]

Rachels also believes that the strong moral intuition about the moral distinction between killing and letting die stems from the selfish motives prevalent in Western countries. The philosophical challenge is to demonstrate that this intuition is morally flawed. According to Rachels, although humans can display certain degrees of altruism, they are more selfish than altruistic and their moral judgment about certain situations is significantly influenced by their personal interests. A cost-benefit analysis suggests that it is more advantageous for affluent countries to enact a stronger prohibition against killing than letting die.

As far as costs are concerned, a prohibition against killing can be accomplished without any significant expenses, whereas the expenses associated with saving lives can be substantial. Treating the prohibitions against killing and letting die as morally equivalent would disrupt the Western way of life and

6 *Id.* at 169–70.

7 Rachels 1975, *supra* note 2, at 117.

8 *Id.* at 115–16. In light of the argument that there is no moral distinction between killing and letting die, Rachels also argues that there is no moral distinction between active and passive euthanasia. If a situation arises where a patient is in severe pain and the physician concludes that it is permissible to let the patient die, there is no reason not to permit active euthanasia. Nevertheless, note that even if a moral distinction exists between killing and letting die, it can still be argued that the distinction between active and passive euthanasia diminishes. Both scenarios involve a situation in which death is intrinsically good and there is no reason not to hasten it. See on this point: Holley Smith Goldman, *Killing, Letting Die and Euthanasia*, 40 ANALYSIS 224 (1980). Also see Chapter 9, which addresses euthanasia.

prohibit spending on luxuries when those funds could be used to save lives. As far as benefits are concerned, citizens of affluent countries face no immediate threats of dying; therefore, a strict prohibition against letting die is not essential. But these countries would suffer if there were no strong prohibition against killing. Therefore, from a self-centered perspective, it is preferable to enforce a more stringent prohibition against killing than against letting die.

Rachels argues, however, that although it seems advantageous for affluent countries to adopt this perspective, this does not establish its moral correctness.[9] He contends that the potential effect of this position on personal liberties and the need to prioritize saving lives over indulgence does not necessarily indicate a moral distinction between killing and letting die.[10] Therefore, it seems that according to Rachels, human freedom may not be an inherent value in its own or may be overridden by significance of human lives.[11] Even if prohibiting letting die affects human freedom, individuals still have a responsibility to make every effort to save others. Failure to do so can be morally equivalent to actively causing someone's death.[12]

2.2 Counterarguments and critiques

Critics have challenged Rachels by presenting alternative cases that suggest the presence of a moral distinction between killing and letting die.[13]

9 Rachels 1979, *supra* note 2, at 171. This argument runs counter to Gilbert Harman's assertion that the distinction between killing and letting die stems from a social contract theory. According to Harman, the rationale for considering killing as more severe than letting die derives from the fact that everyone would accept the prohibition against killing, but not everyone would agree to the prohibition against letting die. Harman argues that everyone would endorse the prohibition against killing because the fear that anyone could cause someone's death is shared by the entire population, regardless of wealth, status, strength, or weakness. By contrast, not everyone would agree to the prohibition against letting die because the wealthy and strong are not at risk and may resist limitations on their freedom. See Gilbert Harman, *Moral Relativism Defended*, 84 PHIL. REV. 3, 13 (1975).

10 Rachels 1979, *supra* note 2, at 169.

11 Rachels dismisses the explanation that distinguishes between killing and letting die and argues that even the absence of bodily movement can be considered an action. For example, if A does not extend a hand to greet B (after B extended his hand), A humiliates B to the same extent as if he insulted him verbally. See *Id.* at 167–69.

12 Bruce Russell, *On the Relative Strictness of Negative and Positive Duties*, 14 AM. PHIL. Q. 87, 94 (1977).

13 See Daniel Dinello, *On Killing and Letting Die*, in *Killing and Letting Die* 192, 195 (Bonnie Steinbock & Alastair Norcross eds., 1994). Additionally, see H. M. Malm, *Between the Horns of the Negative – Positive Duty Debate*, 61 PHIL. STUD. 188, 193–94 (1991). Malm presents cases suggesting that in any situation not involving expense or effort, if all other conditions are equal (intentions, motivations, outcomes), the moral judgment is the same, and it does not change whether the intention in both cases was deliberate harm or indifference. Here are the cases:

Machine 1—A enters a room and sees that if he presses a button, a child will die. A presses the button and the child dies.

Transplant. Joe and Bill are about to die: Joe in two hours unless he receives a heart transplant and Bill in four hours unless he receives a kidney transplant. When Joe dies, his kidney can be transplanted into Bill's body to save him. But Bill's heart can also be transplanted into Joe's body to save him.

It is evident that killing Bill to save Joe is prohibited but allowing Joe to die, consequently saving Bill, is deemed permissible. Therefore, killing is more severe than letting die, otherwise, there would be no difference between the two options.[14]

Rachels argues that there are not two options in this example—killing and letting die—because letting Joe die is not a viable choice. Letting someone die typically implies having the ability to save him but deliberately choosing not to do so. In this case, however, Joe cannot be saved because Bill needs to use his heart. We can claim that the physician let Joe die only if a heart was available, not in use by anyone else, and the physician failed to use it to save Joe. Given that Bill's heart is unavailable, it is inaccurate to say that Joe was left to die.[15] Therefore, this example fails to demonstrate that killing is more severe than letting die.[16]

Machine 2—A enters a room and sees that if he doesn't press a button, a child will die. A doesn't press the button and the child dies.

According to Malm, the moral judgment in both cases is the same. See *Id.* at 191. For Malm's general stance, see also H. M. Malm, *Killing Letting Die and Simple Conflicts,* 18 PHIL. & PUB. AFFS. 238 (1989); H. M. Malm, *Directions of Justification in the Negative-Positive Duty Debate,* 27 AM. PHIL. Q. 315 (1990).

14 Dinello, *supra* note 13, at 195.

15 Rachels' solution is flawed because without a moral distinction, it appears that the effort and expense required to prevent killing and those required to prevent letting die should be identical. See F. M. KAMM, MORALITY, MORTALITY: RIGHTS, DUTIES, AND STATUS (VOLUME 2) 87–99 (1996). Rachels seems to have been aware of this difficulty and notes an alternative solution, proposed by Harris. According to Harris' theory, in this case, it would likely be permissible to kill one person to save another since there is no substantial difference between the two options. See John Harris, *The Survival Lottery,* in KILLING AND LETTING DIE 257 (Bonnie Steinbock & Alastair Norcross eds., 1994) (hereinafter, Harris 1975). See Rachels 1979, *supra* note 2, at 170 (note 16).

16 Rachels did not address additional cases raised by Dinello. For example, if there is no moral distinction between killing and letting die, it seems permissible to kill one person to save five others. Foot offered an example to demonstrate that a moral distinction exists between killing and letting die.

"The Judge"—A culprit urges a judge to sentence an innocent person to death. Unless the judge orders the execution of an innocent person, the culprit is going to kill a greater number of people.

Foot argued that the reason the judge is prohibited from executing the innocent person even if this act would save many lives is that the prohibition against killing is more stringent than that against letting die. Sentencing an innocent person to death constitutes an act of killing, whereas refusing to hand down such a sentence amounts to letting others die. See Philippa Foot, *The Problem of Abortion and the Doctrine of the Double Effect,* in KILLING AND LETTING DIE 266, 270–71 (Bonnie Steinbock & Alastair Norcross eds., 1994).

Lichtenberg countered Foot's argument by stating that the rationale behind prohibiting the execution of one person to save five others does not stem from the fact that killing is more stringent than letting die. Rather, it derives from the fact that in this scenario, we use the individual's fate as a means to rescue five other individuals. See Lichtenberg, *supra* note 2, at 224–25.

Additional criticism has been leveled at the foundational premise of Rachels' approach that from a single pair of cases demonstrating the absence of a moral distinction between killing and letting die, a general rule can be extrapolated, suggesting that in all cases, under equal conditions, there is no distinction between act on omission or between killing and letting die. The meaning of the foundational premise is that if a certain component in a particular case has a moral weight X, that same component in another case has the same moral weight because a moral component is an independent unit whose moral weight does not vary from case to case.[17] Therefore, if in one pair of cases killing is morally equivalent to letting die, then in all cases, when other conditions are equal, there is no distinction. But this line of reasoning appears to contain a flaw, as philosophers like Kamm and Kagan have argued that although there may be instances where no moral distinction exists between killing and letting die, there are many other cases where the distinction becomes evident. For example, it is possible that when the expense required to save the victim is minimal and the intention is malicious, there is no distinction between killing and letting die. But if we slightly alter the case so that the cost of saving the victim is high, and the agent is indifferent to the outcome, killing appears to be more severe than letting die, which proves the existence of an intrinsically moral distinction between these two types of behavior in general.[18]

Furthermore, even if we assume that a general conclusion can be derived from comparing one pair of cases concerning a particular moral component, the moral equivalence between killing and letting die cannot be proven based on the cases presented by Rachels. One may argue that the moral equivalence between the cases stems from the fact that both Smith and Jones desired the same outcome (death) and intended to achieve it in the same way (killing their nephew) rather than from the absence of an inherent moral distinction between killing and letting die. The cases reflect a situation of moral luck, where both intended to kill but Jones did not have to do it because of an accident. This moral similarity aligns with Kant, who argues that luck should not

17 Shelly Kagan, *The Additive Fallacy*, 99 ETHICS 5, 16–17 (1988).

18 See Kamm, *supra* note 15, at 56. "For example, the moral unacceptability of an instance of letting die may depend on the fact that the efforts required to save someone are very small. When the efforts required to save are great, refusing to make the effort and hence letting die may not be unacceptable." See also Kagan, *supra* note 17, at 13; Trammell also raised this argument: Richard L. Trammell, *The Nonequivalency of Saving Life and not Taking Life*, 4 J. MED. & PHIL. 251, 254–55 (1979). Another example that reflects this argument concerns oxygen and nitrogen, which can react similarly when they are in a certain chemical compound, but when placed in a different compound, each of them reacts differently. The fact that oxygen and nitrogen react similarly to certain compounds does not make them identical. The same applies to killing and letting die. The fact that in a given situation there is no moral distinction between the two cases does not prove that categorically there is no moral distinction between the two cases. See Kamm, *supra* note 15, at 56.

play any role in the realm of morality.[19] To show the absence of a moral distinction, Rachels would have needed to present cases in which Smith intended to kill his nephew, whereas Jones intended only to let him die but was unwilling to kill him. Such a scenario may have demonstrated a moral difference between killing and letting die.

3. The comparable reasons argument: overview and logic

Contrary to the first approach, which sought to undermine the moral distinction between act and omission by comparing two cases, the second approach, also developed by Rachels, focuses on analyzing the underlying reasons for the prohibition of killing and letting die. This approach challenges the moral distinction not based on intuitive judgment regarding the comparison of two cases but through a logical process that demonstrates that there cannot be a moral distinction between killing and letting die.

3.1 The logical form of the argument

The argument takes the following logical form:

1. Moral judgment is correct only if it is based on concrete reasons that justify that moral judgment. If there are no reasons justifying a particular action, a person is not obligated to perform it. Furthermore, when faced with various possible actions, the morally appropriate action is the one supported by the best moral reasons.[20]
2. If the reasons against behavior A are identical to the reasons against behavior B, behavior A and behavior B are morally equivalent in their severity.
3. The reasons for prohibiting killing and letting die are the same. Killing is prohibited because it harms the victim by causing his death and distress to his family and acquaintances. Similarly, letting die is prohibited because it has the same consequences as killing.[21]
4. Therefore, the prohibition against killing is morally equivalent in severity to the prohibition against letting die.

Rachels notes that not every case of letting die is morally equivalent to killing. When all other conditions are not equal, there are cases where killing is

19 Immanuel Kant, Groundwork of the Metaphysics of Morals 8 (Mary Gregor trans & ed., Cambridge University Press 1998) (1785). Regarding this critique, see Jean Beer Blumenfeld, *Causing Harm and Bringing Aid*, 18 Am. Phil. Q. 323, 327–28 (1981). On the concept of moral luck, see Thomas Nagel, *Moral Luck*, in Mortal Questions 24 (1979); Bernard Williams, *Moral Luck*, in Moral Luck: Philosophical Papers 20 (1981).

20 See Rachels 1979, *supra* note 2, at 164. Rachels notes that whether or not this is a reason depends on the moral theory one holds.

21 *Id.* at 165.

morally more severe than letting die. Intentionally murdering a healthy individual is morally more severe than letting a terminally ill patient die, when the patient requests the doctor not to provide life-prolonging treatments. Similarly, allowing a person to die intentionally, even when it was possible to save him, is morally more severe than actively killing a terminally ill patient who asks the doctor to do so to alleviate his suffering.[22] According to Rachels, the justifications underlying the prohibition differ, and therefore, the moral severity is also different.

Although Rachels's premises 1 and 2 may be valid, premise 3 is not. In my opinion, the reasons underlying the prohibition against killing are not identical to those underlying the prohibition against letting die. As I elaborate in Chapter 4, a comprehensive understanding of the reasons underlying the prohibition against killing, which I refer to as values or interests, requires us to consider the potential consequences under a regime without any prohibition against killing. Conversely, to grasp the justifications behind the prohibition against letting die, we must contemplate the possible outcomes under a regime where no restrictions exist on allowing others to die. This thought experiment helps us explore the moral situation in each scenario.

In the following, I argue that in the absence of a prohibition against killing, individuals would live in constant fear of being killed at any moment. Such a life would be devoid of security, characterized by perpetual fear, and lacking personal autonomy. Moreover, the significance of the prohibition against killing persists irrespective of a person's ability to defend himself. By contrast, if there were no prohibition against letting die, our societal existence would still be reasonable but would necessitate increased caution. In the absence of a prohibition against letting die, society would still be able to function and individuals would retain their personal autonomy. Chapter 4 delves deeper into this theory, expanding on its alignment with the moral theory of rule utilitarianism and with the social contract theories of Hobbes and Rawls.

3.2 Reframing the debate: the role of attitude and human dignity

It is possible to formulate Rachels's argument slightly differently to address the criticism raised earlier. Unlike Rachels, who argues that the justifications against killing arise from the harm caused to the victim and his family, it can be argued that killing is prohibited because of the disdainful attitude the agent displays toward the victim through the act of killing. This is primarily a Kantian perspective that examines the moral value of an action based on the intention and will that drive the action rather than its outcome. To support this stance, McMahan presented an example, showing the absence of a moral distinction between a scenario where A kills B who had a short time left to live and a scenario where A kills C who had a long time left to live. Evidently, the harm caused to B and C differs, yet we still make no moral distinction between

22 *Id.* at 164.

the two cases. Therefore, it can be concluded that killing is prohibited because of the attitude displayed by the agent toward the individual and his humanity rather than the harm caused to him.[23] According to this approach, there should be no distinction between killing and letting die because in both cases, the attitude exhibited by the agent toward the victim is the same: contempt and lack of respect for human dignity.

In the following, I present an argument that I briefly mentioned earlier, which can explain the moral distinction between killing and letting die, even if we focus on the attitude displayed by the agent toward the humanity of the victim. To understand this argument, it is important to define what constitutes a person's humanity. In my view, a significant aspect of being human is the ability to live without constant psychologic fear and apprehension. Human autonomy, which allows individuals to shape their lives and values, serves as an expression of dignity and humanity. Merely being a living organism does not fully capture human dignity, which is characterized primarily by the capacity for self-directed existence. In contrast to the prohibition against letting die, the prohibition against killing constitutes human autonomy. Because this autonomy is a substantial part of dignity and humanity, act of killing demonstrates a more demeaning attitude toward society as a whole extending beyond the victim, than letting someone die. Violating the norm that constitutes human autonomy and enables the society to live without coercion and fear reflects a deeper sense of alienation and contempt toward human life than letting die, which does not infringe upon that norm.[24]

4. Refuting the moral rationale

In contrast to the previous two approaches, which presented positive arguments against the moral distinction between acts and omissions in general and between killing and letting die in particular, this approach undermines the moral distinction by dismissing various rationales that were raised to differentiate between acts and omissions.[25]

4.1 Refuting the causation rationale

One of the rationales elaborated further here argues that actions directly cause harm, whereas omissions may not cause harm or may do so more indirectly.

23 See Jeff McMahan, The Ethics of Killing: Problems at the Margins of Life 240–42 (2002).

24 The Kantian approach also holds respect for the law to be a significant aspect of moral action. On this matter, see Kant, *supra* note 19, at 45–47. It may be argued that killing, unlike letting die, expresses not only contempt for the victim but also for the law that establishes the person's autonomy.

25 Harris 1975, *supra* note 15.; John Harris, *The Marxist Conception of Violence*, 3 Phil. & Pub. Affs. 192 (1974) (hereinafter, Harris 1974); John Harris, *Bad Samaritan Cause Harm*, 32 Phil. Q. 60 (1982).

For example, when A actively kills B, A directly causes B's death. By contrast, if A lets B die, A's role is not as a direct cause of death but rather a more indirect or even non-contributory factor. Consistent with this rationale, A's culpability is considered higher for an action resulting in death than for allowing someone to die because in the case of an action, the causal connection is more direct.

Harris rejects this rationale, arguing that standing by and doing nothing can be considered an act, thus equating allowing someone to die with murder due to the same causal connection.

Harris's position is radical. In his view, if Y and Z are going to die but can be saved by a physician killing A and removing his organs, failing to kill A would be considered killing Y and Z. If Y and Z could have been saved and this was not done, the inaction is considered to have caused the death of Y and Z as if they had been shot.[26]

4.1.1 The Marxist perspective and societal expectations

According to Harris, the absence of a distinction between act and omission, doing harm and allowing harm, and killing and letting die is based on a Marxist perspective according to which our moral responsibility as a society that allows the exploitation of workers is identical to the moral responsibility of the individuals who created this situation from the outset.[27]

Harris argues that omission can have the same consequences as action, leading to a potential outcome. He challenges Hart and Honoré's viewpoint, which states that omissions can be considered causative only if there was a social expectation for the agent to act in a specific way and he deviated from it.[28] According to Hart and Honoré, determining the main cause of harm requires assessing what is considered normal and reasonable in a given situation and identifying deviations from these standards. The entity that deviates from what is deemed normal and reasonable is regarded as the primary cause of harm.[29] For example, if people are dying of hunger, the government can be

26 Harris 1975, *supra* note 15, at 258.

27 Harris 1974, *supra* note 25, at 192–220.

28 *Id.* at 198–209, Harris also opposes Eric D'arcy, who argues that the absence of action X can lead to outcome Y only when action X could prevent Y and when the agent is expected to perform action X. According to D'arcy, there is an expectation for the agent to undertake action X in one of two cases: (1) X is an action the agent typically takes or is generally performed by the public in the given situation; (2) X is an action demanded from the agent owing to a general or specific moral duty. Without an initial expectation or obligation placed on the agent, there is no connection between the agent and the absence of action X. If the agent is not associated with the absence of action X, there is no causal connection to outcome Y either.

Therefore, if A sees a drunk person about to drown, A has a moral obligation to save him. If A neglects this moral duty, it can be argued that A caused the person's death. Without the initial moral obligation, the resulting death would not be attributed to A. See *Id.* at 199.

29 Hart and Honoré argue that the failure to take an action that could have prevented harm may be a primary cause of that harm. This holds when the prevention of harm has become "second

seen as the cause because governments are expected to care for their citizens and be prepared for such situations.[30]

Harris challenges their position, contending that in cases where harm ensues, a causal link between the omission and the resulting harm can exist independently of any moral or social expectations placed on the agent.[31] The absence of an act X can be a cause of the outcome if the agent could have done X and X would have prevented the outcome, irrespective of the expectation of society.[32]

The key point is that the moral obligation to prevent harm is the product of an objective causal connection between the omission and the ensuing harm, not of the social expectation of preventing harm.[33] Harris argues that if there is a causal link between an omission and harm, there can be no distinction between acts and omissions because both can create a causal link to the outcome.[34]

4.1.2 Counterarguments to Harris: the nature of causality and responsibility

Critics of Harris have argued that only an act can cause an outcome; an omission cannot. Weinryb maintains that only an act that involves a physical movement can bring about a change in the world and therefore cause an outcome, whereas an omission that does not involve physical movement cannot do either. Although in everyday language we use the phrase "consequences of omission," it should not be given the same meaning as the phrase

---

nature" in society, thus establishing a norm. See H. L. A. Hart & Tony Honoré, Causation in the Law 34–35, 37 (1985). I discuss this theory further in Chapter 2.

30 See Harris 1975, *supra* note 15, at 202–03.

31 *Id.* at 205.

32 Harris rejects the question that Hart and Honoré asked to identify the primary cause of harm: Why do these individuals suffer when they usually do not suffer in a similar situation? According to Harris, the question should be: why do these individuals suffer when the harm could have been prevented? The question should not focus on what made the difference but rather on what could have made the difference. *Id.* 206.

33 *Id.* at 200.

34 *Id.* at 211. Harris is not the only one who criticizes Hart and Honoré's position. According to Mack, their stance is problematic because, ostensibly, a positive duty or an expectation from a person cannot establish a causal connection. This can be illustrated by a scenario where A sees B drowning and does not rescue him. According to Hart and Honoré, the failure to save B has a causal link contingent on A having an obligation to save B. Mack questions how a duty or expectation to save alters the causal connection. Let us assume that A has no obligation to save B at time t, that such an obligation arises when C pays A money to save B after time t, that B is drowning before time t, and that A does not save him either before or after time t. According to Hart and Honoré, there is no causal connection before time t because there is no obligation, but there is a causal connection after time t created by the obligation, which seems paradoxical. See Eric Mack, *Bad Samaritanism and the Causation of Harm*, 9 Phil. & Pub. Affs. 230, 238–39 (1980).

"consequences of action" because an act causes harm contrary to an omission, which while not preventing harm, does not cause it.[35]

According to Weinryb, even in cases where a duty to act is imposed on the agent, such as a physician vis-à-vis a patient, and the agent fails to fulfill that duty resulting in the death of the victim, there is no causal link between the omission and the victim's death. In these instances, the physician is convicted not because of the causal connection between the omission and the death but rather because of the failure to fulfill the imposed duty.[36]

Harris's position is criticized from another perspective. According to him, an omission X can be considered a cause of an outcome if the agent could have performed X and X would have prevented the outcome. Mack disputes this by stating that the omission is not a cause of the outcome, because the outcome would occur even without the agent's existence. When the agent actively kills the victim, the act of killing caused the death because without the agent the victim would not have died. But when the agent allows the victim to die, the omission cannot be considered the cause of the outcome because the victim would have died even if the agent never existed, indicating that the absence of rescue did not cause the result.[37]

According to Mack, in a situation where the agent cannot save the victim, as in a case where the victim drowns in the sea because of a whirlpool, it is argued that the sea and the whirlpool were sufficient conditions for the victim's death. If the sea and the whirlpool are sufficient in a scenario where the agent cannot save the victim, they should also be sufficient when the agent can save the victim. Therefore, the omission by the agent cannot be the cause of the outcome.

This criticism can be answered by stating that when the agent cannot save the victim, the failure to rescue is a necessary condition for the victim's death, but the agent is not morally responsible for the outcome because he could not have saved the victim. By contrast, when the agent could have saved the victim, failure to rescue is still a necessary condition, but here the agent is morally responsible because he could have prevented it but chose not to do so.

4.2 *Refuting the intervention rationale*

Contrary to Harris, Kagan raised the possibility that the distinction between doing and allowing harm to occur, as between killing and letting die, relies on the notion of intervention rather than causality. When A shoots and kills

35 Elazar Weinryb, *Omissions and Responsibility*, 30 AME. PHIL. Q. 1, 3 (1980). In relation to Weinryb's approach, see Douglas N. Husak, *Omissions, Causation, and Liability*, 30 PHIL. Q. 318, 324 (1980).

36 Weinryb, *supra* note 35, at 10, and 13–18.

37 Mack, *supra* note 34, at 255. In response to Mack's claim, it may be argued that there are situations of letting die in which, if the agent had not existed, the victim would not have died because someone else (such as another physician) would have saved him.

B, B dies as a result of A's intervention in the normal course of events. But when A allows B to die, B dies as a result of the absence of intervention in the normal course of events. Kagan argued that the concept of intervention is not necessarily linked to causality.[38] Though both killing and letting die involve a causal link between the agent's behavior and the death, the difference lies in the way the victim dies: through active intervention in killing and through non-intervention in letting die.[39]

According to Kagan, the moral significance of the idea of intervention lies in the following reasoning: When the victim dies as a result of the agent's intervention, the agent has made the victim worse off because if the agent had not intervened, the victim would have continued to live. But when the agent does not intervene in the normal course of events but merely allows the victim to die, the agent has not made the victim worse off because even if the agent did not exist at all, the victim would still have died.[40]

4.2.1 Challenging the intervention framework

Despite the aforementioned, Kagan casts doubt on the possibility of distinguishing between doing and allowing harm as well as between killing and letting die, based on the concept of intervention. To illustrate this, he presents four hypothetical cases involving the removal of aid that was on its way to save people from death.[41]

Abdul 1: Food is sent to hungry people, but Abdul steals the food, resulting in the death of the hungry people.

Abdul 2: A check is sent to hungry people so that they can buy food. Abdul steals the check, resulting in the death of those people.

Abdul 3: Abdul writes a personal check and sends it by a private delivery service to help hungry people in need but later regrets his decision and cancels the delivery.

Abdul 4: Abdul writes the check, but before sending it, he regrets it and tears it up.

Kagan argues that in all these cases, Abdul takes an action that prevents aid from reaching the victims. In all these cases, Abdul's intervention in the normal

38 Shelly Kagan, The Limits of Morality 92–94 (1991).

39 *Id.* at 94.

40 *Id.* Kagan argues that at first glance the way to distinguish between cases when an agent intervened and did not is using the following question: What would have happened if the agent hadn't existed? If the victim wouldn't have died, the agent intervened in the victim's death. If the victim would still have died, the agent did not intervene because nothing changed regarding the agent's existence. But Kagan dismisses this approach and contends that if this were the test, it would not provide the correct answer in certain cases. See *Id.* at 96.

41 *Id.* at 106–07.

course of events causes the deaths of the people; if he had not intervened, they would not have died. If the distinction between killing and letting die is based on the concept of intervention, all these cases should be classified as killing (or doing harm) and therefore should be equally prohibited. But it seems that those who agree with the moral distinction between killing and letting die would argue that Abdul 3 and Abdul 4 are morally less severe because they involve letting die, similar to the absence of rescue. Therefore, the distinction based on the concept of intervention is incorrect.

Thus, according to Kagan, the only way to distinguish between killing and letting die is through the concept of intervention, which can lead to prohibitions that proponents of the moral distinction between killing and letting die would not want to impose. Therefore, a distinction based on the concept of intervention may not be tenable.

4.2.2 *Reevaluating Abdul's cases*

Even if we accept that the distinction between doing and allowing and between killing and letting die is based on the concept of intervention, there are still grounds to challenge Kagan's classification of the Abdul cases. It may be argued that Abdul 3 and Abdul 4 should be categorized as letting die rather than killing, given the moral weight of past factors. The history of the case must be considered to determine its classification. In both instances, the victim faced a threat not caused by the agent. The agent initiated assistance but ceased before it reached the victim. Hence, it is more reasonable to classify these cases as an absence of intervention rather than intervention. If Kagan's classification is not necessary, his criticism also loses strength.[42]

5. The neutral definition argument

The last approach defines the concepts of action and omission, as well as killing and letting die, but argues that, according to these definitions, there is no moral basis for distinguishing between them.[43] Bennett is one of the main critics of the distinction between act and omission in general and between killing and letting die in particular. He examines a case in which a woman is giving birth and will die unless a procedure is performed to crush the fetus's head. If the procedure is not performed, the fetus will be born, and the woman will die.[44]

42 See Jeff McMahan, *Killing, Letting Die, and Withdrawing Aid*, in KILLING AND LETTING DIE 383, 395–96 (Bonnie Steinbock & Alastair Norcross eds., 1994).

43 See JONATHAN BENNETT, THE ACT ITSELF 88–96 (1995) (hereinafter, Bennett 1995); Jonathan Bennett, *Whatever the Consequences*, in KILLING AND LETTING DIE 167 (Bonnie Steinbock & Alastair Norcross eds., 1994) (hereinafter, Bennett 1994); KAGAN, *supra* note 38, at 83–127.

44 Bennett 1994, *supra* note 43, at 167.

Should the physician crush the fetus's head and save the woman, or should he do nothing and allow the woman to die? According to Bennett, the only distinction that can be made between these two cases is between killing and letting die. If we crush the fetus's head, we directly cause its death; if we do not, we allow the woman to die but do not kill her. What is the definition of killing and letting die, and can this distinction be a basis for a moral judgment? According to Bennett, when we say that X killed Y, we claim the following:[45]

1. X moved his body.
2. Y died.
3. Among all the possible movements available to X, only a few would have caused Y's death. Most of the movements available to X would not have caused Y's death.

When we say that X let Y die, we claim the following:

1. X moved his body.
2. Y died.
3. Among all the possible movements available to X, most of the movements would have caused Y's death. Only a few movements would not have caused Y's death.

The only difference between killing and letting die lies in the third condition, the number of actions that would have caused Y's death, and this difference lacks a moral basis. Therefore, the alternatives in the presented situation have no moral significance. Crushing the fetus's head would be considered killing because few body movements could lead to the death of the fetus, whereas not performing the procedure would be categorized as letting die because most of the physician's movements would result in the woman's death. According to Bennett, this distinction has no moral significance.[46]

Bennett argues that when A is said to have killed B in the only possible way, then in one of two possible ways, after which another possible way is added, a transition from killing to allowing to die emerges, which lacks moral

45 *Id.* at 180–82. Elsewhere, Bennett makes a semantically different distinction: between positive and negative conduct. See Jonathan Bennett, *Negation and Abstention: Two Theories of Allowing*, in KILLING AND LETTING DIE 230, 232 (Bonnie Steinbock & Alastair Norcross eds., 1994). See also Bennett 1995, *supra* note 43, at 67, 88. For the sake of convenience, I define cases falling in the category of positive conduct as instances of killing and those in the category of negative conduct as instances of letting die. Regarding Bennett's approach, see Fiona Woollard, *Most Ways I Could Move: Bennett's Act/Omission Distinction and the Behaviour Space*, 120 MIND 155, 158–61 (2011).

46 Bennett 1994, *supra* note 43, at 182.

significance. The crucial distinction is between A killing B out of N available options versus A killing B out of N+1 options.[47]

Bennett presents three examples to support his argument. In these examples, a vehicle is on a ground that slopes down to the edge of a cliff.[48]

"Push"—The vehicle stands on the slope, A pushes B who is in the vehicle. The push causes the vehicle to crash and B dies.

"Stay back"—The vehicle is already rolling. A could interpose a rock and stop the vehicle but decides not to do it. As a result, the vehicle crashes and B dies.

"Kick"—The vehicle is rolling toward a place where there is a rock that would stop it. A removes the rock, the vehicle crashes and B dies.

According to Bennett, in "Push," only a few of the actions available to A would lead to B's death, categorizing his action as killing. In "Stay back," most of the actions available to A would cause B to crash, so this behavior is classified as letting die. Finally, in "Kick," only a few of the actions available to A would lead to B's death, similarly to "Push." As noted, according to Bennett, the difference lies in the number of actions that would lead to the outcome and has no moral significance.

Counterarguments to Bennett. Bennett's position on the definition of killing and letting die and his claim that this distinction lacks moral significance has faced criticism. McMahan argues that Bennett's definition of killing and letting die is incorrect; therefore, his theory of the absence of a moral distinction collapses.[49] He brings, among others, the following case:

"Cancel"—A village in Africa is facing a famine. X's bank clerk intends to send a check for a certain amount to save this village. X hears about it and tells the clerk to cancel the check.[50]

According to Bennett, this case would be classified as killing because only some of the actions available to X at this point would lead to the death of the people in the village.[51] According to McMahan, this case is categorized as letting die. McMahan indicates that the main difficulty in Bennett's theory lies in exclusive reference to the action taken at a specific point in time, without considering the moral significance of past elements. In "Cancel," it concerns

47 *Id.* at 183. According to Bennett's theory, it can be inferred that if A sees a person standing at the edge of a cliff and pushes him off, A has only allowed him to die because most of the actions that A could have taken would have led to the person dying anyway. Even if A had done nothing, the person would have fallen. This seems absurd. See Dinello, *supra* note 13, at 193–94.

48 Bennett 1995, *supra* note 43, at 67.

49 Jeff McMahan, *A Challenge to Common Sense Morality*, 108 Ethics 394, 400–03 (1998). For a critique in a similar vein, see Dinello, *supra* note 13, at 192–96.

50 McMahan, *supra* note 49, at 400.

51 Bennett 1995, *supra* note 43, at 103.

resources belonging to X (it is his money), and if these resources reached the village, it may be argued that X saved the residents. In this case, X decided not to continue the rescue and did not prevent the death of the villagers, but it cannot be said that he killed them. The cancellation brought a return to the initial state of failure to carry out the rescue operation. By contrast, if X stops a rescue operation carried out by Y, it could be classified as killing because it is not the cessation of X's own rescue operation.[52]

McMahan also cites the "Interpose and kick" case,[53] in which if the agent placed the rock to prevent the vehicle from crashing but then changed his mind and removed the rock, he allowed the victim to die but did not kill him. Contrary to the conclusion reached by Bennett, this is a cessation of a rescue operation and not an act of killing.[54] These cases prove that Bennett's distinction between killing and letting die is incorrect; therefore, his argument collapses.[55]

In contrast to McMahan, some critics support Bennett's distinction between killing and letting die but emphasize its moral foundation.[56] They argue that the existence of only a few actions resulting in the victim's death signifies a direct causal connection between the agent's behavior and the death. Conversely, the fact that in letting die most of the available actions lead to the victim's death suggests an indirect causal link between the agent's behavior and the death.[57]

In this chapter, I presented various skeptical positions arguing that there is no moral distinction between acts and omissions in general and between killing and letting die in particular. The range of skeptical positions presented shows that this is a contentious approach in moral philosophy, and it deserves careful evaluation. I have shown that these skeptical positions have been criticized and challenged. In the next chapter, I will present arguments that the distinction between acts and omissions is based on a moral rational.

52 McMahan, *supra* note 49, at 402.

53 *Id.* at 403.

54 *Id.* at 402–03. McMahan presents additional cases demonstrating that Bennett's division is incorrect. For example, consider a scenario in which the agent is standing in the path of a vehicle. If the driver continues in his path, he will run into the agent and the driver will survive. The only way to avoid a collision is for the agent to jump aside. According to Bennett, if the agent jumps to the left, it would be considered killing the driver because, of the available actions, only one leads to the driver's death. By contrast, McMahan argues that in this case, the agent allowed the victim to die. This is a situation in which the agent did not save the victim rather than one in which the agent killed the victim. See McMahan, *supra* note 49, at 404.

55 *Id.* at 408.

56 See, for example, Kadri Vihvelin & Terrance Tomkow, *The Dif*, 132 J. Phil. 183 (2005); Tony Honoré, Responsibility and Fault 52 (1999).

57 Vihvelin & Tomkow, *supra* note 56, at 190–91. Vihvelin & Tomkow refer to the distinction between causing harm and allowing harm to occur as "The Dif." For a different critique, see Woollard, *supra* note 45, at 164–69.

2 The moral rationales

1. Introduction

In this chapter, I analyze the approaches that base the distinction between acts and omissions in criminal jurisprudence on moral rationales.[1] Theses rationales base the distinction on moral reasons that justify the duty requirement in omissions. They focus either on the agent's blameworthiness in relation to an act that causes harm as opposed to an omission or on particular moral values that the law aims to protect by this distinction.

Given that the examination of the distinction is common in both philosophical and legal literature, the chapter integrates the discussion of various rationales. This synthesis is intended to enrich both criminal law and moral perspectives, as philosophical insights can shed light on distinctions within criminal law while legal perspectives may offer valuable insights for moral-philosophical differentiation.

This chapter proceeds as follows:

In Section 2, I examine rationales that highlight the differential harm experienced by agents concerning acts and omissions. I begin by exploring the liberty rationale, which explains the varying degrees of harm caused to agents when acts are prohibited compared to omissions. Next, I analyze the "agent as a means" rationale, which argues that the duty to rescue involves using a person as a means to save another, contrasting with the prohibition against acts.

In Section 3, I examine the causation rationale, which argues that acts are considered more severe than omissions because of the distinct causal relationship they have with the resulting harm.

In Section 4, I explore the "harm to the victim" rationale, according to which the harm inflicted on the victim in the case of acts differs in nature from that inflicted in the case of omissions.

1 As I noted, the distinction between act and omission appears to apply to conduct and result offenses, yet the primary focus of this distinction is on result offenses.

DOI: 10.4324/9781003380405-4

In Section 5, I analyze the dominance rationale, according to which the distinction between acts and omissions is not based on a single consideration but on multiple factors.

2. The harm to the agent

2.1 The liberty rationale

In this section, I explore a well-established and widely accepted theory that addresses the distinction between acts and omissions, with emphasis on the agent's liberty. According to this theory, the moral justification for distinguishing between these two types of prohibitions stems from the different degrees to which each prohibition limits the agent's liberty.

Two interpretations of the liberty rationale, the narrow theory of liberty and the liberal theory of liberty, have been proposed. In my analysis of these theories, I will explore how the concept of duty serves to bridge the gap between acts and omissions. Additionally, I provide a clear elucidation of the definition of an act and an omission derived from this rationale.

2.1.1 The narrow theory of liberty

According to Fitzgerald, the difference between the prohibition against causing harm by an act and by an omission arises from the fact that the prohibition against an act prevents the agent from doing one thing but leaves him with the possibility of doing many others. By contrast, the prohibition against an omission requires the agent to perform one act but prevents him from performing many others at the same time. For example, regarding the distinction between killing and letting die, the prohibition against shooting someone prevents the agent from shooting a person but leaves him the possibility of performing many other acts. By contrast, the duty to help a person drowning allows the agent to perform one act, the rescue, and at the same time prevents him from performing many other acts.[2]

The narrow theory of liberty explains the legislative reluctance to enact laws concerning direct omission offenses,[3] where the duty to act is explicitly defined in the offense itself. Instances of such offenses included the duty to render aid to an individual in certain situations, to prevent the commission of a crime, or to file a report to the tax authorities.[4] Ostensibly, an individual's

2 P. J. Fitzgerald, *Acting and Refraining*, 27 Analysis 133, 138 (1967).

3 This is in contrast to indirect omission offenses (like in result offences), where the agent's omission conduct can lead to criminal liability, subject to the identification of a duty to act that is external to the result offense itself.

4 Direct omission offenses do not present unique challenges in their definition because convicting the perpetrator requires only proving his failure to perform the act specified in the offense.

involvement in a direct omission offense is infrequent. But Fitzgerald argues that even in such situations, there is a restriction on the individual's liberty because when he is required to act, he is prevented from performing many other possible actions.

This position is flawed because it mistakenly assumes that direct omission offenses inherently infringe upon liberty more than offenses that prohibit specific acts. The extent to which liberty is impaired depends on the precise definition of the offense and the individual's personal preferences. For example, a ban on smoking significantly restricts the freedom of an individual who greatly enjoys smoking, although he is still able to engage in activities like singing or dancing during the time he does not smoke.[5]

Moreover, if the requirement to perform a particular act is rare, it does not significantly violate one's liberty. For example, being required to throw a life buoy to a potential drowning victim or submit a report to the tax authorities does not impose a significant limitation on freedom, although it prevents the individual from engaging in countless other actions during that particular period. The harm to liberty is determined by the frequency of the infringement rather than by preventing the agent from performing various other actions within a given timeframe.[6]

2.1.2 The liberal theory of liberty

To address the challenges I raised regarding the narrow theory of liberty, I now examine the liberal theory of liberty, which seeks to reconcile these issues and offer a comprehensive understanding of the distinction. According to this theory, the prohibition of a specific act does not significantly restrict an individual's liberty because it simply requires refraining from that act. However, the prohibition against omissions that cause harm imposes a notable restriction on liberty because it necessitates the individual to cease his activities at any moment to prevent harm to others. If it were possible to convict individuals for causing harm by omissions without a specific duty to act, it would necessitate relinquishing all regular activities to dedicate oneself entirely to various rescue missions. Because the legal system must allow individuals to lead their regular lives without constantly being required to abandon their activities and engage in various rescue tasks, criminal law stipulates that a person will be convicted of an omission offense only if a duty to act is identified. This approach enables people to carry on with their

5 See George P. Fletcher, *Moral Irrelevance of Bodily Movements*, 142 U. Pa. L. Rev. 1450–51 (1994).

6 Yitzhak Kugler, *Criminal omissions*, 20 Bar-Ilan L. Rev. 201, 216 (2003) (hereinafter, Kugler 2003).

daily lives without being overwhelmed by endless intervention and rescue responsibilities.[7]

According to this theory, the distinction between acts and omissions is derived from the combination of two assumptions: first, the prohibition against an act requires citizens to refrain from performing that particular action, but they are free to perform countless others. By contrast, when a person has a duty to prevent harm, he is allowed to perform only that particular action and is prevented from performing any other. Second, the need to prevent harm is a recurring one.[8]

This can be illustrated by the following case:

"Anxiety": Person A lives in proximity to an elderly person who suffers from anxiety and depression that may lead to his death. Every day, the elderly person calls A and asks him to come to his house to talk to him; otherwise, the elderly person may die.

If A believes the elderly person, whenever he receives such a request, he will have to abandon his regular activities such as watching television, reading a book, or playing with his children, and go to the elderly person's home; otherwise, he risks being criminally charged with manslaughter or negligent homicide.[9] Imposing criminal responsibility in such cases without identifying a duty to act would severely limit citizens' choices.

The duty to act, therefore, aims to limit the instances in which a citizen is obligated to intervene to prevent harm or death, minimizing the encroachment on his liberty. Thus, the obligation of a father to save his son does not significantly harm his liberty because it does not contain an unlimited number of cases demanding such acts. But if there were no concrete obligations for individuals to act in cases of omission offenses, and every citizen were compelled to rescue others whenever feasible, it would significantly encroach on citizens' liberty.

The distinction between the narrow and the liberal theory of liberty is clear. The liberal theory posits that the violation of human liberty occurs when a cumulative series of obligations to assist others is imposed. The restriction on freedom is not significant in the case of a concrete and well-defined situation where the need to aid arises, even if it limits the individual's range of possible actions. Conversely, the narrow theory maintains that even in a single instance where a person is required to help another by a simple action, there is still an

7 A. P. Simester, J. R. Spencer, F. stark, G. R. Sullivan & G. J. Virgo, Simester and Sullivan's Criminal Law – Theory and Doctrine 75–76 (2019). ("If d buys a piece of furniture for his home, why is he not held responsible for the lives that money would save in, say, Ethiopia? One factor is our widespread acceptance that people are to some extent entitled to prefer their own interests, and the interests of those near to them, above the interests of others.")

8 Kugler 2003, *supra* note 6, at 212.

9 *Id.* at 213.

infringement on human liberty because, in that particular situation, the individual is precluded from a range of possible actions.

The liberal theory of liberty presented here is not exclusive to criminal justice, and it is also used by researchers dealing with the moral question of whether killing is morally more severe than letting die. For example, according to Trammell,[10] there is a moral difference between A who knows that B could be killed in a shooting but apathetically does nothing, leading to B's death, and A who, while shooting for practice, sees B walk into the line of fire and, unconcerned, shoots him.[11] Trammell argues that the distinction lies in the consideration of liberty between the two cases. For a person to lead his life reasonably, a distinction must be made between the prohibition against killing and the prohibition against letting die. A moral system that is not based on this moral distinction cannot be reasonable because it is so demanding that no citizen can comply with it.

> If the duty to save is solemnized to the same degree that the duty not to kill is, the moral agent either will lead the life of a John the Baptist or else will become demoralized (i.e., cease to take the rule so seriously) or else will be a miserable human being.[12]

As I show in Chapter 9, basing the distinction on the consideration of liberty also has implications for cases of euthanasia. In these cases, because the physician does not raise the liberty argument (he does not argue that the patient's duty to be connected to the respirator violates his freedom), the distinction between injecting poison into the patient and not connecting him to

10 See Richard L. Trammell, *Tooley's Moral Symmetry Principle*, 5 PHIL. & PUB. AFFS. 305, 309 (1976) (hereinafter, Trammell 1976); For additional cases, see Richard Trammell, *Saving Life and Taking Life*, in KILLING AND LETTING DIE 290 (Bonnie Steinbock & Alastair Norcross eds., 1994) (hereinafter, Trammell 1975); See also Richard L. Trammell, *The Nonequivalency of Saving Life and not Taking Life*, 4 J. MED. & PHIL. 251 (1979) (hereinafter, Trammell 1979).

11 Trammell 1976, *supra* note 10, at 309. In this example, Trammell opposes the cases that Tooley used to demonstrate that there is no distinction between killing and letting die. The cases Tooley presented involved intentional wrongdoing and minimal effort in both killing and letting die. Trammell argues that when there is intentional wrongdoing, it becomes difficult to see the distinction even if it exists. This is similar to mixing two types of wine with green persimmon juice, making it difficult to distinguish the flavor of the wines. See Trammell 1975, *supra* note 10, at 291.

12 Trammell 1979, *supra* note 10, at 261. See also Trammell 1975, *supra* note 10, at 293: "The problem is that, even though fulfillment of one particular act of aid involves only minimal effort, it sets a precedent for millions of such efforts. If one maintains as a general principle that we have an equal duty not to kill as to save, then either one must uphold an ethic so strenuous that asceticism is the only morally defensible way of life; or else one must be willing to allow Smith to harm someone with his car for lack of a simple repair." See also Roni Rosenberg, *Between Killing and Letting Die in Criminal Jurisprudence*, N. ILL. U. L. REV. 391, 394–400 (2014).

the respirator is irrelevant for identifying a duty to act. The two cases appear to be legally and morally identical because the liberty rationale is not relevant here. Hence, the courts that permit the disconnection of a patient from a respirator, framing it as an omission, and relieve the physician of any duty to act in the case of a terminal patient, are mistaken. In the relationship between physician and patient, especially in these situations, the liberty consideration is not relevant; therefore, it does not matter how the behavior is defined, as an act or an omission. If, for example, in certain cases, it is desirable to allow the physician not to connect a patient to a respirator, this should be accomplished within a separate framework of defense, not as part of the regular distinction between acts and omissions.

2.1.2.1 DEFINITION OF ACTS AND OMISSIONS

According to the liberal theory of liberty, the accepted criterion for defining an act and an omission regarding the need to establish a duty to act is the bodily movement test. Under this test, a bodily movement resulting in harm is categorized as an act, whereas the absence of such movement resulting in harm is categorized as an omission.[13] When considering the difference between killing and letting die, a bodily movement resulting in death is classified as killing, whereas the absence of a bodily movement resulting in death is classified as letting die.

The bodily movement test appears to have a strong connection with the underlying principle of liberty. When an act is prohibited and defined as bodily movement, it does not significantly violate an individual's liberty because he still retains a range of alternative actions. By contrast, when an omission is prohibited and defined as the absence of bodily movement, it encroaches upon an individual's liberty because it necessitates him to perform particular actions. When such cases are frequent (as in result offenses), they significantly disrupt the normal course of life.

If a general duty were imposed on an individual to prevent harm, he would be required to exert effort whenever he becomes aware of potential harm. But because a person cannot be physically present in multiple locations simultaneously and cannot concurrently perform numerous actions with his muscles, trying to comply with such a duty would disrupt his regular course of life. This disruption becomes particularly pronounced when dealing with highly frequent cases, significantly limiting the individual's ability to lead a normal life.

Note that the categorization of a behavior as an act or an omission is unaffected by the terminology we use to describe it. For example, if a father fails

13 Simester and Sullivan's Criminal Law, *supra* note 7, at 85; Jean Beer Blumenfeld, *Causing Harm and Bringing Aid*, 18 Am. Phil. Q. 323, 324 (1981); Paul H. Robinson, Criminal Law 202–03 (1997); Itzhak Kugler, *Two Concepts of Omission*, 14 Crim. L. Forum 421, 437 (2003).

to provide nourishment to his young son for a certain period, resulting in the child's death, we argue that the father starved the child. Initially, the term "starved" may imply some form of active engagement. However, since starving the child did not involve any bodily movement, it is categorized as an omission rather than an act. Consequently, the father incurs criminal liability not because starving the child is defined as an act but rather because of a legal duty to act in this particular situation.

2.1.2.2 THE LIBERTY RATIONALE, THE GOOD SAMARITAN LAW, AND HOMICIDE OFFENSES

At first glance, the liberty rationale appears to argue that one can be convicted for causing harm by omission not only when there is a special relationship to the victim but also when violating a duty toward strangers, as in the Good Samaritan law. This is justified by two reasons: first, the Good Samaritan law applies to limited circumstances, minimizing the infringement on personal liberty; second, when an omission falls under a direct omission category, the legislature has already ruled that action is necessary, overriding considerations of liberty. Consequently, the distinction between acts and omissions collapses, allowing for convictions in the relevant offense. But this view raises questions because our moral intuition suggests a significant difference between someone who actively causes harm and someone who fails to intervene, especially in cases involving strangers, as opposed to a duty that derives from the relationship between the accused and the victim, or the source of danger, or from responsibilities of his role.[14] If a substantial moral distinction remains between these instances, the liberty rationale runs into difficulty explaining this difference. Can it explain this distinction without having to argue that there is no moral difference between the two cases?

Trammell contends that the absence of specific limitations on the prohibition against killing, in contrast to the narrow range of cases included in the prohibition against letting die, indicates a moral distinction between the two kinds of conduct, even within these limited scenarios. Thus, even when it is stipulated that an individual must fulfill the duty to save strictly in the concrete cases listed by the Good Samaritan law, a significant moral distinction between killing and letting die persists, even for the cases on the list. The fact that the number of cases in which a person is required to save has been reduced turns the duty to save into a morally less burdensome obligation. Trammell's position stems from the logic that two main parameters determine whether a

14 Wayne R. LaFave, Criminal Law 423 (2017); Helen Silving, Constituent Elements of Crime 90 (1967); Jacobo Dopico Gomez-Aller, *Criminal Omissions: A European Perspective*, 11 New Crim. L. Rev. 419, 421 (2008); Jesus-Maria Silva Sanchez, *Criminal Omissions: Some Relevant Distinctions*, 11 New Crim. L. Rev. 452, 453 (2008).

moral law carries weight and achieves recognition: the scope of the law and the feasibility of complying with it.

Scope of the law. The law should have universal applicability, remaining in effect at all times. In principle, it should be applicable to everyone and complied with even when it exacts a high cost. When a law is applicable only partially and contains many exceptions, it fails to be perceived as a serious moral law.

Feasibility of compliance. To ensure that a law is perceived as a meaningful moral imperative, it must be realistically attainable and embraced by the general public. Merely having a law that applies universally is insufficient; it should also align with people's practical abilities. When a law appears excessively stringent and cannot be fully upheld, its significance tends to diminish.

These parameters apply also to the two prohibitions under consideration. The prohibition against killing is universally applicable, with minimal exceptions such as self-defense, and it remains in force regardless of the financial or physical costs required to prevent death. Moreover, compliance with this prohibition can be achieved through mere abstention from action, allowing individuals to lead relatively normal lives. Consequently, people perceive it as a substantial moral prohibition and treat it with due reverence.

Conversely, complete compliance with the prohibition against letting die faces challenges because of its significant encroachment on individual liberty. Full enforcement of this prohibition would require individuals to abruptly cease all activities and assist others, resulting in an untenable lifestyle. Consequently, the law must be limited. This limitation results in the law not always being applicable, containing numerous exceptions, and relieving individuals from moral obligations when substantial costs or efforts are involved. Therefore, the restriction on rescue cases does not diminish the moral disparity between killing and letting die. It merely demonstrates the varying moral severity of the two prohibitions, indicating that even in cases necessitating rescue, a moral distinction between killing and letting die is apparent.[15]

2.1.2.3 REEVALUATING THE LIBERTY RATIONALE

The liberty rationale is susceptible to several difficulties:

First, if Trammel's approach were correct, there should be a significant moral difference not only in cases where someone violates the duty of a Good Samaritan, but also in cases where a specific duty to act is breached, such as the duty between a parent and his child or between a doctor and a patient. However, morally, there is no significant difference between an act and an omission when the duty to act arises from the relationship between the actor and the victim.

15 Trammell, *supra* note 10, at 260–61.

Second, the duty to act according to the liberty rationale appears to have greater relevance where the mental element of the offense is negligence or recklessness. If omissions were convicted without imposing a duty to act, individuals would be at risk of being convicted whenever they failed to assist someone in need. Given the potential frequency of such cases, which necessitate only awareness or negligence, convicting them would significantly curtail personal liberty. But in offenses requiring specific intent, this concern does not apply because individuals cannot be convicted for failing to provide aid unless they intended the prohibited outcome, which is uncommon. As criminal law does not differentiate between acts and omissions in its mental element requirement, it follows that the liberty rationale cannot be the exclusive argument for this distinction.

Third, if we considered liberty as the sole rationale for the distinction between acts and omissions, it would be inappropriate to convict an individual of homicide if refraining from a lethal act significantly curtailed his freedom. Although, as noted, refraining from an act of killing generally does not severely restrict one's liberty, there may still be cases when doing so results in a significant infringement on liberty. Although the liberty rationale may suggest a less stringent duty to abstain from killing in these instances, such an interpretation is legally flawed because the legal prohibition against killing does not lose its weight based on the limitation it imposes on an individual's freedom.[16]

Last, according to this approach, the distinction between acts and omissions does not reflect an inherent difference between causing harm by an act as opposed to an omission. Rather, it hinges on the relative ease of complying with the prohibition concerning actions compared to omissions. Yet it seems that if this difference covers the entire distinction between acts and omissions, it is insufficient to explain the sharp distinction we make legally between these two types of behavior. As Honoré notes:

> If it turns out that, apart from considerations of cost, not contributing to the relief fund is morally just as bad, or almost as bad, as poisoning the relief food, we shall have to ask whether law and conventional morality are justified in making so sharp a distinction between acts and omissions on the basis of cost alone.[17]

The argument can be refined as follows: In a liberal democracy, we uphold the critical principle that the use of coercive measures through law requires justification. It is therefore appropriate to resist coercion whenever we possess a compelling argument against it. This principle, applied in criminal law, acknowledges that criminal prohibitions curtail an individual's freedom, requiring justification. This perspective has implications for the distinction

16 See Roni Rosenberg, *Two Concepts of Freedom in Criminal Jurisprudence*, 6 Brit. J. Am. L. Stud. 279, 284 (2017); Victor Tadros, Criminal Responsibility 198–99 (2007).

17 Tony Honoré, Responsibility and Fault 43 (1999).

between acts and omissions in criminal law. Regarding an act prohibited by law, the event prompting intervention is typically within the agent's control, as he has the choice not to engage in the prohibited conduct (A can choose not to shoot B). Conversely, in cases of an omission prohibited by law (A's obligation to save B from drowning), the event necessitating intervention is imposed on the agent and lies beyond his control (B's drowning is not caused by A, but it is instead imposed on A and beyond his control). Because of this distinction, the justification for restricting liberty is greater in the case of acts than omissions. Thus, a conviction for an omission offense requires the identification of a specific duty to act.

This argument, however, also presents a challenge. the prohibition of an act extends not only to situations where the agent has exclusive control but also to instances where the circumstances are imposed on the agent. In these cases, the restriction on liberty is akin to that experienced in omission offenses. Despite the similar limitation on freedom, a distinction is still maintained between acts and omissions in such circumstances. For example, consider a scenario in which A is driving a car and suddenly encounters B on the road. If A has sufficient time and opportunity to swerve and avoid hitting B, he is obligated to take such action and cannot invoke the defense that he lacked initial control over the situation.

The liberty rationale faces challenges when it comes to the definition of acts and omissions based on the bodily movement test. Some cases involving bodily movement should be categorized as omissions and vice versa.

Motion 1: C shoots at A. A is wearing body armor or is inside a vehicle and would not have been harmed by the bullet, but A moves, causing the bullet to hit and kill B.

Although the bodily movement test would categorize A's movement as an act because it involved the movement of his muscles resulting in the death of B, it may be more appropriate to classify this behavior as an omission. Consequently, convicting A would be justified only if a duty to remain in place and not move can be identified.

Death by hypothermia 1: B is about to die from hypothermia and wants to enter A's house. A does not want to let B in (he is not afraid of B) and locks the door. As a result, B dies.

Despite assuming that B would have been saved if A had not locked him out, it remains legally incorrect to convict A of homicide. This scenario aligns more closely with a failure to rescue situation rather than one of intentional killing.

Inaction: B runs toward A to evade C, who intends to harm him. A's refusal to move out of B's way results in B colliding with A and subsequently dying.

This case does not involve bodily movement but it seems that we need no duty to act to convict A for manslaughter.

Silent threat: A and B are sitting together near C. B threatens C, claiming A intends to harm C's family. A, a known criminal and aware that C will take the threat seriously, remains silent and continues sitting alongside B and C.

In this scenario, distinguishing between a threat conveyed verbally and one implied by A's silence is challenging; therefore, convicting A would not require a specific duty to act.

These examples illustrate the complexities that arise when applying the liberty rationale and the bodily movement test to differentiate between acts and omissions, suggesting a need for further examination and refinement of the legal understanding of this distinction.

2.2 The agent as a means rationale

Kimberly Ferzan contends that the distinction between acts and omissions in criminal law is also rooted in the divergent effects on the agent, although not in the same way as the liberty rationale suggests.[18] According to Ferzan, this distinction arises from the deontological constraint that individuals should not be treated merely as a means to an end. The problematic aspect of imposing a duty to act in omission offenses, such as the duty to provide aid, is that it transforms the individual's body into a mere instrument for saving another person, unlike the prohibition against an act that causes harm, which does not use the individual's body as a means of rescue. As a result, the justification for restricting liberty is stronger when we prohibit an act as opposed to an omission.[19]

Ferzan argues that the deontological prohibition against using a person as a means explains additional cases unrelated to the distinction between acts and omissions. This is exemplified by the case presented by Judith Thomson to justify abortion in certain circumstances. A person wakes up connected to a violinist who suffers from a fatal kidney disease. Disconnecting the violinist from the person would result in the immediate death of the violinist. Thomson asks whether it is morally permissible to disconnect the violinist in this situation.[20] Another case reflecting a similar point is raised by Boorse and Sorensen. Alex and Bruce confront a bear. Alex prepares by putting on his running shoes. Bruce tells Alex, "You can't outrun the bear." Alex responds, "I don't need to outrun him. I only need to outrun you."[21] This case falls under the category known as "ducking" cases. Michael Moore argues that Alex's right to run arises from his right to defend himself against the bear. Ferzan argues that Alex's right stems from the relationship between him and Bruce, unrelated to the bear. Alex is not obligated to make his body a means to save Bruce by allowing the bear to eat him. A similar argument arises concerning the case of the violinist: the person should be permitted to disconnect the device

18 Kimberly Kessler Ferzan, *Omissions, Acts, and the Duty to Rescue*, in THE ETHICS AND LAW OF OMISSIONS 217–18 (Dana Kay Nelkin & Samuel C. Richless eds., 2017).

19 *Id.* at 220–21.

20 *Id.* at 223. Judith Jarvis Thomson, *A Defense of Abortion*, 1 PHIL. & PUB. AFFS. 47 (1971).

21 Christopher Boorse & Roy A. Sorensen, *Ducking Harm*, 85 J. PHIL. 115 (1988).

attaching him to the violinist because there is no obligation to make his body a means to save the violinist.[22]

Ferzan points out that the prohibition against using a person as a mere means explains additional cases. Regarding the trolley problem, it is generally accepted that it is permissible to divert a train from its track if it is set to kill five people tied to the railway if the diversion would result in the death of only one person. The rationale behind this is based on a utilitarian calculation that prioritizes saving five individuals over saving one. But it seems impermissible to intentionally push a heavyset person off a bridge to stop the train and save five other people. The accepted rationale for the prohibition is that causing the person's death, in this case, involves using him as a means, contrary to the case where the train was diverted and caused the death of one person because his death was not necessary to save the other five.[23]

The prohibition against using a person as a means is reflected in other cases as well.

Paralyzing attacker: A dangerous attacker attempts to paralyze Alice. If Alice tries to defend herself, the attacker becomes so enraged that he will paralyze two other individuals.[24]

Clearly, Alice has the right to defend herself against the attacker to prevent becoming paralyzed, despite the resulting harm to two innocent people. Ferzan argues that the underlying justification is that Alice is not compelled to make her body a means to save the two innocent individuals by sacrificing herself. The two individuals lack the right to demand that Alice sacrifice herself. Conversely, if Alice had a prior agreement or commitment to save the two individuals, it is conceivable that she would be prohibited from defending herself because she had consented to make her body a means for their rescue.[25]

The same applies to the following case:

Bob: A rescuer is on his way to save two individuals. The rescuer sees a person named Bob whom he despises and wishes to kill. The rescuer pulls out a gun to kill Bob. The only way Bob can save himself is by killing the rescuer, an act that would result in the death of the two individuals in need of assistance.

Ferzan argues that Bob has the right to save himself, even if it resulted in the deaths of two individuals. The fundamental rationale behind it is that Bob is not obligated to sacrifice himself for the sake of the other two individuals. Imposing such an obligation would effectively reduce Bob to being a means for saving the other two.[26]

22 Ferzan, *supra* note 18, at 223–25.

23 *Id.* at 222. See also Larry Alexander, *The Means Principle*, in LEGAL, MORAL, AND METAPHYSICAL TRUTHS: THE PHILOSOPHY OF MICHAEL S. MOORE 251 (Kimberly Kessler Ferzan & Stephen J. Morse eds., 2016).

24 *Id.* at 227–28.

25 *Id.* at 228–29.

26 *Id.* at 231–32.

2.2.1 Definition of acts and omissions

Ferzan does not directly attempt to define acts and omissions but argues that a prohibition against an act that causes harm does not turn the agent into a means of saving another person, whereas a prohibition against an omission that causes harm does make the agent a means for the other person's rescue. Therefore, according to Ferzan, there may be cases where an individual performs bodily movements resulting in the death of another person, and yet the case is categorized as an omission, and the individual is held liable only if there was a duty to act because imposing criminal responsibility in such a situation entails making the person a means for the other's rescue. For example, Alex's duty to stay put and not flee the bear implies that he is becoming a means for the rescue of Bruce. In this situation, Alex should stay put only if a legal duty to save Bruce exists. Similarly, the person who disconnects himself from the violinist is held criminally liable only if there is a duty to act, even if the action results in death because this case is categorized as an omission rather than an act.

2.2.2 The duty requirement in omissions

Ferzan challenges the liberty rationale, which claims that the duty to act in cases of omission is intended to protect the agents' liberty, obligating them to act only when there is a recognized legal duty. In Ferzan's view, the duty requirement signifies cases in which the legislature allows using an individual as a means to save another person, overriding the general constraint against such usage. Thus, when an individual assumes the role of a lifeguard, he cannot refuse to use his body as a means of saving another person because he willingly undertook the mission and is obligated to do so. Similarly, when a parent is required by law to rescue his young child from danger, the legislator determined that the prohibition against using a person as a means of saving another is suspended in this particular situation.[27]

Ferzan's position provides an intriguing explanation of the distinction between acts and omissions in criminal law. Moreover, in most cases involving omissions, where there is no dispute, the prohibition does indeed turn the person into a means of rescue. Ferzan's position, however, runs into difficulty when confronted with scenarios involving the withdrawal of aid, as in the "interpose and kick" case,[28] where B will drive his vehicle off the cliff and die if he continues on his path. A interposes a rock to save B but then regrets it and kicks away the rock, resulting in B's death. In this case, A is criminally liable for B's death only if a duty had been imposed on A to save B. Yet, according to

27 *Id.* at 221.
28 Jeff McMahan, *A Challenge to Common Sense Morality*, 108 Ethics 394, 402 (1998).

Ferzan, this case should be categorized as an act that does not require a duty to act because the prohibition on A kicking away the rock does not turn A into a means to save B but rather turns A's property into a means for B's rescue. It is reasonable to argue that B's right to life should take precedence over the prohibition of using A's property as a means for his own rescue.

3. The causation rationale

3.1 Introduction

In this section, I examine one of the most intuitively plausible rationales for differentiating between acts and omissions from a moral standpoint. It relies on establishing a causal distinction between an act that directly causes harm and an omission that leads to an identical harmful outcome. According to this perspective, acts are deemed more severe than omissions because they can directly cause harm, whereas omissions either cannot produce an outcome or involve a more indirect causal process. Specifically, in distinguishing between killing and letting die, this rationale contends that killing is more severe because it exhibits a direct causal link between the act and the victim's death, whereas letting die lacks a causal connection or involves a more indirect one. The structure of this section is as follows: I begin by presenting an overview of the fundamental inquiries that any causal theory seeking to address the distinction between acts and omissions must consider. I proceed with an analysis of three theories of causation that potentially support the proposition that the distinction between acts and omissions is rooted in causal reasoning. Next, I examine an intermediate theory of causation that diverges from previous theories by claiming that omissions can cause certain outcomes, although not always. Consequently, the distinction between acts and omissions becomes less sharp under this theory. Finally, I examine two additional theories of causation, arguing that there is no intrinsic difference between acts and omissions regarding causation, although a moral distinction may be made between them.

3.2 Fundamental questions of causation

According to the view that the distinction between acts and omissions is based on causal reasoning, an act can cause harm but an omission cannot. For example, when A throws B off a cliff, causing his death, the act of throwing by A directly causes B's death. By contrast, when A witnesses B drowning in the sea and does nothing to save B, although A could have done so, it is the sea, not A, who stood by doing nothing, that causes B's death.

The issue of causation is not definitively resolved in legal discourse, and the philosophical debate on the matter is complex and multifaceted; therefore, it is appropriate to present the main issues relating to causation. To begin with, it is necessary to differentiate between two fundamental inquiries: (1) What constitutes the causal relationship, that is, what are the elements comprising it? (2) How should we define and characterize a causal relationship, specifically, when can we assert that X caused Y to occur?[29]

The first query pertains to the nature of the components of a causal relationship. Assuming that a causal relationship exists between a cause and an effect, a question arises about the ontological nature of the cause and the effect. Are they limited to events or can they include facts, states of affairs, and other entities? The second query concerns the essence and characterization of the causal relationship. Even if we assume that the components of the causal relationship are events, we must investigate when one event can be said to have caused another. Two schools of thought have sought to characterize the causal relationship: one characterizes the cause of a given effect based on the presence of necessary and sufficient conditions; the other requires that the necessary or sufficient condition also generates or produces the effect in some way.

Causality theories can agree on the components of the causal relationship while differing in their characterization, and conversely, they can differ on the components but find common ground in the characterization. For example, some may argue that the characterization of a causal relationship is based on the but-for test so that A causes C if and only if, without A, C would not occur, but disagree on the components comprising the causal relationship. Conversely, some may argue that the components of the causal relationship are events but contest the claim that a causal relationship is based on the but-for test.

3.3 *Basing the distinction between acts and omissions on a causal rationale*

The following three approaches differentiate between acts and omissions based on a causal rationale. The first approach bases the differentiation on the components of the causal relationship; the second extends it to both its components and characterization; and the third approach confines it solely to the characterization of the causal relationship.

3.3.1 *Causal components as events and omission as non-event*

According to this approach, the distinction between acts and omissions stems from the initial question about the components of the causal relationship. From this perspective, the components of a causal relationship are limited to events, so that a causal relationship can occur only between one event (the cause) and another (the effect). There is no clear consensus on the definition

29 Jonathan Bennett, *Event Causation: The Counterfactual Analysis*, 1 SUPPLEMENT NOUS 367–68 (1987).

of an "event," but Mellor's definition appears reasonable:[30] an event is an occurrence that happens both in space and time. An event necessitates a particular occurrence in time and space, as it brings about a change in the world. This occurrence can range from brief instances, such as taking a photo, to lengthy situations such as battles during wartime. An event is theoretically distinct from other objects that can be localized in space but lack temporal localization.[31] An event does not necessarily require human intervention; natural phenomena such as earthquakes also qualify as events. But when it comes to comprehending the causal distinction between acts and omissions, it is crucial to highlight that bodily movements are considered events because they satisfy the criteria of being an occurrence unfolding in time and space.

When A shoots B, it instigates a modification in the world, leading to the conclusion that the gunshot caused B's death. By contrast, omission does not qualify as an event because it lacks spatial existence and consequently cannot cause a specific effect. For example, when A fails to water B's flowers, and they wither, it is the resulting dryness that causes the wilting and not A's omission because the absence of watering does not bring about any change in the world.

The position whereby omission cannot cause harm garners support from the philosophy of science, moral philosophy, and legal scholarship. From a science philosophy standpoint, Helen Beebee argues that omission cannot cause a specific effect because a non-action does not qualify as an event:

> The reason I deny that there's any such thing as causation by absence is that I want to uphold the view that causation is a relation between events . . . and I assume in what follows that there are no negative events—which is to say, more or less, there are no events whose essence is the absence of a property or particular.[32]

According to Beebee, in everyday language, we attribute causal relationships to omissions and the absence of action as well. For example, not closing fire doors caused the fire to spread and destroy the building, and not watering the flowers caused their wilting. Beebee argues, however, that a distinction should be made between the common language in which we attribute causality

30 The definition of an event has been a source of ambiguity regarding causality, and as Mellor put it: "In discussions of causation the word event has become a term of art which different artists use in different ways." See D. H. MELLOR, THE FACTS OF CAUSATION 121 (1995). Although I use Mellor's definition of an event, Mellor disputed the view that events are the basic components of causal relations. According to him, the fundamental components are facts rather than events.

31 *Id.* at 122.

32 Helen Beebee, *Causing and Nothingness*, in CAUSATION AND COUNTERFACTUALS 291(John Collins, Ned Hall & L. A. Paul eds., 2004).

to omissions and the objective fact that in reality, omission does not cause anything.[33]

From a moral philosophy perspective, Mack argues that a "Bad Samaritan" who chooses not to save someone when he is capable of doing so is not the cause of death. According to Mack, the omission itself does not contribute to the particular outcome, and therefore, it cannot be claimed as its cause.[34]

In the legal realm, Feller maintains that in a scenario where B drowns in the sea while A stands by without acting, the cause of death lies in the relationship between the relative density of B's body and that of the sea, resulting in respiratory impairment. Feller argues that the omission itself, as a non-action, cannot be a cause,[35] but he acknowledges that a causal relationship can exist in cases of non-action when there is a legal duty to act, which, if unfulfilled, leads to an outcome. For example, when A, serving as B's physician, fails to provide life-saving medication, withholding the medication is the cause of B's death.[36] This contradicts Mack and Beebee, who argue that an omission cannot cause an outcome regardless of the existence of a legal duty to act.

For the characterization of the causal relationship, this approach can be based on the but-for test, which states that event A causes event C if A and C are distinct events, and if A had not occurred, C would not have occurred either.[37]

By combining event causation and the but-for test we can conclude that A shooting B is the cause of B's death. The shooting is an event that is necessary for the outcome. But the failure to water the flowers by A is not the cause of their wilting. Although the absence of watering is necessary for the wilting, it is not an event and therefore does not cause it.

In conclusion, according to this perspective, the distinction between an act and an omission for causality does not arise from the failure of an omission to pass the but-for test but rather from the fact that an omission is not an event and therefore cannot be a cause.

33 *Id.* at 304.

34 Eric Mack, *Bad Samaritanism and the Causation of Harm*, 9 Phil. & Pub. Affs. 230, 259 (1980). See also: Elazar Weinryb, *Omissions and Responsibility*, 30 Phil. Q. 1, 2–5 (1980).

35 S. Z. Feller, Elements of Criminal Law (Volume 1) 429 (1984).

36 *Id.*

37 See David Lewis, *Causation*, 70 J. Phil. 556–67 (1973). Although Lewis believes that a cause is a necessary condition for an effect, in the sense that if the cause did not exist, the effect would not occur, he holds a different view regarding omissions causing effects because he has a different position on the first question. See David Lewis, *Causation as Influence*, 97 J. Phil. 182 (2000); David Lewis, *Causation as Influence*, in Causation and Counterfactuals 75 (John Collins, Ned Hall & L. A. Paul eds., 2004) (hereinafter, Lewis 2004a). See also David Lewis, *Void and Object*, in Causation and Counterfactuals 277–90 (John Collins, Ned Hall & L. A. Paul eds., 2004) (hereinafter, Lewis 2004b); regarding the but-for test, see also Joshua Dressler, Understanding Criminal Law 180–81 (2022) for the but-for test in the case of homicide crimes, see, for example, Fleming v. United States, 224 A.3d 213, 221 (D.C. 2020) "the actual-cause requirement means that the [prosecutor] must prove that, if one subtracted the defendant's actions from the chain of events, the decedent would not have been killed."

3.3.1.1 DEFINITION OF ACTS AND OMISSIONS

Based on the philosophical framework presented earlier, it is reasonable to argue that the distinction between acts and omissions is based on the bodily movement test: an act is a bodily movement that constitutes an event, whereas an omission is the absence of bodily movement that is not an event. Applying this test to the distinction between killing and letting die, A kills B when A performs a bodily movement that results in B's death (e.g., shooting A). Conversely, A allows B to die when A refrains from undertaking any bodily movement to save B, resulting in B's death.

The underlying rationale for distinguishing between killing and letting die stems from the difference in the causal relationship in these two cases. In cases of killing, A is responsible for the death by creating an event that led to the fatal outcome. Conversely, in letting die, A is not responsible for the death because a non-action cannot cause anything. This distinction implies that the degree of responsibility and culpability is heightened in the case of a causal relationship between the act and the ensuing harm, in contrast to situations where no such causal link exists between the agent's conduct and the harm.

3.3.1.2 THE DUTY REQUIREMENT IN OMISSIONS

According to the theory that denies a direct link between omission and harm, it becomes clear that there is a need to establish a duty to act in cases involving omissions. Typically, a causal relationship assigns responsibility to the person who caused the harm by establishing a clear connection between the action and the resulting harm. This person naturally becomes the primary candidate held accountable for the consequences. The duty to act in cases of omission serves as a substitute for the direct causal relationship by creating a distinct connection to the relevant harm. Under this approach, if parents fail to provide food for their child, leading to the child's death from starvation, they are held responsible for the death (their degree of culpability depending on their mental state). This responsibility is not based on a causal link between the absence of feeding and the death but rather on the breach of their legal duty arising from the unique connection between parents and their children. Similarly, when a qualified rescuer chooses not to assist a drowning person, he is considered culpable for the death because of his unique connection to the harm, demonstrated by his failure to fulfill the duty rather than the existence of a causal relationship.[38]

38 See Weinryb, *supra* note 34, at 3, 15. The need to identify a duty to act, as mentioned here, is common to all three theories that argue that omission cannot cause an outcome. Therefore, I did not specify this need within the framework of these theories and mentioned this need only here.

Additionally, according to Weinryb, not every duty to act can serve as a basis for criminal liability in the relevant result or conduct offenses. For example, the duty arising from the Good Samaritan law cannot serve as a basis for manslaughter because it does not create a unique connection to the harm. See the discussion in Chapter 6 about which duties can serve as a basis for criminal omissions.

This perspective faces several challenges. One line of criticism is directed at the claim that omissions cannot directly cause outcomes because they are not events in the same sense as actions are. Yet there are numerous cases where we attribute causation to omissions and non-actions. For example, when A fails to pay taxes, which leads to the confiscation of his belongings, we state that the non-payment is the cause of the confiscation. Likewise, when A stops showing up for work, resulting in his termination, we claim that the failure to attend work is the cause of his dismissal.[39] Therefore, omissions can indeed have causal effects, undermining the exclusive reliance on a causal element to distinguish between acts and omissions.[40]

Beebee addresses this criticism by drawing on Davidson's distinction between the concepts of causation and causal explanation. According to Davidson, causation pertains to the relationship between two events expressed in the statement "A caused C," whereas causal explanation involves a relationship between two facts expressed in the statement "A because of C."[41] Although omission may not cause an outcome, it can provide a causal explanation for a specific outcome. For example, when we say that Brutus stabbing Julius Caesar

39 Moreover, not only can omissions and non-actions appear to cause a particular outcome, but they can also constitute the outcome itself. For instance, if A had the flu and therefore did not attend an event, his absence becomes the outcome. For a position that discusses the critique emphasizing that in ordinary language omissions can cause harm, see E. Garrard & S. Wilkinson, *Passive Euthanasia*, 31 J. MED. ETHICS 64–68 (2005). For criticism of this article, emphasizing the causal distinction between killing and letting die as well as between active and passive euthanasia, see H. V. McLachlan, *The Ethics of Killing and Letting Die: Active and Passive Euthanasia*, 34 J. MED. ETHICS 636 (2008).

40 Some have raised the argument that while there are cases involving omissions referred to as "causes" in common language, there are also other cases that are not fundamentally different from the previous ones as far as causality is concerned, yet they are not labeled "causes" in everyday language. For example, although the Queen of England did not water the flowers, we do not claim that her failure to water them caused them to wilt. We argue that A, whose duty it was to water the flowers, caused them to wilt. Superficially, there seems to be no fundamental difference between the Queen of England and A failing to water the flowers. Regarding this argument, see Beebee, *supra* note 32, at 294–98. See also Sara McGrath, *Causation by Omission: A Dilemma,* 123 PHIL. STUD. 125, 126–28 (2005). But this argument still does not explain the strong intuitions we have regarding omissions that we often see as causes.

Regarding this matter, see also JUDITH JARVIS THOMSON, THE REALM OF RIGHTS 237–39. Thomson also believes that it is difficult from a causal perspective to distinguish between the two aforementioned situations but maintains that intuitively, when there is an obligation and the agent does not fulfill it, we can say that he caused harm. Nevertheless, she acknowledges that this distinction is problematic.

41 Beebee argues: "In "Causal Relations" (1967), Davidson argues for a distinction between causation and causal explanation by concentrating on the logical form of causal statements. He argues . . . that causation is a relation between events rather than facts: in other words, that the canonical form of causal statements is 'c caused e', where c and e are events and caused is a two-place relation, rather than 'E because C', where C and E are facts and 'because' is a sentential connective." Beebee, *supra* note 32, at 301. See also Donald Davidson, *Causal Relations*, in ESSAYS ON ACTION AND EVENTS 149, 161–62 (2001).

caused his death we express a statement of causation. By contrast, when we say that Brutus opposed Julius Caesar because he was ambitious we express a statement of causal explanation rather than an objective causation. Similarly, according to Beebee, we cannot contend that A's failure to water the flowers caused them to wither, even if A had an obligation to do so. The accurate statement would be that the flowers wilted because A did not water them, providing a causal explanation for their wilting.[42]

Contrary to Beebee, Lewis and Bennett argue that omissions can indeed produce outcomes, including instances such as the Queen of England's failure to water the flowers leading to their wilting. The decision not to explicitly designate it as a cause is primarily due to pragmatic factors rather than principled ones. Not all causes are deemed pertinent to our analysis; therefore, we mention A's failure to water the flowers as the reason for their wilting, calling attention to A's obligation in contrast to that of the Queen of England.[43]

The second line of criticism focuses on the characterization of the causal test as a necessary condition. As noted, according to this perspective, A causes C if A and C occurred, and if A had not existed, C would not have occurred. But there are cases where even if A had not occurred, C would still have occurred, and still, we would argue that A caused C. The following are two examples:

1. Alternative causes for the outcome. A and B both intend to kill C, but each is unaware of the other's intention. A shoots C first, and C dies. But if A had not shot C, B's shot would have killed C.
2. Sufficient causes coexisting in the relevant situation. A and B shot C together and each shot could kill C. C dies.[44]

In the first case, it is argued that A caused C's death although his act is not a necessary condition for the outcome. In the second case, shots by both A and B appear to have caused C's death, although their actions are not necessary conditions for the outcome. If A had not shot him, C would still have died by B's bullet, and vice versa. These cases indicate that the characterization of factual causation based on the but-for test is not accurate.[45]

A possible solution is to argue that the concept of causation is based not only on the general but-for test but rather on a more sensitive one, so that if A's action had not occurred, C's death would not have occurred when it did or in the same manner. Regarding the first case, if A had not shot, C would have died a second later, being shot by B. The second between A's and B's shots turns the event into a later and different one. In the second case, it may be said

42 Beebee, *supra* note 32, at 304.

43 See Lewis 2004a, *supra* note 37, at 101. See also Jonathan Bennett, The Act Itself 130–31 (1995).

44 Dressler, *supra* note 37, at 183–84.

45 *Id.* See also Simester and Sullivan's Criminal Law, *supra* note 7, at 92–93.

that if B had not shot, C would have died, but the death would have occurred at a different time or in a different manner.[46]

Lewis proposes a slightly different approach, arguing that the concept of causation is grounded in causal influence rather than causal dependence. According to Lewis, A causes the death of C not because the absence of A's shot would have prevented C's death but rather because A influenced C's death. In the first case, for example, this influence is expressed in the fact that if A had shot differently while B used the same shot, C's death would have been different. Conversely, if A had shot as he originally did but B had changed his shot, C's death would have been unaffected.[47]

The third line of criticism challenges the foundation of the distinction between acts and omissions based on causation. Even if we agree that omission cannot cause an outcome, it is not necessarily clear that the moral distinction between acts and omissions is grounded exclusively on a causal distinction; there are situations where the agent performs an act that has a causal connection to the victim's death, yet the case is categorized as an omission rather than an act. Consider the following scenario:

Death by hypothermia 1:[48] B is about to die from hypothermia and wants to enter A's house. A does not want to let B in (he is not afraid of B) and locks the door. As a result, B dies.

I argue that although locking the door caused B's death, this case should be categorized as an omission rather than an act. From a moral perspective, there appears to be no distinction between this case and a failure to provide aid from the beginning. Therefore, the general distinction between acts and omissions, as well as between killing and letting die, cannot rely strictly on the causal distinction.

3.3.2 The process theory

It may be argued that the distinction between acts and omissions is not based exclusively on the fact that an omission, unlike an act, cannot be a component in a causal relationship, but also on the notion that the characterization of a causal relationship cannot include an omission. Supporting this perspective is the process theory, which was developed by Wesley Salmon and Phil Dowe.

To simplify the theory, I begin with its main conclusion, then provide a more detailed explanation. According to the process theory, an outcome can occur only when there is a direct interaction between two processes that simultaneously contribute to it. If event X occurs in one room and event Y

46 *Id.* at 184; State v. Montoya, 61 P. 3d 793, 797 (N.M. 2002). See also ROLIN M. PERKINS & RONALD N. BOYLE, CRIMINAL LAW 772–73 (1982); L. A. Paul, Keeping *Track of the Time: Emending the Counterfactual Analysis of Causation*, 58 ANALYSIS 191 (1998); Glanville Williams, *Causation in Homicide*, CRIM. L. REV. 429, 435–37 (1957).

47 See Lewis 2004a, *supra* note 37, at 90–93.

48 This case was mentioned earlier as a critique of the liberty rationale.

in another, a causal relationship between them cannot exist without a direct connection between X and Y. Therefore, if A kidnaps B's son and as a result, B suffers a heart attack and dies, there is no causal relationship between the act of kidnapping and B's death because there was no direct encounter between A's action and B's body. But when A shoots B and B dies, there is a causal relationship between A's shot and B's death because the death occurs as a result of a direct encounter between A's action and B's body.

According to Salmon's early approach, two fundamental concepts regarding causality arise: causal process and causal interaction. A causal process refers to the continuous state of an object characterized by its ability to transmit a mark. Examples of causal processes include phenomena like light beams, sound waves, and material particles in motion. Salmon notes that a causal process can be distinguished from a pseudo-causal process by its capacity to transmit a particular mark, whereas a pseudo-causal process cannot. A brief pulse of light traveling from the beacon to the wall is an example of a causal process. If we place a red filter in the path of the light beam, we can observe that the color of the light beam changes to red and remains red from the point of insertion to the wall without any further intervention. By interposing a red filter between the source and the beam a mark is introduced, which is then transmitted along the beam.[49] Conversely, the shadow of a moving car is not considered a causal process because the shadow itself cannot transmit any mark.[50] A causal interaction occurs when at least two causal processes meet, resulting in a change beyond the point of their encounter.[51]

From this theory, a clear distinction arises between an act and an omission. If A shoots B and causes his death, a causal interaction occurs. The bullet fired from the gun is a causal process, as well as B's standing. The encounter between the fired bullet and B's body is a causal interaction because a change, B's death, occurs beyond the point of their encounter.[52] By contrast, A's failure to warn B about falling off the cliff is not causally linked to B's death, because A's omission is not a causal process, thus lacking causal interaction.

Even Salmon's later theory about causation does not allow for causality in omission. According to his later account, causes and effects are connected through spatiotemporally continuous causal processes and interactions. A causal process is defined as the worldline of an object transmitting a conserved quantity, while "transmission" implies the possession of that quantity at every spacetime point along the process. Causal interaction involves the exchange of a conserved quantity. This theory, however, does not account for

49 Wesley C. Salmon, *Causality Without Counterfactuals*, 61 Phil. Science 297, 302 (1994) (hereinafter, Salmon 1994).

50 *Id.* at 301–02. See also Wesley C. Salmon, *Causality and Explanation: A Reply to Two Critiques*, 64 Phil. Science 461, 468 (1997) (hereinafter, Salmon 1997).

51 Salmon 1994, *supra* note 49, at 298, 300.

52 Wesley C. Salmon, *Causality: Production and Propagation*, in Causation 154, 168–69 (Ernest Sosa & Michael Tooley eds., 1980).

omissions because they do not link to effects through this type of connection. For example, there is no set of causal processes and interactions involving conserved quantities that connect A's failure to warn B about the danger of falling off a cliff to B's subsequent death.

3.3.2.1 THE DISTINCTION BETWEEN THE PROCESS THEORY AND THE BUT-FOR TEST

The process theory, proposed by Salmon, provides an alternative perspective to the traditional but-for test. In this view, A causes B not simply because A is a necessary condition for B as seen in the but-for test, but rather because A generates a causal interaction that brings about a change.[53] Considering this, cases involving alternative causes do not challenge the process theory. For example, if A shoots C and C dies, one can argue that if A had not shot C and caused his death, B would have shot him, resulting in his death anyway. According to process theory, the causal relationship between A's shot and C's death is evident because it is A's bullet that generates the causal interaction rather than B's bullet.

Similarly, in cases involving cumulative causes, where both A and B shoot C simultaneously, the process theory may state that both are responsible for C's death because their respective bullets create a causal interaction that leads to a change. We can analyze the effect caused by each individual's action in accordance with the laws of physics, without dwelling on hypothetical scenarios where A or B did not fire their shots.

3.3.2.2 THE DEFINITION OF ACTS AND OMISSIONS

Drawing on the process theory to elucidate the causal reasoning that distinguishes between acts and omissions and between killing and letting die inevitably affects the definition of these terms. An act is defined as a bodily movement that generates a causal interaction leading to harm, whereas an omission is defined as a lack of bodily movement that results in harm without causal interaction. When examining the distinction between killing and letting die, it can be argued that killing is a bodily movement that generates a causal interaction leading to the victim's death, whereas letting die refers to cases where the victim dies without the agent producing a direct causal interaction. Note that this definition differs from the previously mentioned theory, as it acknowledges cases involving bodily movement that would not be classified as killing owing to the absence of a causal interaction.

The process theory, however, runs into difficulty in relation to the act-omission distinction. As noted earlier, there are many cases where omissions are deemed to cause the outcome. For example, A fails to pay taxes,

53 Phil Dowe, *Causation and Misconnections*, 71 PHIL. SCIENCE 926 (2004).

leading to the seizure of his assets, or neglects to show up for work and is subsequently fired. Dowe, a prominent advocate of the process theory (although he proposed different definitions for causal processes and interactions), acknowledged the problem involving omissions. According to him, significant intuitions suggest that omissions can indeed be causative; it is reasonable to perceive the father's failure to prevent his son from running into the road as the cause of the son's death.[54] In answering criticism concerning omissions, Dowe made a distinction between two types of causality: genuine causation and quasi-causation.[55] He argued that omissions reflect a quasi-causation rather than a genuine one.[56] Therefore, the true cause of the accident lies in the causal interaction between the child running onto the road and the passing car. The father's lack of protection, according to Dowe, represents a quasi-causation in relation to the accident that emerges because, had the father grabbed his son, the causal interaction would not have occurred.[57]

Even if we accept Dowe's distinction between the two types of causality, there may not necessarily be a correlation between genuine causation, which manifests as a causal interaction between two causal processes, and moral or legal causation. It is plausible that from a "scientific" standpoint, omissions do not directly cause the outcome, as they lack a causal interaction. But from a moral or legal perspective, omissions are regarded as causing the outcome because moral or legal causality includes different connections between events or facts in reality. The characterization of quasi-causation proposed by Dowe may align with the causality manifested in law and ethics.[58]

According to Dowe, there is no distinction between the moral or legal implications of genuine and quasi-causation. The distinction between the two types of causation remains purely theoretical. The father not grabbing his son, thereby contributing to the accident, reflects quasi rather than genuine causation, yet this should not alter the moral or legal implications of the event.[59] Thus, even if we concur with the process theory from a scientific standpoint,

54 See Phil Dowe, *A Counterfactual Theory of Prevention and 'Causation' by Omission*, 79 Austl. J. Phil. 216 (2001). "There is, no doubt, a temptation to treat preventions, such as 'the father's grabbing the child prevented the accident', and cases of 'causation' by omission, such as 'the father's inattention was the cause of the child's accident,' as cases of genuine causation."

55 *Id.* at 217.

56 *Id.*

57 *Id.* 222.

58 In another context, Dowe makes a similar distinction, distinguishing between "actual causation," which is rooted in an empirical analysis of the actual world and validated by scientific theories, and "conceptual causation," which aims to explain how individuals in society perceive causation. It appears that the framework I previously mentioned as "quasi-causation" aligns with this "conceptual causation" that operates in legal and ethical contexts. See Dowe, *supra* note 53, at 927.

59 Dowe, *supra* note 54, at 225.

it cannot fully account for the legal and moral distinction between acts and omissions.

3.3.3 *Authorship and creating the threat theory*

3.3.3.1 FOOT'S THEORY

Unlike previous theories that distinguished between acts and omissions in the causal relationship components as well, the approach presented in this section situates the difference strictly in the characterization of the causal connection. According to this approach, even if the absence of an act can serve as a component in the causal relationship (unlike in previous theories), it generally does not lead to the outcome. Prominent representatives of this approach are Foot and McMahan. Because McMahan disagrees with Foot on the categorization of certain cases, I present first Foot's position, then McMahan's.

According to Foot, the distinction between acts and omissions is based on the agency of the agent.[60] The distinction lies in whether the person created or generated the threat that caused the harm or simply allowed the threat to occur. If the actor created the threat that caused the harm, he is considered the agent of the harm, and the behavior is classified as an act. If, however, the actor did not create the threat that caused the harm but merely allowed it to happen, he is not the agent of the harm, and the behavior is classified as an omission.[61] This distinction also underlies that between killing and letting die. If the agent created or generated the threat that caused death, the behavior is categorized as killing, but if he only allowed the threat to materialize, the behavior is categorized as letting die.

For example, when A shoots B and causes his death, this act is classified as killing because A created the threat that led to B's death. To determine who created the threat that caused death, two stages must be examined. First, the cause of the person's death is identified, and second, it is determined who created the threat that caused the death. In this case, the first stage identifies that B died as a result of being hit by the bullet, and the second stage identifies A as the one who shot the bullet that hit B. By contrast, if C witnessed the incident but did not assist B, it would be categorized as letting die because although the absence of aid is a necessary condition for the outcome, it is not the generator of the threat that led to it.[62]

60 See Philippa Foot, *The Problem of Abortion and the Doctrine of the Double Effect*, in KILLING AND LETTING DIE 266, 273 (Bonnie Steinbock & Alastair Norcross eds., 1994) (hereinafter, Foot 1967). See also Philippa Foot, *Killing and Letting Die*, in KILLING AND LETTING DIE 280, 281–82 (Bonnie Steinbock & Alastair Norcross eds., 1994) (hereinafter, Foot 1984).

Foot's general stance is also expressed in: Philippa Foot, *Morality, Action and Outcome*, in MORALITY AND OBJECTIVITY 23 (Ted Hondrich ed., 1985) (hereinafter, Foot 1985).

61 Foot 1984, *supra* note 60, at 281–82.

62 *Id*. For an elaboration of Foot's theory, see Fiona Woollard, *The Doctrine of Doing and Allowing I: Analysis of Doing/Allowing Distinction*, 7 PHIL. COMPASS 448 (2012).

3.3.3.2 DEFINITION OF ACTS AND OMISSIONS

Based on what was given earlier, according to Foot, an act is a situation in which the agent created the sequence of events that led to the harm; When A pushed B off a cliff, A created the sequence of events that caused B's death.[63] By contrast, an omission can fall into two categories: non-intervention and removal of a safeguard.

1. In cases of non-intervention, a sequence of events that could cause harm was set in motion, and the agent did nothing to prevent the outcome. For example, A could have warned B about the cliff but failed to do so, resulting in B's death.
2. In cases of removal of a safeguard against the threat, there is a threat that could cause harm but also a shield to prevent it, and the actor removes that shield. For example, A opens the door, allowing a predator to enter and kill B.[64] According to Foot, it does not matter who initially placed the shield or removed it. In any case, the removal of a shield is classified as an omission or allowing harm to happen.

Based on Foot's perspective, the definition of the concepts of act and omission, as well as killing and letting die, does not rely on the physical movement of the agent. There may be situations where A allows B to die by removing a shield against harm. Furthermore, according to Foot, an actor can cause a certain outcome without taking any action. For example, a singer who fails to show up for a performance causes the failure of the show rather than merely allowing it to fail.[65] This perspective differs descriptively from the causal theories previously presented because it does not rely on bodily movement as the basis for the distinction between acts and omissions.

3.3.3.3 MCMAHAN'S THEORY

McMahan shares Foot's view that the key factor in distinguishing between acts and omissions is whether the agent created or generated the threat, but he differs regarding the circumstances under which the agent is considered the

63 Foot 1985, *supra* note 60, at 24. Foot also notes that cases of sustaining an action can also fall within the definition of killing because they can be seen as creating a threat. In such cases, without the sustaining action, the action would cease, as in the case of causing a car to continue driving by pressing the accelerator, creating a new threat. For criticism of Foot's position, see Warren S. Quinn, *Actions, Intentions, and Consequences: The Doctrine of Doing and Allowing*, in KILLING AND LETTING DIE 355 (Bonnie Steinbock & Alastair Norcross eds., 1994).

64 Foot 1967, *supra* note 60, at 273.

65 *Id.*

creator of the threat.[66] This contrast can be observed in the Dutch boy 1 and Dutch boy 2 cases presented by McMahan.

Dutch boy 1: A boy places his finger in the dam to prevent it from breaking and endangering the residents of the city. Later, he removes his finger, and tragically, the dam breaks, causing the death of all the residents.

According to Foot, both cases would be regarded as letting die because in both cases the agents (the boy and the father) removed the shield against harm. By contrast, McMahan categorizes the father's action in Dutch boy 2 as killing, not as letting die. The underlying reasoning lies in the fact that the father as remover is not the same as the one who laid the shield in the first place, which is the boy. Had the father not intervened, the boy's action would have saved the residents.[67] Therefore, the father's intervention is seen as creating a new threat that led to the residents' death and it is classified as killing. Nevertheless, McMahan categorizes Dutch boy 1 as letting die[68] because the one who removes the finger is the same as the one who initially placed it: the boy himself. The removal of the finger does not create a new threat, it merely returns the situation to where it was had the boy not intervened initially.

McMahan's viewpoint suggests that the question of what would have happened had the agent not been present, determines whether the agent is considered the creator of the threat.[69] In Dutch boy 1, the boy's absence would not have changed the tragic outcome, as the dam would still have burst; therefore, the boy cannot be considered the creator of the threat. In Dutch boy 2, in the father's absence, the child's action would have saved the residents;

66 Jeff McMahan, *Killing, Letting Die, and Withdrawing Aid*, in KILLING AND LETTING DIE 383, 389 (Bonnie Steinbock & Alastair Norcross eds., 1994) (hereinafter, McMahan 1993); For McMahan's general stance, see also JEFF MCMAHAN, THE ETHICS OF KILLING: PROBLEMS AT THE MARGINS OF LIFE 378–92 (2002) (hereinafter, McMahan 2002). Jeff McMahan, *A Challenge to Common Sense Morality*, 108 ETHICS 394 (1998) (hereinafter, McMahan 1998).

67 A similar distinction was raised by Alan Donagan, as noted by Bennett. Donagan distinguishes between killing and letting die because in killing there is intervention in the regular course of nature, whereas in letting die there is no such intervention. It can be argued that McMahan's theory is a development of this idea. For example, according to McMahan, when the Dutch boy removes his finger, there is no intervention in the regular course of nature. The removal of the finger is only a return to the natural state before the intervention of the boy. By contrast, when a father removes his son's finger, there is intervention in the regular course of nature, without which the residents would have survived. See Bennett 1995, *supra* note 43, at 105–18. See also ALAN DONAGAN, THE THEORY OF MORALITY 42–43 (1977).

68 McMahan 1993, *supra* note 66, at 389.

69 A similar position, distinguishing between acts and omissions using this question, can be found in: LEO KATZ, BAD ACTS AND GUILTY MINDS: CONUNDRUMS OF THE CRIMINAL LAW 14 (1987).

therefore, the father is seen as the creator of a new threat that caused their death.[70]

McMahan explicitly argues that the moral rationale for the earlier theoretical distinction is rooted in causal differentiation.

> This intuition may be articulated in rough and general terms as follows. If the situation is such that a person will live in the absence of any further intervention in his life by a certain agent, then, if the person nevertheless dies, the agent has killed him. In these cases, we identify the agent's intervention as the primary cause of the person's death. If, by contrast, a person dies who would not have lived without some present or future intervention in his life by a certain agent, and if the agent neither caused the person's need for aid nor caused a further, independent threat to his life, the agent has let the person die. In these cases, we trace the cause of the person's death to conditions that are independent of any intervention by the agent.[71]

Regarding the distinction between killing and letting die, from a moral standpoint, in cases involving killing, the agent's intervention is viewed as the primary cause of the victim's death. Conversely, in cases of letting die, the cause of the victim's death is attributed to conditions independent of the agent's intervention.[72]

70 Despite the earlier discussion, according to McMahan, there are cases in which the one who removed the shield is the one that initially placed it and yet this action is still classified as killing. For example, consider the following case:

Gas leak: In a certain factory, a gas valve leaked, posing a threat to the lives of many workers. An employee of the factory closed the valve and saved the workers. A year later, he reopened the valve and many workers died.

McMahan classified this case as killing rather than letting die although the person who closed the valve was the one who subsequently opened it. This is because the question is focused not only on the identity of the remover of the shield but also on the type of protection or aid in question, in this case, whether the shield was perfect and did not require further maintenance or whether it was a shield that needed additional maintenance. In the case of the gas leak, no further action or intervention was required from the agent beyond closing the valve to remove the threat. Therefore, reopening the valve is considered the creation of a new threat that caused the workers' death, an action classified as killing. Thus, the reopening of the gas valve was not a cessation of rescue that began and did not end because, at this stage, the workers were already living without any intervention from the agent who closed the gas valve and were no longer relying on his assistance. See: McMahan 2002, *supra* note 66, at 381.

Another position claiming that the distinction between killing and letting die rests on a causal distinction can be found in: O. H. Green, *Killing and Letting Die*, 17 AM. PHIL. Q. 195 (1980); Mathew Hanser, *Why are Killing and Letting Die Wrong?* 24 PHIL. & PUB. AFFS. 175 (1995).

71 McMahan 1993, *supra* note 66, at 411.

72 McMahan cites theories of causation according to which even the absence of an action can cause an outcome. According to these theories, the distinction between killing and letting die cannot be based on a causal distinction. See McMahan 1993, *supra* note 66, at 411–12.

McMahan correctly criticizes Foot's theory for classifying certain cases as letting die when a shield against harm is removed, but his own position also raises questions. Consider these instances:

Death by hypothermia 1: B is about to die from hypothermia and wants to enter A's house. A does not want to let B in (he is not afraid of B) and locks the door. As a result, B dies.

Death by hypothermia 2: The case is the same as Death by hypothermia 1 but in this case, B wants to enter his own house, and A, who is inside B's house, locks the door, resulting in B's death.

Despite the identical actions, Death by hypothermia 1 is likely to be classified as letting die and Death by hypothermia 2 as killing based on ownership of the house. This difference seems difficult to justify causally because A's actions are the same in both cases.

Another challenge to McMahan's position arises in cases where the agent removes a shield not initially laid by him. McMahan categorizes such cases as killing rather than letting die but I argue that there are instances where although the agent removes a shield he did not originally set, the behavior should be classified as letting die.

Hunger: A sees C throwing a loaf of bread into the garbage. A eats it, resulting in B's death from hunger.

McMahan would categorize this case as killing because A did not place the shield (the bread) initially, and without A's intervention, B would have survived because of the aid provided by C. Nevertheless, it seems that this case should be classified as letting die, not killing.

Furthermore, even if we assume a causal distinction between an act and an omission, the question remains whether this distinction has moral significance. The primary concern should be preventing harm, regardless of whether it is achieved through an act or an omission. Consequently, even if there is a causal distinction between an act and an omission, it may not provide a moral rationale for differentiating between the two.

3.3.3.4 SIMESTER'S THEORY

Simester argues that the distinction between acts and omissions is based on the concept of authorship; when a person causes harm by act, he is the author of the outcome, making the victim's harm a part of his life. By contrast, when he fails to prevent harm, he is not the author of that outcome and the result cannot be attributed to him.[73] For example, Simester describes a scenario involving D, who faces a trolley dilemma: if he does nothing, Tom will die, but if

73 A. P. Simester, *Why Omissions Are Special*, 1 LEGAL THEORY 311, 329–31 (1995).

he diverts the trolley, Sam will die instead.[74] In his view, D should not divert the trolley because by doing so, he makes Sam's death a part of his life and becomes its author, contrary to having done nothing. In such a case, D can say to Tom's parents, "I do not have to justify my not saving Tom, for his death had nothing to do with me."[75] Simester does not deny that there is a causal link between D's inaction and Tom's death, but this does not make him the author of Tom's death, and thus, it cannot be attributed to him.[76]

However, it is challenging to separate causality from authorship. If a person's failure to save another still causes death, why should the death not be attributed to him and why is he not considered the author? If the argument is that in the case of omission the causal link is indirect, the main argument rests on a causal distinction and not on authorship. Even if the issue of causality can be separated from the claim of authorship, why cannot a person be the author of certain outcomes when he refrains from an action? For example, if I decided to go to a movie with a friend and later changed my mind, it is difficult to argue that I am not the author of the disappointment caused to my friend.[77]

3.4 *The "intermediate" theory*

3.4.1 The position of Hart and Honoré

In contrast to the theories discussed earlier, according to which an omission cannot cause a particular result, and contrary to the theories arguing that causation is a necessary condition for the outcome, Hart and Honoré, in their book *Causation in the Law*, argue that an omission can indeed lead to harm in certain cases and distinguish between mere conditions for harm and the cause of harm. For example, when someone tosses a burning match into a paper recycling bin, causing a fire, we claim that the act of tossing the match into the bin is the primary cause of the harm, although there are other necessary conditions for the fire to erupt, such as the presence of oxygen in the air and of paper in the recycling bin.[78]

Similarly, when A shoots B, causing B's death, there are several necessary conditions for B's death to happen, such as A's mother giving birth to him and B's mother giving birth to B. Yet it is important to distinguish between these conditions and the primary cause of B's death, which is A shooting him.

74 *Id.* at 330.

75 *Id.* at 331.

76 *Id.*

77 See also Tadros, *supra* note 16, at 190–96; Mark Dsouza, Against the Act/*Omission* Distinction, 73 Northern Ireland Legal Quarterly 103, 117–18 (2022).

78 H. L. A. Hart & Tony Honoré, Causation in the Law 34–35 (1985); for further discussion regarding Hart and Honoré's stance, see Geoffrey Mead, *Contracting into Crime: A Theory of Criminal Omissions*, 11 Oxford J. Legal Stud. 147, 149–52 (1991).

Hart and Honoré cite the need to differentiate between mere conditions and the primary cause, making it possible to assign responsibility for the occurrence of the harm. They argue that a cause for harm, as opposed to a mere condition, must meet two cumulative criteria:[79] pass the but-for test and deviate from what is considered normal and reasonable in a given situation.

The but-for test has been explained earlier; therefore, I elaborate here only on the second criterion. In our daily lives, questions of causality arise mainly when something happens that deviates from the usual course of events. For example, when a young person dies, it prompts us to question the reason behind the death because in normal circumstances young individuals typically do not die. Similarly, in the example mentioned earlier, we inquire about the cause of the fire because fires of this type do not usually happen.

According to Hart and Honoré, the mere conditions for a specific harm exist even when the harm does not occur. In the case of tossing a burning match into a paper recycling bin, the presence of oxygen in the air is a mere condition for the resulting harm but not the primary cause because oxygen exists in the air even when the fire does not start. Nor is the presence of papers in the paper recycling bin the primary cause of the harm because it is normal and reasonable to find papers in the bin. Tossing the burning match into the bin is the primary cause of the harm because usually, people do not toss burning matches into it. Therefore, we can consider the act of tossing the burning match as the difference maker.[80]

Hart and Honoré point out that at times the presence of oxygen can be the primary cause of the harm and not only a mere condition, for example, when a fire occurs in a laboratory where oxygen is not supposed to be present, and the presence of oxygen deviates from the normal and expected conditions.[81]

There can also be situations where, as part of a single event, an occurrence can be both a mere condition (and not the cause) and a primary cause (and not only a mere condition), depending on the observer's perspective. When there is famine in India and people die as a result, Indian citizens may see the lack of rainfall as the cause of the harm while the US government may see the Indian government as the cause of the deaths. The argument here is that Indian citizens perceive the behavior of their government as normal and reasonable, whereas the US government does not.

Hart and Honoré argue that a departure from normal and reasonable behavior does not always require active intervention; it can also result from an omission, a failure to act. Such omissions can also be the cause of harm, as for example, failure to intervene in certain situations can lead to negative outcomes. To prevent harm, societies establish norms, laws, and customs. When someone deviates from these established standards and causes harm, his

79 *Id.* at 109–11.
80 *Id.* at 34.
81 *Id.* at 35.

behavior becomes the cause of the harm, not merely a necessary condition for it.[82] For example, when A fails to water the flowers despite being obligated to do so, failure to water the flowers is not merely a necessary condition for the wilting of the flowers but also the primary cause of it because A's failure is a deviation from normal and expected behavior in this case. But the fact that the Queen of England did not water the flowers is not the cause of their wilting, but merely a condition for it, because the Queen's failure to water the flowers is not a deviation from normal and expected behavior.[83]

At first glance, it is possible to argue that, according to Hart and Honoré's analysis of causation, there is no significant causal distinction between an act and an omission, as both can be the cause of harm. Similarly, there seems to be no causal difference between killing and letting die, as both types of behavior can deviate from normal and reasonable conduct under certain circumstances.[84]

In a different book, however, Honoré claims that there is a causal distinction between acts and omissions, and the difference lies in whether the relevant behavior brings about a tangible change in the world. Often, an act can be considered the cause because it constitutes a deviation from normal and expected behavior under given circumstances. But in most cases, an omission does not create a change in the world; therefore, it is not a cause of harm. The few cases where omissions are deemed causative of harm are situations where there was an expectation for the agent to act, but he failed to do so. If a lifeguard fails to rescue a drowning person when he could have done so, the omission is considered the cause of harm because the societal expectation was for the lifeguard to save the drowning person, and he deviated from this expectation. In cases of this type, it would be possible to impose criminal liability on the person who failed to act.[85]

Contrary to Beebee and Mack, who argued for a strict causal distinction between acts and omissions, according to Hart and Honoré, there is indeed a causal distinction between the two, although not a sharp one because there are cases when omissions can cause harm.

82 *Id.* at 37–38.

83 *Id.* at 38.

84 Hart and Honoré have argued that the distinction between necessary conditions and the primary cause for an outcome is based on objective causal considerations rather than policy considerations. See *Id.* at 24–27. This position is not without controversy, however, and some contend that the distinction between necessary conditions and the main cause for harm is based on policy considerations rather than objective causal ones. See DOUGLAS N. HUSAK, PHILOSOPHY OF CRIMINAL LAW 164–65 (1987). Similarly, criticism of Hart and Honoré's position can be found in: R. W. Wright, *Causation in Tort Law*, 73 CALIF. L. REV. 1737, 1745–47 (1985).

85 Honoré, *supra* note 17, at 53.

3.4.1.1 DEFINITION OF ACTS AND OMISSIONS

According to Honoré, the distinction between acts and omissions is based on the bodily movement test: an act is a bodily movement whereas an omission is the absence of such movement. When the agent moves his body and harm occurs, we can usually attribute the harm to the agent because there is a departure from normal and reasonable behavior. But when the agent does not move his body and harm occurs, we generally cannot hold him responsible unless it is an inaction that deviates from normal and reasonable behavior in specific circumstances. This distinction also distinguishes between killing and letting die: when the agent moves his body and the victim dies as a result, it is usually categorized as killing because of a departure from normal and reasonable behavior. Conversely, when the agent does not move his body, it is typically categorized as letting die because it usually does not deviate from normal and reasonable behavior. When the absence of an act is a departure from the routine, it is considered letting die with a causal link to death, which is not morally different from killing.[86]

3.4.1.2 THE DUTY REQUIREMENT IN OMISSIONS

According to Hart and Honoré's theory, I can propose three reasons why criminal law requires a duty to act to convict for omissions:

1. The duty to act enables criminal liability even when there is no causal connection in omission. This is reasonable when the duty to act does not reflect common practice.
2. The purpose of the duty to act is to inform citizens that, in certain cases, there is a causal connection through omission. The cases identified as duties to act are those that reflect routine practices and are considered normal and reasonable behavior. The purpose here is to inform citizens that in such cases, if they fail to fulfill their duty, they will be considered one of the causes of harm.[87]
3. The duty to act creates the expectation, which in turn establishes the causal connection in omission. According to this perspective, the duty to act is not required merely to inform citizens about the existence of a causal link between the omission and the harm. Rather, its purpose is to create the accepted routine for establishing a causal connection between the omission and the harm.

86 *Id.* at 52–53.

87 It is not clear, according to Honoré, whether the causal connection in cases of omission is qualitatively the same in its "strength" as the causal connection in cases of action. In a particular section of his book (*Id.* at 53), it can be understood that even when an omission causes harm, there still exists a qualitative distinction between an act and an omission from a causal perspective. It can be argued that according to Honoré, there are two types of causation: strong, which is carried out through an action that inevitably creates a change in the world, and weak, which is carried out through an omission that deviates from a certain routine.

3.4.2 *Fletcher's theory*

Fletcher argues that the distinction between acts and omissions, as well as between killing and letting die, is based on a causal analysis inspired by the theories developed by Hart and Honoré.[88] According to Fletcher, if the but-for test were accurate, criminal law would convict individuals for omission without even establishing a duty to act. But criminal law cannot rely on a theory claiming that omission cannot cause harm because it would result in no liability for manslaughter or murder, even if a duty to act were identified. Therefore, Fletcher suggests that omission causes harm only when there is a departure from normal and reasonable behavior in the given situation. In cases where inaction aligns with reasonable expectations, there is no causal connection to the harm. The need for a duty to act in omissions arises from the distinct causal relationship between act and omission; the list of duties to act reflects situations where there is a moral or social expectation to do so, establishing a causal connection between the omission and the harm.[89]

But Fletcher maintains that even when a causal link is established in omission, there remains a distinction between acts and omissions. He argues that when there is a duty to act, the causal link is less direct than in the case of an act that directly caused the harm.[90] This distinction may have implications for the level of punishment in acts and omissions.[91]

3.4.2.1 DEFINITION OF ACTS AND OMISSIONS

The primary difference between Fletcher's approach and that of Hart and Honoré lies in the definition of acts and omissions. Whereas Honoré and Moore (mentioned further here) argued that the definition is based on the bodily movement test, Fletcher's definition is not tied to this test. According to him, the physical movement of the agent's body carries no intrinsic moral significance. Consequently, some cases can be classified as acts from a legal perspective although the agent did not move his body, and vice versa.

88 For Fletcher's causal approach, see George P. Fletcher, Rethinking Criminal Law 593–602 (1978) (hereinafter, Fletcher 1978). See also George P. Fletcher, Basic Concepts of Criminal Law 59–70 (1998) (hereinafter, Fletcher 1998).

89 Fletcher 1998, *supra* note 88, at 67–68.

90 *Id.* at 67. According to Fletcher, when it is unclear whether to classify a particular case as killing or as letting die, we must use everyday language. Fletcher argues that everyday language makes a distinction between cases of killing and letting die even when a causal connection exists. This linguistic distinction has moral significance. See Fletcher 1978, *supra* note 88, at 597 and at 600–01. Fletcher maintains that in everyday language, when a physician does not administer medication to a patient, it is considered letting die rather than killing. Conversely, if someone fails to feed his child and he dies, language frames the act as killing. This linguistic categorization of withholding medication as letting die has moral implications, especially in cases of punishment. Punishment in cases of killing may be more severe than in cases categorized as letting die, even if a duty to act exists.

91 See discussion in Chapter 7.

For example, Fletcher maintains that if a physician disconnects a terminally ill patient from a life-support machine, it constitutes an omission that allows the patient to die. If, however, A stood in a certain place and B bumped into him and died, A caused B's death, assuming that A could have stepped aside. In this scenario, we do not view A's standing put as an omission that requires a duty to act for conviction. Additional examples could include a stubborn motorist who refuses to move from a traffic lane or a pilot who stops moving and refuses to fly the aircraft. According to Fletcher, these types of behaviors are not considered legal omissions but rather acts.

> There is certainly no correlation between activity or motion, on the one hand, and the use of affirmative verbs of killing, on the other. A parent might starve a child to death by refusing to feed it. One can kill by standing still; and as we shall see later, one can let die by moving one's body. The issue is not motion, but the particular link that exists between the act and the occurrence of death.[92]

3.4.2.2 FLETCHER'S THEORY AND THE ACT REQUIREMENT IN CRIMINAL LAW

Fletcher's causal approach, together with his position that standing still in a certain situation should be regarded as an act, fits well with his perspective on the nature of the act requirement in criminal law, arguing that the act requirement should not be treated as a metaphysical abstraction separated from its context. Human conduct invariably serves as a form of expression or meaningful communication between individuals. Because human action is a form of intersubjective communication, the key factor in defining an act should be the understating of the social context in which it was carried out. Consequently, the interpretation of the terms "act" and "omission" should not be confined to a strictly biological or physical understanding and should not be inherently linked to the bodily movement test.[93] For example, from a biological standpoint, when

92 Fletcher, 1978, *supra* note 88, at 601–02. See also Fletcher, *supra* note 5, at 1442, 1445. "I mean to challenge this conventional view . . . with the radical suggestion that bodily movements have no bearing on the act/omission distinction. Movement, as such, has no moral relevance."

93 See George P. Fletcher, The Grammar of Criminal Law: American, Comparative, International 283 (2007). Fletcher argues against Moore's position. Even those who have written about Fletcher and his aforementioned book understood that the emphasis lies in the connection between an individual's actions and the societal communication between human beings.

"For Fletcher, the first thing that needs to be noticed in the concept of action is that human conduct is always a form of expression or of relevant communication between human beings. Consequently, if we consider the concept of action from the point of view of the traditional theories (causal or teleological), we ignore precisely the only thing that really characterizes human action in general, and human criminal action in particular: that, regardless of any external assessment that can be made of it, human action is, above all, a form of intersubjective communication and not a simple causal or teleological process." See Francisco Munoz Conde & Luis Ernesto Chiesa, *The Act Requirement as Basic Concept of Criminal Law,* 28 Cardozo L. Rev. 2463–64 (2007).

a psychologist sits in front of a patient without moving a muscle, it may not be considered an act. But in the realm of criminal law, there should be no distinction between this case and one where the accused moves his muscles. Similarly, attentive listening by students to a lecturer without physical movement should not be treated differently from regular acts in relevant legal contexts.[94]

From this perspective, we can understand Fletcher's position that standing still can at times be regarded as simply allowing someone to die, while in other cases, it may be classified as killing. Moreover, there are situations in which bodily movement can be deemed as killing and others in which it may be seen as simply allowing death to occur. According to Fletcher, categorically classifying the absence of bodily movement as always letting die is not feasible because the agent's behavior cannot be detached from the social context in which it occurred.[95]

In conclusion, the crux of the matter lies in the understanding of the causal link between the agent's behavior and the victim's death rather than in strict focus on whether or not it involves bodily movement.

3.5 *Theories claiming that there is no causal distinction between acts and omissions*

I outlined earlier the main options for causal differences between acts and omissions. I now proceed to explore the approaches arguing that omission can lead to a result even without constituting a deviation from normal and reasonable behavior. According to these approaches, if an omission can cause harm, there can be no causal distinction between acts and omissions. This view is not negligible, and it crosses boundaries. For example, legal scholars such as Perkins[96] and Leavens,[97] as well as philosophers in the fields of science and ethics, such as Lewis,[98] Bennett,[99] Melor,[100] Kagan,[101] Harris,[102] and Mackie[103] argue that omission can cause harm just as an act can.

94 Fletcher, *supra* note 93, at 272–72. Another well-known example is that of the palace guard of the Queen of England. Although standing still may not be considered a biological action, from a legal or moral perspective, in relevant cases, this conduct should not differ from that of a regular action.

95 See Conde & Chiesa, *supra* note 93, at 2469.

96 Perkins, *supra* note 46, at 773.

97 Arthur Leavens, *A Causation Approach to Criminal Omissions,* 76 Calif. L. Rev. 547 (1988).

98 Lewis 2004b, *supra* note 37.

99 Bennett 1995, *supra* note 43, at 126–30.

100 Mellor, *supra* note 30, at 130–35.

101 Shelly Kagan, The Limits of Morality 92–94 (1991).

102 See John Harris, *The Survival Lottery*, in Killing and Letting Die 257–65 (Bonnie Steinbock & Alastair Norcross eds., 1994). See also John Harris, *The Marxist Conception of Violence*, 3 Phil. & Pub. Affs. 192 (1974) (hereinafter, Harris 1974).

103 J. L. Mackie, *Causes and Conditions*, 2 Am. Phil. Q. 245 (1965).

3.5.1 *Causal components: events or facts?*

In contrast to the perspective according to which an omission cannot cause harm because the causal elements involve events, and omission is not considered an event, an alternative viewpoint posits that an omission can lead to harm. This is either because the causal elements are not events but rather facts or because the causal components are events, and an omission is indeed an event. In the following I present two options based on this perspective: omission is an event and causal components are facts.

3.5.1.1 OMISSION IS AN EVENT: DAVIDSON'S POSITION

Contrary to the position that omission cannot cause harm because it is not an event, Donald Davidson argues that omission is an event. According to Davidson's theory of action, just as there is a causal connection between two events when the first one is the cause and the second the effect, there is also a causal relationship between a person's mental action and physical actions.[104] For example, when A shoots B, there is a causal connection between the mental action, which is the decision to shoot B, and the physical action, which is the act of shooting. The decision to shoot B is the cause of the shooting action. Mental actions that lead to results are events, and they are varied, such as deciding to take action, making a specific calculation, judging, and so on.[105] Thus, when A shoots B and B dies, two causal connections are established: one between A's mental decision to shoot B and the shooting action, and the other between A's shooting and B's death.[106]

I argue that just as there is a causal relationship between a person's intention or decision and his actions, there is also a causal relationship between a person's intention and his omissions. When A fails to warn B about the cliff and B dies as a result, we can explain the case as follows: the mental event manifested in A's intention not to warn B about the cliff led to B's death. The mental event of A's decision not to warn B resulted in A not warning B, which led to B's death.[107] Davidson regarded omissions as entities capable of causing outcomes.

> The word "action" does not very often occur in ordinary speech, and when it does, it is usually reserved for fairly portentous occasions.

104 See Donald Davidson, *Mental Events*, in ESSAYS ON ACTION AND EVENTS 207, 208 (2001) (hereinafter, Davidson 1970). See also Donald Davidson, *Actions, Reasons, and Causes*, in ESSAYS ON ACTION AND EVENTS 3 (2001) (hereinafter, Davidson 1963).

105 Davidson 1970, *supra* note 104.

106 *Id.*

107 In analyzing this case, two possibilities can be raised:

The first is to argue that the conduct of not warning is itself an event manifesting in staying in place.

The second is to argue that the conduct of not warning is not an event, but we can still attribute the cause of B's death to another event, which is the mental decision that led to the choice not to warn and save B. Thus, a causal connection is established between A's decision not to save B and the event in which he dies.

> I follow a useful philosophical practice in calling anything an agent does intentionally an action, including intentional omissions.[108]

We can strengthen Davidson's argument that omissions could cause an outcome by stating that he attributed agency to individuals if they acted with intention. For example, when a person intentionally pours coffee, we can argue that he is the agent of the act of pouring coffee. But if someone accidentally knocks over the coffee because someone else pushed his elbow, he is not the agent of the spill because no intention can be attributed to him in that act.[109] Similarly, if A intentionally fails to warn B about the cliff, we can argue he is the agent of the omission not to warn B. Thus, it is reasonable to say that omissions can also be events and cause harm.

3.5.1.2 CAUSAL COMPONENTS ARE FACTS

According to Melor, Lewis, and Bennett, causal components can be facts rather than events. Melor provides an illustrative case to demonstrate this point:

Fall: A's fall caused his death because his bones were fragile.

In this case, the fact that A's bones were fragile caused his death following a fall. Because the fragility of A's bones is not an event but a fact, it is clear that facts can cause results.[110] Another case presented by Hart and Honoré reflects this position:

Ice: The accident occurred because the road was covered in ice.

The fact that the road was covered in ice is not an event, but we still regard it as the cause of the accident.[111]

Melor reinforces his argument by considering negative cases as well. He states that if we can claim that A's falling caused his death, we can also claim that A not falling caused him not to die.[112]

Lewis supports this idea by presenting a hypothetical scenario in which a person is in a complete void and dies because of a lack of air. The void does not suck the air like a magnet. Instead, air molecules collide, exerting repulsive forces on each other. These forces create a pressure that, if unopposed, leads to the expansion and dispersion of the air. The void applies no force to counter this pressure, resulting in the air departing from the lungs. In short, Lewis

108 Davidson 1963, *supra* note 104, at 5 (note 2); see also John Kleinig, *Criminal Liability for Failure to Act*, 49 LAW & CONTEMP. PROBS. 161, 173–74 (1986).

109 Donald Davidson, *Agency*, in ESSAYS ON ACTION AND EVENTS 43 (2001).

110 Mellor, *supra* note 30, at 106–09.

111 Hart and Honoré, *supra* note 78, at 27.

112 Mellor, *supra* note 30, at 132. Dowe disagrees. According to him, this constitutes quasi rather than genuine causation. See Dowe, *supra* note 54, at 217.

demonstrates that a void is deadly "not because it exerts forces and supplies energy, but because it does not."[113] According to Lewis, the absolute void represents the most extreme form of "absence."[114] If we accept that the absolute void can cause a person's death, it becomes even more apparent that a regular omission can also lead to harm.[115]

Bennett, who also addressed the distinction between acts and omissions, as well as between killing and letting die, contends that the difference cannot rely exclusively on a causal distinction because causal components can be facts, and an omission is also a fact capable of causing harmful consequences. Thus, when he refers to a case where an agent failed to divert a rock to save the victim ("Stayback"), he argues:

> My account of causation makes it impressively weak. It implies that in Stayback the causes of the vehicle's demise include its momentum, the slope of the ground, the presence of the cliff, the stillness of the ground, and agents not moving in a certain way. That is the crux: the agent's not interposing the rock is a cause of the vehicle's destruction; so the causal analysis of our distinction fails.[116]

To summarize, if we accept that omissions can also serve as causal components, and if the definition of the causal connection relies on the but-for test, there is reason to claim that omissions can cause harm in the same way as acts can. Consequently, the moral distinction between act and omission cannot rely on a causal difference but lies elsewhere.

4. The harm to the victim rationale

4.1 Introduction

In this section, I introduce two theories concerning harm to the victim.

According to the entitlement theory, the rationale for the distinction between an act and an omission is based on the different harm suffered by the victim in each case. In all cases of harm caused by an omission, there is an essential characteristic: the victim loses a life or property that could have been preserved only if the agent offered aid. By contrast, in most cases where harm

113 Lewis, 2004b, *supra* note 37, at 277.

114 *Id.*

115 *Id.* at 282. It should be noted that Harris and Rachels, who were discussed earlier within the context of skeptical approaches, argued that there is no significant causal distinction between A killing B and A not saving B when A could do so. Harris explicitly asserts that not saving is a negative action that results in death. See Harris 1974, *supra* note 102, at 208.
See also the discussion in Chapter 1 within the framework of skeptical approaches.

116 Bennett 1995, *supra* note 43, at 129–30.

is caused by an act, the victim loses a life or property that would have been preserved independently from the agent's aid.

For example, in a scenario where A drowns B, B loses life that could have been preserved independently from the agent's aid because he could have continued to live without any action from A. But in the case where A fails to save B, B loses a life that could have been preserved only with A's help.[117]

The metaphysical theory states that the harm caused to the victim by an act is greater than the harm caused by an omission. The reasoning is that an act aggravates the victim's state, whereas an omission, although it may not improve it, does not worsen it. This perspective is based on a causal approach, suggesting that only an act can cause an outcome, whereas an omission cannot; therefore, it cannot be said that the agent made the victim's state worse.[118]

4.2 *The entitlement theory*

Methodologically, Frances Kamm, representing the entitlement theory, goes beyond merely presenting two cases, one involving harm by an act and the other by an omission, to demonstrate the moral distinction between them. Kamm argues that it is not always easy to intuitively discern moral distinctions, especially when both cases involve harmful intentions and minimal efforts to prevent harm. Simply presenting two cases is not enough to fully reveal the core factor that makes causing harm through omission morally different from causing harm through action.

Kamm proposes a different methodological approach that highlights both the moral distinction between the cases and the significant component that creates this moral divide between act and omission in general and between killing and letting die specifically.

To illustrate this difference regarding the moral distinction between killing and letting die, Kamm analyzes the essential components (referred to as "conceptual components") of each. An essential component is a fundamental element present in every instance of a particular concept.

According to Kamm, the essential components of killing are as follows: (1) The agent creates the threat that leads to the victim's death, such as shooting

117 F. M. Kamm, Morality, Mortality: Rights, Duties, and Status (Volume 2), Part 1 (1996) (hereinafter, Kamm 1996).
F. M. Kamm, *Action, Omission, and the Stringency of Duties*, 142 U. Pa. L. Rev. 1493 (1994) (hereinafter, Kamm 1994).
Frances Myrna Kamm, *Killing and Letting Die: Methodological and Substantive Issues*, 64 Pac. Phil. Q. 297 (hereinafter, Kamm 1983).
Frances Myrna Kamm, *Harming, Not Aiding, and Positive Rights*, 15 Phil. & Pub. Affs. 3 (1986) (hereinafter, Kamm 1986).

118 Michael S. Moore, Act and Crime: The Philosophy of Action and Its Implications for Criminal Law 28–30 (1993) (hereinafter, Moore 1993).

the victim, or in more complex cases, removing the victim's shield. (2) The victim dies as a result of direct harm to him or his belongings.[119]

The essential components of letting die are as follows: (1) The victim is under threat without any connection to the agent's actions. (2) The victim loses a life that could have been preserved only with the agent's aid. For example, when A fails to save B, who is about to fall off a cliff, B loses a life that could have been preserved only with A's assistance. (3) The agent's assistance would prolong the life of the victim. (4) The agent controls only the means related to him.[120]

Kamm points out that essential components of letting die can be applied to cases of killing without altering their classification. For example, the component that the victim loses a life that could have been saved only with the agent's aid, which is essential to letting die, is also present in certain cases of killing: when B is already receiving lifesaving aid from A but simultaneously A shoots B and kills him. In this case, A kills B by shooting, but B still loses a life that could have been saved only if A had assisted.[121]

The technique of comparing cases in which an essential component of letting die appears in killing can explain the moral distinction between the two. If we can prove that a typical case of killing (without an essential component of letting die) is morally more severe than one that includes an essential component of letting die, and that this latter case is more severe than a standard case of letting die, we can conclude that a typical case of killing is morally more severe than a regular case of letting die. In this way, we can identify the moral component that distinguishes between killing and letting die.[122]

According to Kamm, it appears that the component that makes letting die morally less severe than killing is the fact that in letting die, the victim loses a life that could have been preserved only with the agent's assistance. This component is crucial to letting die but not an essential aspect of killing because in most cases classified as killing, the victim loses a life that could have been preserved without the agent's aid. The moral significance of this particular component can be observed by the technique of comparing two cases of killing, one that includes this essential element and one that does not.

Shooting 1: B is attached to A's body to save B's life, without A's consent. The only way to detach B from A is to shoot B. A shoots B, causing his death.

119 Kamm analyzes primarily the essential components of letting die, but from the definition she provides for letting die, it is possible to infer the crucial elements of killing. See Kamm 1996, *supra* note 117, at 29–30.

120 *Id.* at 31; Kamm 1983, *supra* note 117, at 301.

121 Kamm 1996, *supra* note 117, at 36–37.

122 "That is, for example, introducing a property conceptually true of letting die into a case of killing might make the particular killing more easily justified than killing in a case which lacked the property." Kamm 1983, *supra* note 117, at 301; see also Kamm 1996, *supra* note 117, at 32.

Shooting 2: B is not attached to A's body and does not rely on A to live. A shoots B, killing him.

Both cases deal with the death of B caused by A's action. But Shooting 1 contains an essential component of letting die because B loses a life that could have been preserved only with A's assistance, unlike in Shooting 2, where B loses a life that could have been preserved were it not for A because B could have continued living independently from A's aid. Kamm argues that this essential element makes Shooting 1 morally less severe, and at the same time, it is morally more severe than a regular case of letting die. Therefore, it can be concluded that a regular case of killing is morally more severe than a regular case of letting die.[123]

According to Kamm, the essential element pertaining to the victim losing a life that could have been preserved only with the agent's aid has moral significance. Every individual is entitled only to what he possesses independently, unrelated to the actions of others. Whatever is not within their independent control, they are not entitled to. Hence, when the agent allows the victim to die, the victim loses a life to which he was not entitled because he could not have continued living independently, without the agent's intervention. Conversely, in most cases of killing, the victim loses a life to which he is entitled because he could have continued living were it not for the intervention of the agent.[124]

This fact explains why, from a moral standpoint, there is no significant difference between a typical case of letting die and the case of Shooting 1, where B was not entitled to assistance from A in the first place. Therefore, there is no reason to prevent A from ceasing his rescue efforts, even by an act of killing.[125]

Kamm indicates that the moral distinction between killing and letting die, as shown in these cases, is not based on the bodily movement test. A physical action is involved in Shooting 1 but according to Kamm, this alone does not create a significant moral difference from a typical case of letting die. Moreover, the difference between killing and letting die is not determined by whether the agent caused the harm or intervened in the victim's life. In Shooting 1, the

123 Kamm explains that the proof based on the comparison of two cases of killing is subject to the condition that this essential component does not function differently when it is present in a case of regular letting die. If it did function differently, it would not be possible to prove the moral distinction between killing and letting die, and it would not be possible to demonstrate that this particular component is the relevant moral component. See Kamm 1983, *supra* note 117, at 305.

124 "[T]he Entitlement Thesis—emphasizes that relative to a particular person, you are entitled only to what you have independently of the other person, and she is entitled to the efforts which she could make on your behalf." See Kamm 1994, *supra* note 117, at 1496. See also Kagan, *supra* note 101, at 116–21.

125 Kamm 1983, *supra* note 117, at 304.

agent caused the harm but there is no fundamental difference from a regular case of letting die.

> Notice that the conceptual distinction between killing and letting die focused on in these examples is not that between action and omission, of interference and noninterference, since action and interference occur in both cases of killing. Rather the conceptual characteristic of letting die thought to be morally significant, and so introduced into one case of killing, is that the person who dies loses only a life he would have had via the aid of the agent in question . . . rather than independently of his aid.[126]

4.2.1 Definition of acts and omissions

The distinction between acts and omissions can be inferred from Kamm's classification of killing and letting die cases. Cases categorized as killing include:

1. Directly causing death, such as when A shoots B, resulting in B's death.
2. Removing a shield against death, where the person removing the shield did not provide it initially. For example, when A takes off a protective vest from B, knowing that it will expose B to harm.[127]

Cases classified as letting die are:[128]

1. Allowing death by non-intervention, for example, when A observes B drowning but chooses not to save him despite being able to do so.
2. Removing a shield against death, where the person removing the shield is the one who initially provided it, or when the person removes a shield that belongs to him, even if he was not the one who initially deployed it. This is the case, for example, when A uses a protective shield belonging to B to protect C, but then B removes the shield, leading to C's death. This case is considered letting die because the shield belonged to B and he removed it.[129]

Kamm challenges the liberty and causation rationales that support the bodily movement test. According to her, there could be cases where the victim dies because of the agent's bodily movement, but these would still be categorized

126 Kamm 1986, *supra* note 117, at 7.

127 According to Kamm, even preventing rescue by controlling the means available to the victim may be classified as killing. For example, if B is in a life-threatening situation and C is about to help B, whereupon A intervenes to stop C, A has effectively killed B. See Kamm 1994, *supra* note 117, at 1497.

128 Kamm 1996, *supra* note 117, at 43.

129 *Id.* at 28–29.

as letting die. This occurs when the agent terminates the assistance he previously provided or removes a protective measure belonging to him.

4.2.2 *The duty requirement in omissions*

Although Kamm did not directly address the legal distinction between acts and omissions but focused on the moral distinction between killing and letting die, her analysis suggests why a legal distinction exists. When harm is caused by an act, the victim loses property or life that could have been preserved independently from the agent's aid, making the victim rightfully entitled to that property or life. By contrast, in omissions, the victim loses property or life that could have been preserved only with the agent's aid; therefore, the victim is not rightfully entitled to them.

Because of this distinction, to hold someone liable for causing harm by omission it is necessary to establish the duty to act. Contrary to the liberty rationale, which claims that the duty requirement in omissions seeks to minimize the cases where a person is obligated to act, Kamm argues that the duty requirement aims to address the moral weakness present in omissions compared to acts. The duty to act makes causing harm by omission morally more severe because although the victim loses property or life that he could have only with the agent's assistance, the victim was entitled to this assistance by virtue of the legal obligation to act. This turns certain cases of harm by omission into something morally analogous, albeit not identical, to harm caused by an act.[130]

Kamm's position faces some challenges. First, concerning the moral rationale of the distinction, Kamm notes that in letting die the victim loses a life that could have been saved only with the agent's assistance, and because the victim is not entitled to this assistance, he loses a life he is not entitled to. But this argument begs the question because it assumes what needs to be proven. Kamm starts from the premise that every individual is entitled only to what he can have independently, which makes letting die morally less severe. But if we consider that the victim is entitled to the agent's assistance, the distinction between killing and letting die may not be significant.[131]

Additionally, Kamm argues that when the agent stops saving the victim by killing him, as in Shooting 1, the situation is not morally different from a regular case of letting die because in both cases, the victim loses what could have been preserved only with the agent's aid. Contrary to Kamm, I contend that the case is not severe, not because the victim loses a life that could have

130 Kamm indicates that morally, killing is still more severe than letting die even when a duty to act exists. The rationale behind this is that as opposed to killing, in letting die, the victim still loses a life that could have been saved only with the agent's aid, although the duty to aid is imposed on the agent. See Kamm 1994, *supra* note 117, at 1496–97.

131 Kagan, *supra* note 101, at 120.

been preserved only with the agent's aid but rather because A's right over his body was massively violated. In certain situations, where the violation of bodily ownership rights is substantial, it may be permissible to kill the attacker and neutralize the harm, which is a form of self-defense of one's body. It may be argued that the victim losing a life that could have been preserved only by the agent is not a morally significant factor in the following case:

Swimming: B is drowning and can save himself only if he holds onto A's leg. A doesn't want B to hold onto his leg, so he reaches for his underwater firearm and shoots B, resulting in B's death.

In this case, B loses a life that could have been preserved only with A's assistance, but this situation appears significantly more severe morally than a regular case of letting die. The difference between Swimming and Shooting 1 is that in Swimming, the harm to A's right of bodily ownership is not significant; therefore, A has no right to harm B's right of bodily ownership. By contrast, in Shooting 1, A's right of bodily ownership is significantly violated; therefore, he has the right to harm B's body to neutralize the threat.[132]

Kamm's approach is problematic also when it comes to the definition of killing and letting die. For example, consider the following case:

Starvation: B is dying of hunger and sees a loaf of bread that could save him. A, who is also hungry, takes the loaf of bread and eats it.

Kamm would classify this case as killing because B's life could have been preserved without A's help. If A had done nothing, B would have been saved. In this case, A could be convicted of homicide without the need to identify a duty to act. But I would categorize this case as letting die rather than killing. This scenario is akin to one in which A purchased a medicine from C to make a profit, and as a result, B, who needed this medicine, died. In this case,

132 I am doubtful whether the following scenarios that Kamm presented can prove the significance of the element that in letting die the victim loses a life that could have been preserved only with the agent's aid:

Blood 1: As a result of a freak of nature, blood flows from A's body to B's body. Without the blood flow to B's body, B would die. The blood flow to B's body causes harm to A. A can stop the blood flow only by killing B. A kills B.

Blood 2: The situation is the same as in Blood 1, except that A can stop the blood flow only by killing an innocent bystander who is not involved in the situation.

According to Kamm, killing B in Blood 1 is morally less severe than killing the innocent bystander in Blood 2 because in Blood 1, B loses a life that could have been preserved only with A's aid, whereas in Blood 2, the uninvolved bystander loses a life that could have been preserved independently from A's aid. See Kamm 1996, *supra* note 117, at 47–48.

I do not think it is permissible for A in Blood 1 to kill B. The argument that B could raise is as follows: "I'm not responsible for the flow of your blood into my body. You are not allowed to stop the blood flowing into my body by means or resources that belong to me. Therefore, you are not allowed to kill me as a means to the blood flow. "

Even if we assume that killing B in Blood 1 is permissible, the only justification for doing so would be the harm caused to A. But if we assume that the blood flow into B's body does not cause any harm to A, it is clear that A is not allowed to kill B merely because B would lose a life that could be preserved only with A's help.

A cannot be convicted of homicide merely for purchasing the medicine unless a specific duty was identified prohibiting A from buying the medicine in the first place.

4.3 The metaphysical theory

Moore argues that the distinction between acts and omissions arises from a moral distinction between positive and negative duties, based on a fundamental causal distinction between action and inaction. When an agent commits an act that causes harm, he violates his negative duty toward the victim. Conversely, when an agent refrains from a certain act and harm occurs, he violates his positive duty toward the victim. According to Moore, violating a negative duty is more severe than violating a positive one because it worsens the victim's situation, whereas violating a positive duty merely preserves the current state. This distinction relies on a causal theory that distinguishes between acts and omissions. An act can produce a change in the world; therefore, it has the potential to cause harm, aggravating the victim's situation. An omission cannot produce change; therefore, it cannot aggravate the victim's situation.[133]

> Omissions do not cause anything. Then when I omit to prevent some harm I do not make the world worse . . . only when I cause that harm to occur—through my actions—do I worsen the world.[134]

Moore does not argue that the absence of aggravation in the victim's situation implies that omissions should be excused from punishment. He distinguishes between two types of omissions: significant ones, which involve the violation of a substantial positive duty stemming from a direct relationship between the agent and the source of danger or the victim, and weak ones, which lack a connection to the source of danger or the victim.[135] An example of a substantial positive duty is a parent's obligation to rescue his young child. Although the non-rescue of the child does not worsen the victim's situation, the omission still merits punishment because it represents a substantial moral duty based on the relationship between the agent and the victim. By contrast, weak

133 Moore 1993, *supra* note 118. See also Michael S. Moore, MICHAEL S. MOORE, CAUSATION AND RESPONSIBILITY – AN ESSAY IN LAW, MORALS AND METAPHYSICS 139–42 (2009) (hereinafter, Moore 2009). Moore's theory of causality relies on the preceding causal theory, which argues that omission, which does not involve bodily movement, cannot cause an outcome. Despite this reliance on causal differentiation, the distinction serves as a foundation for a more fundamental distinction between making the victim's situation worse and not making it better.

134 Moore 1993, *supra* note 118. See also Moore 2009, *supra* note 133, at 53. "First, generically, an omission is literally nothing at all. An omission to kill is not some ghostly kind of killing. It is like an absent elephant, which is no elephant at all."

135 Moore 1993, *supra* note 118, at 54–57.

positive duties entail obligations to provide aid when unrelated individuals are involved. According to Moore, this type of omission does not cause harm to the victim and involves a weak obligation; therefore, individuals should not be held liable for violating such duties, which would impinge upon their liberty.[136] Moore argues that the liberty argument is relevant only to explain why criminal liability should not be imposed for violations of weak positive duties rather than serve as an explanation of the fundamental distinction between acts and omissions. This distinction, as noted, is based on the notion that acts worsen the victim's situation whereas omissions simply fail to improve it.[137]

According to Moore, there is a hierarchy of behaviors. The first type includes acts that cause significant harm and warrant punishment because they infringe upon the victim's negative rights, leading to a worsened situation. The second type involves the violation of significant positive duties, based on the relationship between the agent and the source of danger or the victim, such as the parents' duty to save their child. Moore contends that the second type is less severe than the first because it does not worsen the victim's situation, but it still justifies punishment because it represents a violation of a significant moral duty. The third type pertains to violations of weak positive duties, obligating a person to aid an unrelated individual. As noted, Moore holds that such violations should not be subject to punishment because of the liberty consideration. At the same time, the liberty consideration is not strong enough to prevent the criminal liability of offenses of the second type, and it surely also lacks the strength to prevent the criminal liability of offenses of the first type.[138]

Both Kamm and Moore focus on the victim's harm but their approaches differ. Kamm maintains that a causal link can exist in both acts and omissions, whereas Moore argues that omissions lack a causal link. Regarding the distinction between killing and letting die, Kamm's argument concerns the victim's entitlement to continue living. In most cases of killing, the victim loses a life to which he was entitled because he could have continued living independently from the agent's aid. In cases of letting die, however, the victim loses a life he was not entitled to because he could have continued living only with the assistance of the agent. By contrast, Moore focuses on the fact that the victim's situation worsens in cases of killing, whereas in cases of letting die, the victim's situation remains unchanged because omissions do not bring about any changes in the world.

4.3.1 The duty requirement in omissions

Moore argues that the duty requirement in case of omission arises from the absence of a causal connection between the omission and the resulting harm.

136 The liberty rationale was introduced in Section 2.1.
137 Moore 1993, *supra* note 118, at 57.
138 *Id.* at 58.

For example, when a physician fails to administer insulin to a patient, resulting in the patient's death, there is no causal link between the failure to provide the medication and the death. To convict the physician of the patient's death, even without a causal link, a legal duty to act must be established. Moore does not claim that the duty to act creates a causal connection in omissions: If there is no causal link without the duty, the duty cannot change that fact.[139] The agent is convicted for the violation of duty rather than causing the harm.[140]

4.3.2 Definition of acts and omissions

Moore's definition of acts and omissions is similar to that provided by the liberty rationale, which is based on the bodily movement test. According to Moore, an act is a voluntary bodily movement, whereas an omission is the absence of such movement. In the matter of killing and letting die, this means that the agent physically moving and causing the victim's death is classified as killing, and there is no need for a duty to act to convict the agent. But when the agent did not physically move and the victim died, a duty to act is required for conviction.[141]

The definition based on the bodily movement test is logically derived from Moore's rationale for distinguishing between acts and omissions. This rationale is based on causal theory whereby an act causes harm and makes the victim worse off, whereas an omission does not create any change in the victim's situation and causes no harm.

Although Moore endorses the definition of acts and omissions based on the criterion of bodily movement, he still agrees that when individual A fails to rescue individual B from drowning while simultaneously walking, singing, or whistling, this behavior would be categorized as an omission rather than an act. This is because if A had remained in place and not moved, B would still have died, rendering A's bodily movement inconsequential to B's death.[142] But if A placed his hands over his ears to avoid hearing B's cries for help as B drowns, this behavior would be classified as an act rather than an omission because, without this action, A could have saved B.[143]

Despite the similarity between Moore's approach and the liberty rationale in the definition of acts and omissions, the rationale for the definitions differs. According to the liberty rationale, the prohibition against an act defined as a bodily movement does not significantly impede human liberty because other options for action remain available. By contrast, the prohibition against an omission, defined as nonaction, does affect human liberty because it compels the person

139 Michael S. Moore, *More on Act and Crime,* 142 U. Pa. L. Rev. 1784–85 (1994).

140 *Id.*

141 *Id.* at 1785–87.

142 Moore 1993, *supra* note 118, at 29–30.

143 *Id.* at 87. For example, according to Moore, if a person ties both hands together to avoid eating, he is not committing an omission but rather performing an action that prevents eating.

to take action, which often prevents the person from living a reasonable life. Moore's rationale for the definition, however, stems from a causal perspective, where acts can cause harm unlike omissions defined as nonactions that cannot.[144]

Moore's approach has been criticized both for the proposed rationale and for the definition of acts and omissions. First, even if we agree that there is a significant difference between making the victim worse off and not making him better off, it is still not clear why not preventing harm does not make the victim worse off. For example, when A fails to rescue a drowning baby, why is it not considered making the baby worse off? It is possible to argue that the baby's fate was aggravated by A's inaction. If we accept that in such cases, A makes the baby's situation worse, Moore's rationale for distinguishing between acts and omissions weakens.[145] According to Moore, the reason for the difference is the causal distinction between an act and an omission. As shown earlier, this point is debatable, and many think that even an omission can cause harm and make the victim worse off.[146]

Even if we agree that omissions cannot cause harm, the moral validity of Moore's distinction remains uncertain. Feinberg provides an insightful perspective on different types of "benefits."[147] The first type involves improving a person's normal state, such as giving a gift to a friend, which elevates his situation above the norm.[148] The second type entails elevating a person to his normal state, like rescuing a drowning baby and bringing him back to his previous state before the incident.

Feinberg argues that these two types of benefits have distinct moral implications. Although individuals do not have a right to the first type of benefit, which elevates them beyond their normal state, they do have a right to the second type, which brings them back to their normal state. I argue that Moore's distinction may hold true concerning the first type of benefit. There may be

144 *Id.* at 28–29.

145 Simester, *supra* note 73, at 322.

"Conversely, might not non-interventions often be said to make things worse or create a risk that they will be worse? Peter's lot is worsened, and the risk of his drowning increased . . . , by my non-intervention."

146 See Chapter 2, Section 3.3; see also Alec Walen, *More Contra Moore on Omissions as Causes*, 58 CRIM. L. BULL. 375 (2022); Jonathan Schaffer, *Disconnection and Responsibility*, 18 LEGAL THEORY 399 (2012).

147 JOEL FEINBERG, HARM TO OTHERS: THE MORAL LIMITS OF THE CRIMINAL LAW 30–43 (1984). For further critique, see Michael Corrado, *Is There an Act Requirement in the Criminal Law*, 142 U. PA. L. REV. 1529 (1994); Samuel Freeman, *Criminal Liability and the Duty to Aid*, 142 U. PA. L. REV. 1455 (1994); Ron Shapira, *Structural Flaws of the "Willed Bodily Movement" Theory of Action*, 1 BUFF. CRIM. L. REV. 349 (1997).

148 Defining the normal state of a person is a complex task. For example, when a friend loses $10,000 in a certain deal, am I obligated to restore him to the state he was in before the loss? Does it matter why he lost it? Or $10,000 is stolen from my friend; am I obligated to restore him to his state before the theft? I assume that the normal state of a person is one in which he can function without any devices or assistance. This is not an exhaustive definition but to distinguish between two types of favor, I believe it is sufficient.

a moral difference between causing harm and aggravating the situation of the victim, as opposed to not elevating the victim beyond his normal state. But it remains unclear whether there is a moral distinction between causing harm and making the victim worse off compared to not elevating the victim to his normal state. Is there a difference between lowering a person to state X (which is much worse than his normal state) and not elevating him above state X?

Moore's definition of acts and omissions is also problematic, and the critique proposed by the liberty rationale is relevant here as well. There are cases involving bodily movement that are classified as omissions, requiring a duty to act for imposing criminal liability, for example, Motion 1 and Death by hypothermia 1, discussed earlier. Conversely, some cases do not involve bodily movement and are classified as acts, therefore not requiring a duty to act for imposing criminal liability (e.g., "Inaction" and "Silent threat").[149]

5. The dominance rationale

Kremnitzer and Segev argue that there are several differences between acts and omissions.[150] Act-related offenses impose fewer restrictions on individual liberty than omission-related ones. Moreover, acts establish a direct causal link to the harm, whereas mere omissions lack a clear causal connection or possess a more speculative link. Similar to Moore's approach, acts worsen the victim's condition whereas omissions do not alter his state. Additionally, the active agent exercises control over events and the ensuing harm, a degree of control that does not apply to omissions. Even if an individual has a duty to save a drowning person or extinguish a fire, refraining from doing so does not constitute control in the accepted sense, as in managing or influencing the sequence of events.[151]

5.1 The duty requirement in omissions

Kemnitzer and Segev argue that the duty requirement in omissions aims to establish a moral equivalence between acts and omissions. They contend that because omissions are generally considered less severe than acts in their antisocial energy, determination to act, and the causal distinction between the two, it is necessary to identify a specific duty that arises from a particular connection between the agent and the source of harm or the victim rather than relying on

149 Moore believes that even if A places his hands over his ears not to hear B's cries and avoid having to rescue him, A's action is classified as an act and not an omission because of A's bodily movement. I believe this is a counterexample to Moore's theory because it is more accurate to view this scenario as letting die rather than killing.

150 Mordechai Kremnitzer & Re'em Segev, *Omission in Criminal Law*, in TAMIR BOOK 197, 199–204 (Yosef Tamir & Ora Hirsh eds., 1999).

151 *Id.* at 203–04.

a general obligation.[152] This position contrasts with the liberty rationale, which posits that the duty to act seeks to limit the infringement on the agent's liberty. According to the liberty rationale, any duty to act, whether stemming from a general or specific duty, could form the basis for criminal liability in conduct or result offenses. By contrast, Kremnitzer and Segev's distinction between acts and omissions takes into account additional considerations, making it problematic to use a general duty to act for imposing criminal liability for omission.

5.2 Definition of acts and omissions

Kremnitzer and Segev argue that most cases can be accurately classified using the bodily movement test, but in complex scenarios involving both an act and an omission, the classification should be based on the dominance test. According to this test, if the dominant behavior leading to the outcome was an act, the behavior is classified as an act, but if the dominant behavior leading to the outcome was passive, the behavior is classified as an omission. Determining whether the behavior is active or passive relies on the rationales that differentiate between acts and omissions.[153]

Kremnitzer and Segev examined several cases demonstrating the application of the dominance test. One such case involves a placebo scenario where a physician provides a patient with a placebo (having no effect) instead of the curative medication, resulting in the patient's death.[154] Kremnitzer and Segev classify this as an omission rather than an act because the patient's death resulted from the omission of receiving the beneficial medication. But after analyzing the characteristics they consider relevant for identifying acts vs. omissions, it is still not clear why the dominant rationale should be the passive one in this case. First, from a causal point of view, the case involves active behavior that resulted in death. Providing the placebo caused the patient to forgo seeking the cure that could have saved his life. Although the physician did not cause the illness, he effectively prevented the patient from saving himself. This situation is analogous to a scenario where a physician steals a patient's medicine, resulting in the patient's death. Second, the administration of the placebo worsened the patient's condition, as without it, the patient would have received the curative medication and survived. Given these points, it is unclear why, according to the dominance test, this behavior should be classified as an omission.

Bullet firing incident: B is seriously injured by a bullet and is rapidly losing blood. Bystanders approach A, who is standing nearby, and inquire about the situation. Intentionally attempting to deceive them, A falsely states that B died.

152 *Id.* at 218–19.
153 *Id.*
154 *Id.* at 210.

Kremnitzer and Segev argue that from a causal perspective, this incident can be seen as an omission because it involves the failure to provide aid rather than directly causing the outcome. It also involves hypothetical causality. At the same time, A's behavior worsened B's situation because, with the approach of the bystanders, a new situation arose that could have enabled the victim's rescue. This new situation also represents the regular course of events that would have occurred; therefore, changing it exacerbates the status quo. Consequently, they classified this case as an act, not an omission.[155]

If so, why not classify the placebo scenario also as an act and not an omission? In the placebo scenario, the physician deceived the patient by providing a neutral medication that prevented the patient's rescue. It may be argued that the placebo case is more severe than the bullet-firing incident: if the agent misleading others to prevent the victim's rescue is considered an act, the physician deceiving the patient himself should also be regarded as an act rather than an omission. Moreover, it is difficult to understand why, from a causal perspective, it is not considered an act given that A caused the outcome and performed an act that led to the fatal result. The distinction between whether the outcome occurred by preventing rescue or as a direct result of the threat itself appears to be blurred.

Kremnitzer and Segev also discuss the legal implications of an agent withdrawing his rescue action, such as pulling back a rope thrown to someone in distress. According to their analysis, if the rescue action does not reach the victim, the positive and negative behaviors cancel each other out, resulting in an omission. But if the rescue action reaches the victim and is later withdrawn, it is considered an act, for otherwise the person who initially rescued the victim but then threw him back into the water would be viewed as merely omitting to help. The underlying rationale is that in the first case, the victim's situation remains unchanged, whereas in the second, the behavior worsens the victim's situation.

By contrast, when it comes to preventing rescue by another person, it does not matter whether the rescue action reached the victim or not. For example, if A threw a rescue rope to save B and C removed the rope, they classify this as an act by C, not an omission of not rescuing.[156]

In my opinion, the distinctions proposed by Kremnitzer and Segev may not necessarily align with the characteristics they presented to determine whether a certain behavior is classified as an act or an omission. It is unclear why removing assistance upon reaching the victim is considered a worsening of the existing situation, whereas it is seen as preserving the status quo when assistance is withdrawn before reaching the victim. It is possible to argue that if it is seen as a worsening of the existing situation when assistance reaches the victim, then assistance not reaching the victim should also be considered a worsening of

155 *Id.* at 212.
156 *Id.* at 213.

the existing situation. Furthermore, if the question whether or not the assistance reached the victim is significant, it should be relevant even when a third party obstructed the assistance. But according to Kremnitzer and Segev, when it comes to a third party obstructing the assistance, it does not matter whether or not the assistance reaches the victim.[157]

157 In my opinion, the more accurate distinction is the one proposed by McMahan. The relevant question is whether the shield still requires additional maintenance by the agent or not. If the shield still necessitates further maintenance (defined as ongoing actions by the agent to ensure that the shield continues to function as a protector), the removal of the shield is regarded as an omission; if the shield does not require additional maintenance, its removal is defined as an act. Additionally, in my opinion, the distinction is not related to causation or aggravating the current state but it is grounded in the fundamental concept of "interference" or "intrusion" into the safeguarded realm of the victim. When the agent prevents the victim or anyone else from taking items that rightfully belong to him, it is not seen as interfering or intruding into the victim's domain; therefore, it should be classified as an omission. For example, if C removes a rope (that belongs to him) thrown by A to rescue B, it can be seen as an omission rather than an act, because C isn't intruding into the victim's domain but merely withholding his own property. In contrast, if the rope thrown by A for B's rescue belongs to A or B and C removes it, this action constitutes interference or intrusion into the victim's domain, because the item providing assistance belongs to the victim or the helper.

3 The legal rationales

1. Introduction

In this chapter, I analyze the theories suggesting that the distinction between acts and omissions is rooted in legal reasoning rather than moral considerations. According to these viewpoints, even if there is no moral disparity between acts and omissions, it is appropriate for criminal law to differentiate them based on internal legal reasoning.

Five distinct legal rationales form the foundation for distinguishing between acts and omissions in criminal law. The first rationale argues that the duty requirement in omissions is necessary to resolve problems that may arise from the principle of legality. The second rationale states that the duty to act in omissions is derived from the principle of lenity, which favors interpretations of criminal laws that are more favorable to defendants.[1] According to the third rationale, the duty requirement in omissions is needed to resolve coordination challenges that indirect omission offenses may present.[2] The fourth rationale posits that the duty to act is essential to limit the potential criminalization of individuals in cases of omission.[3] The last rationale emphasizes the duty to act as a means to minimize encroachments on individual freedom,[4] and it was listed among the moral rationales presented in Chapter 2. Nevertheless, even if the liberty consideration does not constitute a moral factor, a legal system still needs to differentiate between acts and omissions to allow citizens to manage their lives according to their preferences.

1 Gideon Yaffe, *The Duty Requirement*, in THE ETHICS AND LAW OF OMISSIONS 199 (Dana Kay Nelkin & Samuel C. Richless eds., 2017).

2 JOEL FEINBERG, HARM TO OTHERS: THE MORAL LIMITS OF THE CRIMINAL LAW 159–81 (1984).

3 GEORGE P. FLETCHER, RETHINKING CRIMINAL LAW 604–05 (1978).

4 Yitzhak Kugler, *Criminal omissions*, 20 BAR-ILAN L. REV. 201, 214 (2003).

DOI: 10.4324/9781003380405-5

2. The principle of legality rationale

2.1 Leavens' critique of the duty requirement in omissions

As noted, according to certain causation theories, there is a distinct difference between acts and omissions. Acts can cause harm, whereas omissions do not. According to these theories, the duty to act serves as a substitute for the causal link in an omission. Furthermore, even within the causation theory proposed by Hart and Honoré, there are arguments supporting the continued distinction between acts and omissions, making omission culpable only if a concrete duty to act has been identified. From this viewpoint, the duty to act establishes or reveals the causal connection in cases of omission. Some, however, draw upon the same causation theory proposed by Hart and Honoré to argue that there is no real distinction between acts and omissions.

Hart and Honoré's causation theory focuses primarily on distinguishing between mere conditions for harm and the primary cause of it. According to this theory, a certain component is a mere condition but not the cause of harm when it does not deviate from what is normal and reasonable in a given situation. Conversely, a component is regarded as the primary cause of harm when it deviates from what is normal and reasonable in a given situation. For example, tossing a burning match and causing a house fire is considered the primary cause of harm because it deviates from what is normal and reasonable in the relevant situation. By contrast, the presence of oxygen in the air is a mere condition and not a primary cause because it exists regardless of whether the house catches fire. According to Hart and Honoré, the component that deviates from the normal and reasonable is the one that makes the difference, as it intervenes in the regular state of affairs and brings about change. As noted, Hart and Honoré argue that not only physical movement but also the absence of movement can deviate from what is normal and reasonable.[5] Thus, when a certain routine already prevents harm and an individual acts contrary to this routine, the omission caused the harm because it is the absence of action that deviates from what is normal and reasonable.

Thus, the distinction between acts and omissions is not a sharp causal difference, as both can lead to harm. Although there may be a greater number of acts than omissions that cause harm, this difference is quantitative rather than qualitative.

Based on Hart and Honoré's causation theory, Arthur Leavens argues that the duty requirement in omissions is unnecessary.[6] According to his approach, this doctrine rests on a false perception that there is a causal distinction between causing harm by an act and by an omission. If we acknowledge,

5 H. L. A. Hart and Tony Honoré, Causation in the Law 37–38 (1985).
6 Arthur Leavens, *A Causation Approach to Criminal Omissions*, 76 Calif. L. Rev. 547, 551 (1988).

however; that there is no qualitative difference between these types of causation, there is no genuine need for this doctrine in omissions.[7]

When a father does not feed his son, he causes the son's death. Similarly, when a person parks his car on a hill, the normal situation calls for using the brakes to prevent the car from rolling downhill. If the person does not use the brakes, he changes the existing routine or habit, causing a change in the world by the absence of physical movement.[8]

The question we ask regarding acts and omissions is the same: Is there a deviation from the normal and the reasonable? If there is a deviation, we can argue that the omission caused the harm, and if there is no deviation, the omission did not cause it.[9] Thus, even if there was no specific obligation imposed on the father to feed his son, if the son dies as a result of not being fed, the father may be charged with manslaughter or murder (depending on his mental state), having caused the son's death without any physical movement. In this case, the failure to feed the son deviates from the normal, the reasonable, and the status quo; therefore, it is the cause of the son's death. Thus, Leavens argues that the duty requirement in omissions only creates confusion regarding causation and should be abolished.

2.2 *The duty requirement in omissions*

Although Leavens argues that there is no need for a duty to act in omissions as there is no causal difference between acts and omissions, I maintain that a duty requirement in omissions is made necessary by the principle of legality. Because causation is rooted in a deviation from what is normal and reasonable, citizens must be aware of what is considered normal and reasonable and of the existing routine. The legislator, however, cannot assume that citizens indeed have such awareness. For example, although a citizen may be aware that if he does not rescue a person drowning in the sea, the person may die, it is not clear whether the citizen is aware that the failure to provide aid constitutes a deviation from the reasonable or the routine, and may not be conscious of the causal link in this case. Therefore, legislation is needed to warn citizens and clearly inform them in which cases they are exposed to prosecution and in which cases not. Simply informing the citizens that they are liable if a causal connection exists in an omission, based on an accepted routine or convention, does not constitute sufficient warning.

In the case of acts that cause harm, however, it may be assumed that the citizens are aware that they are the ones causing the change. Thus, when this change causes harm, they may be culpable because the regular perception of people is that an act is a change occurring in the world. Therefore, it may be

7 *Id.*
8 *Id.* at 572–75.
9 *Id.* at 583.

said that the duty to act defines for citizens what is the norm that has become a routine, allowing them to conduct themselves accordingly when, following this routine, a causal connection exists.

3. The rule of lenity rationale

3.1 Interpretation of the rule of lenity in result offences

Gideon Yaffe argues that the distinction between acts and omissions does not rely on a causal rationale because both can cause harm. He further argues that even without a duty to act, if A fails to save B from death and intends for B to die, it is equivalent to committing murder, just as if A actively carried out the murder by shooting B.[10] In the case of omission, however, criminal law provides a defense in the absence of a duty to act. Contrary to the causation approach, Yaffe contends that the duty requirement does not expand the possibility of criminal liability in omission; rather, it narrows it.[11]

According to Yaffe, the duty requirement in cases of omissions stems from the rule of lenity, which favors interpretations of criminal laws that are more lenient toward defendants.[12] For example, if an offense simply prohibits causing harm to another person, the straightforward interpretation is that the offense involves a physical action and the defendant can avoid committing the offense by doing nothing. But if we interpret the offense to also impose a duty on the defendant to take positive action to prevent harm, even without explicit instructions to do so, we would be stretching the interpretation beyond what the offense explicitly states, placing a heavier burden on the defendant. Such an expansive interpretation would go against the rule of lenity, which calls for a narrower understanding of the offense and a more lenient approach toward defendants.[13]

Consider a hypothetical scenario where we interpret the murder offense in a way that A can be held accountable for murdering B not only through direct acts like shooting or poisoning but also by failing to provide food to B, even if the offense does not explicitly relate to omissions. In this situation, A's conviction for murder, even without a specific duty to act, suggests that the omission of not feeding B indicates a disregard for the legal and moral considerations underlying the crime of murder. To support this argument, we would need to contend that the murder offense not only requires individuals to refrain from actions causing death but also imposes an obligation to take rescue actions. Adopting this interpretation, however, would conflict with the rule of lenity, which advocates an interpretation that minimizes the burden on the defendant.[14]

10 Yaffe, *supra* note 1, at 202.
11 *Id.*
12 *Id.* at 210–15.
13 *Id.* at 211.
14 *Id.* at 211–12.

3.2 The duty requirement in omissions

Therefore, Yaffe argues that to convict for omission behavior in an offense that does not explicitly mention the possibility of culpability in omission, a specific duty to act must be identified. For example, if a duty is imposed on a parent to feed his child, a reasonable interpretation of the murder offense would be that the accused can be convicted both when the harm is caused by an act and when it is caused by an omission to feed the child. This is a reasonable interpretation that does not violate the rule of lenity by minimizing the burden on the defendant. In cases where the parent did not feed his child, it may be argued that the omission to provide sustenance reflects a failure to ascribe sufficient weight to the legal and moral reasons underlying the crime of murder.[15]

The difficulty with this theory begins with the lack of clarity regarding why according to Yaffe, when it comes to prohibiting harm or death, the simple interpretation is not to perform a specific act. If the rationale is that refraining from a particular act imposes fewer restrictions on freedom than when a person is required to take rescue actions, this rationale appears to be similar to the liberty rationale. Moreover, according to Yaffe, if an offense explicitly prohibits omissions there is no need for a specific duty to act. For example, if the offense is formulated as "causing death or injury by an act or omission" or "harming by an act or omission," the accused could be convicted for any situation where he could have prevented the harm to the person and failed to do so, even without identifying a specific duty to act. In such cases, the interpretation would not narrow the scope because the provision explicitly allows convicting for omissions. This position is problematic because even when the offense is formulated as "act or omission," there is still a need to identify a specific duty to act in cases of omission.

4. The coordination problem rationale

4.1 The efficiency and justice challenges in a general duty to aid

Feinberg argues that there is no moral distinction between causing harm by action or by omission, nor is there a moral distinction between killing and letting die. When someone refrains from doing X although he could have done so and harm occurs as a result, the omission can be seen as the cause because that person had control over the occurrence of the harm.[16]

15 *Id.* at 212–13.

16 *Id.* at 174–75. According to Feinberg, for the failure to prevent harm to be considered a cause of the harm it must be an omission, and not every failure to prevent harm is considered an omission by Feinberg. Thus, A omitted doing X when:

1. A did not do X.
2. There was a reasonable opportunity for A to do X, and he was aware of this opportunity. This condition narrows the number of those who can be described as having omitted. It excludes those who were not present at the scene. If A was not present at the scene or if he was present but not aware that he could help B, it cannot be said that he failed to do X; therefore, we also cannot claim that he caused a specific harmful outcome.

Feinberg argues further that even if it is claimed that an omission cannot cause a harmful outcome, there is still no moral distinction between acts and omissions.[17] If we compare two cases in which the harm is significant and preventing it does not require high effort, we can see that there is no moral difference between them. In cases where preventing harm requires significant cost or effort, a moral distinction may be apparent,[18] but according to Feinberg, the difference lies not in moral considerations but in a legal-pragmatic distinction.[19]

Feinberg's primary argument centers on the notion that the absence of a general duty to rescue (beyond the scope of Good Samaritan laws), as opposed to the duty not to kill, arises from an internal legal problem that can be referred to as a "coordination problem."[20] He suggests dividing the coordination problem into two aspects: the efficiency and the justice problem.[21]

The efficiency problem is characterized by the lack of coordination between people if everyone were required to rescue another in need of help. This would lead to absolute inefficiency in the allocation of rescue resources, with many means and efforts going to waste. Thus, society should arrange for the duty of rescue to be performed in an organized and efficient manner through taxation, with the state allocating rescue resources according to need.

The justice problem arises from the fact that if a general duty of rescue were imposed, some citizens would invest more effort than others in rescue efforts. This problem can also be solved by the state allocating rescue resources through taxation.

When it comes to enacting a general prohibition against a certain act, such as the prohibition against killing, the matter of coordination between individuals does not arise. Generally, a person can easily comply with the rule not to kill, as refraining from killing usually does not require complex means or substantial expenses. By contrast, when dealing with a general rule to save lives, a coordination problem arises because it may lead to a situation where

---

3. It was reasonable to expect A to do X based on the existing circumstances for one of the following reasons:

a. People in A's position generally do X.
b. The duty to do X was imposed on A owing to a professional obligation or the existing relationship between him and the victim.
c. A moral obligation to do X was imposed on A owing to an early agreement or promise.
d. A moral obligation was imposed on A for another reason to carry out X.

Feinberg, *supra* note 2, at 159–61.

17 *Id.* at 166. "Assuming then that one causes harm to another by initiating a causal process that leads directly to a harmful result unless it is stopped short, and that one 'allows' or fails to prevent harm when one does not intervene to stop a causal process already begun . . . what does it matter morally whether A causes harm to B or fails to prevent harm to B when it is easy to do so?"

18 For example, I will have to pay $10,000 to avoid killing someone, but I will not have to pay $10,000 to prevent someone from dying. *Id.* at 167.

19 *Id.* at 169.

20 *Id.*

21 *Id.* at 169–71.

many people focus on a single rescue case, necessitating communication and cooperation between individuals.

According to Feinberg, when dealing with an unexpected duty to rescue, individuals are obligated to help, and this duty is not less severe than the duty not to kill. In such cases, resource allocation by the state is not useful. But when it comes to an expected duty to rescue, such as saving hungry people from starvation or people in dangerous situations where it is known that they may die or need help, the duty to rescue is imposed on the state through designated agents and we fulfill it through our tax payments.[22]

4.2 The duty requirement in omissions

As noted, according to Feinberg, there is no moral distinction between acts and omissions, nor is there a moral distinction between killing and letting die. But in cases involving death or bodily harm, it is not sensible to impose a general duty of rescue on citizens because such a duty would lead to challenging problems of coordination, inefficiency, and injustice.

It seems that according to Feinberg the duty requirement in cases of omission does not aim to resolve the issue of liberty or bridge the moral gap caused by the causal distinction between acts and omissions but to address the problem of coordination between citizens. By enacting a duty to act, the legislature clarifies the citizens' responsibilities more logically and reasonably, avoiding inefficiency and injustice.

Hence, the legislature imposes the duty to safeguard children from potential dangers specifically on their parents, not on other individuals, as this obligation is more efficient. In a similar vein, the duty to extinguish fires is assigned to firefighters, who specialize in these tasks, rather than to all citizens. Additionally, the legislature imposes specific duties on police officers to assist people in dangerous situations. Imposing particular duties on certain individuals in specific situations is often more effective and, at times, even more just than a general duty to prevent harm.

According to this perspective, even someone like Rachels, who finds no moral distinction between killing and letting die and claims that significant efforts are required to prevent the death of others, may consider that from a legal standpoint, it is appropriate to distinguish between acts and omissions.

5. Minimizing the number of defendants rationale

5.1 The asymmetrical challenge in identifying the primary wrongdoer

Fletcher raises an additional argument for distinguishing between acts and omissions in general and between killing and letting die in particular. The argument is rooted in the need for a duty to act when prosecuting omissions,

22 *Id.*

addressing the legal problem of identifying the primary wrongdoer among multiple potential offenders. When someone directly causes harm by an act, like A shooting B resulting in B's death, it is relatively easy to identify A as the primary offender because of his close causal connection to the outcome. But in situations of letting someone die, it becomes challenging to pinpoint the primary offender among all individuals involved. For example, if B drowns, and 100 people were aware of the situation but did nothing, it is difficult to determine who should be held primarily responsible. Without a doctrine of the duty to act, the legal system would need to rely on criminal law excuses, like necessity or duress, to establish the culpability of these individuals, but these excuses might not be suitable in many cases. Thus, the most efficient and effective approach to identify the primary offenders in omissions is through the duty requirement.[23]

5.2 *The duty requirement in omissions*

According to this rationale, we do not want to convict every bystander who did nothing to save the victim; therefore, we need a doctrine of duty to act in omissions. This doctrine enables us to identify the primary offender among potential offenders, just as a physical action allows us to identify the person with the closest causal connection to the outcome. The duty to act serves as a mechanism for ascertaining who bears the responsibility for rescuing a person, effectively isolating the primary offender among potential candidates.

In a slightly different context, Williams describes the minimizing the number of defendants rationale, explaining why a general duty to prevent harm is not imposed.

> Fifthly, and perhaps most important of all, the law enforcement agencies (including the courts) have their work cut out to deal with people who offend by active conduct. The prisons, it is scarcely necessary to recall, are packed with them. To extend the campaign by attempting to punish all (or large groups of) those who contribute to the evil result by failing to co-operate in the great endeavour of producing a happier world would exceed the bounds of possibility.[24]

Williams refers to the Good Samaritan law, but based on the points discussed earlier, it may be argued that the duty requirement in omissions also stems from this rationale.

23 Fletcher, *supra* note 3.

24 Glanville Williams, *Criminal Omissions—The Conventional View*, 107 LAW Q. REV. 86, 88–89 (1991).

6. The legal liberty rationale

6.1 The curtailment of liberty in prohibitions on omissions

The last approach explaining the distinction between acts and omissions in criminal law is based on the liberty rationale. As noted in Chapter 2, prohibiting an act that causes harm does not significantly affect the liberty of the agent. All the agent needs to do is refrain from performing a certain act, which does not substantially limit his liberty, as he usually retains the ability to continue with his routine activities. By contrast, a prohibition against omissions that cause harm does indeed impede the individual's liberty, as it would require the individual to cease his usual activities at any given moment to prevent harm to others. I presented this rationale as part of the moral rationales that differentiate between acts and omissions.[25]

Yet we need not regard the liberty rationale strictly as a moral one. Even if we argue that liberty is not an intrinsic moral value, we can still maintain that, from a legal perspective, there is a need to distinguish between acts and omissions due to pragmatic considerations. Thus, even if there is no moral distinction between acts and omissions, it is still not justifiable from a legal standpoint for criminal law to always impose a duty to act for the benefit of others, which would significantly curtail the individual's liberty to conduct his day-to-day life and spend his money however he wants.[26]

6.2 The duty requirement in omissions

From the point of view of the liberty rationale, the duty requirement in omissions arises from the understanding that without it, criminal law would infringe upon the individual's liberty to live his regular life and pursue his plans according to his choices and understanding.[27] Establishing a duty to act reduces the number of cases in which individuals would be compelled to take action and consequently minimizes the infringement on their freedom.

6.3 Implications of categorizing the liberty rationale as legal rather than moral

It may be asked whether it is justified to classify the liberty rationale as either moral or legal because the main argument is the same: the prohibition against omissions harms the individual's liberty more than does the prohibition against acts. In my opinion, from a moral perspective, this issue carries significant weight. When liberty is viewed not as a moral value but as a pragmatic-legal

25 See, among others, Richard Trammell, *Saving Life and Taking Life*, in KILLING AND LETTING DIE 290 (Bonnie Steinbock & Alastair Norcross eds., 1994); Kugler, *supra* note 4, at 211.

26 Kugler, *supra* note 4, at 214 (note 28).

27 *Id.* at 212–15.

one, citizens are legally required to aid others only in situations specified by law. This legal framework lists concrete circumstances for intervention. Morally, however, our actions should often extend beyond the confines of legal obligations. For example, even without a legal duty to rescue a stranger trapped in a fire, moral principles impel us to act and save the potential victim. Similarly, even if there is no legal requirement to donate money for someone's medical procedure, moral principles may obligate us to donate. At the same time, if we regard liberty as a moral value, in certain life-threatening situations, moral duty might not always demand that we intervene. In these cases, the moral value of liberty may take precedence over the imperative to preserve human life.

All theories based on legal rationales face challenges from various directions. First, if proponents of these rationales indeed maintain that there is no moral distinction between acts and omissions at all, they are susceptible to the criticism raised against the skeptical theories discussed in Chapter 1. Additionally, it is difficult to assume that the distinction between acts and omissions, which applies to all types of offenses, including those where the protected interest is of utmost importance, relies exclusively on a pragmatic-legal analysis.

Second, based on all these perspectives, the distinction between acts and omissions and between killing and letting die, from a descriptive standpoint, relies on the bodily movement test. For example, Feinberg argues that the duty to act in omissions arises from the coordination problem discussed earlier. The waste of resources can occur only when the legislature obligates individuals to physically intervene, move their bodies, and take action. In such a scenario, an absolute duty to rescue in all circumstances could result in a significant waste of resources, as everyone would be compelled to abandon their activities to save one person. Yet when it comes to prohibiting certain actions, according to Feinberg, there is no coordination problem; therefore, it is reasonable to expect citizens to adhere to such prohibitions.

If the definition of an act and an omission is based exclusively on the bodily movement test, it appears to contradict the legal rationale in certain cases. This is evident in Death by hypothermia 1, where B, who is on the brink of death from hypothermia, seeks to enter A's house to save himself. According to Feinberg, if A were to lock his door and prevent B from entering, A could be charged with manslaughter or even murder, depending on his mental state. Convicting A in this scenario, despite the lack of a specific legal duty to keep the door unlocked, does not lead to coordination problems or resource wastage. In my opinion, as explained earlier, this case is not fundamentally different from a typical non-rescue scenario, and A should be held accountable only if he had a legal duty to open his door.

This challenge also emerges in the case of Motion 1, where C fires a bullet at A but A is wearing body armor or is inside a vehicle, making him impervious to harm. A moves, leading to B's death. According to Feinberg, A could be held responsible for B's death despite the absence of any specific legal obligation for

A to remain stationary. This is because enforcing a rule requiring everyone in such scenarios to stay put would not create a coordination problem.

These legal challenges also arise concerning the rationale of minimizing the number of defendants, where the problem lies in identifying the main offender. In cases involving bodily movement, the offender can be identified, but as I have shown in Chapter 2, many of the cases involving bodily movement are not fundamentally different from those of initial non-rescue. Therefore, in my view, these rationales face significant difficulties when applied as an inclusive distinction to all types of offenses. This critique is also relevant to the legal liberty rationale, as discussed in Chapter 2.[28]

28 Another problematic point arising from these positions is that according to all of them, when we narrow down the number of cases in which a person is required to rescue, it would be possible to convict someone of homicide. For example, based on this view, if A saw B drown and did not save him despite being able to do so easily, A could be convicted of homicide or murder, depending on his mental element. I claim, however, that this contradicts our basic intuition regarding these cases.

4 The autonomy-based theory

1. Introduction

In this chapter, I argue for an alternative perspective that departs from the approaches examined in Chapters 2 and 3. This divergence manifests in both the rationale and the methodology employed to discern between acts and omissions. To illustrate this, I will explore the distinction between the prohibition against killing and the prohibition against letting die as a test case.

From the rationale standpoint, I argue that the key to this distinction lies in understanding the values (or interests) these prohibitions aim to protect. Previously mentioned theories often assumed that both prohibitions sought to protect the same values. I propose that the values underlying these prohibitions are distinct. The prohibition against killing encompasses broader and more significant values, particularly safeguards human life, constitutes our personal autonomy as individuals and as a society and enabling us to lead secure lives free from fear. By contrast, the prohibition against letting die does not guarantee our personal autonomy, although in certain instances, it may expand it.

Methodologically, my approach to distinguishing between killing and letting die diverges from the paths taken by many scholars in this field. Other scholars have sought to determine the moral distinction between the two by presenting specific instances of killing and letting die, then assessing their moral differentiation. My approach differs: rather than scrutinizing individual cases of killing and letting die to reach an explanation of the severity of the prohibition against killing compared to letting die, I argue that the severity of the prohibition should be derived from the values that form the basis of the prohibitions against killing and letting die. I show that comprehending the severity of the prohibition based on the values underlying it aligns both with rule utilitarian theory and the Hobbesian and Rawlsian social contract theory. I also point out the differences and similarities between the proposed rationale and others.

DOI: 10.4324/9781003380405-6

2. Presenting the argument

As noted, the distinction between the prohibitions against killing and letting die should be examined in light of the interests and values underlying these prohibitions. The prevailing assumption of the rationales presented is that the interests and values underlying the prohibition against killing are similar to those underlying the prohibition against letting die. But I contend that this foundational assumption is mistaken. The former are broader and more significant than the latter, and these values are at the basis of the distinction between the two prohibitions.

To assess the interests and values at the core of these prohibitions, we must ask two fundamental questions: First, what would happen in a world where there is no prohibition against killing? Second, what would happen in a world where there is a prohibition only against killing, and it was enforced, but not against letting die? These questions can clarify what each prohibition safeguards.

2.1 A world without a prohibition against killing

Without the prohibition against killing, humanity would deteriorate to a life of fear and self-defense, with constant dread of injury and death. Even if people managed to preserve their lives and avoid death, autonomy would be severely curtailed by constant fear and apprehension of death. This fear would undermine a different aspect of human autonomy, making it difficult for individuals to pursue their aspirations and plan their lives reasonably.

I do not refer here to Kantian autonomy, according to which a person is autonomous if he is rational and capable of legislating moral laws that can become universal principles, that is, a person who subordinates his will to moral principles of reason.[1] The autonomy I refer to includes two components: the ability of a person to live a life without constant fear and the need to defend himself, and the capacity to plan and realize his life, in accordance with Raz's idea that an autonomous person can be the author of his life.[2] Within

1 IMMANUEL KANT, GROUNDWORK OF THE METAPHYSICS OF MORALS 52–57 (Mary Gregor trans. & ed., Cambridge University Press 1998) (1785). For a critique of the Kantian concept of autonomy, see JOEL FEINBERG, HARM TO SELF: THE MORAL LIMITS OF THE CRIMINAL LAW 94–96 (1986). Feinberg challenges Kant's interpretation of the term "autonomy" because it is dissociated from the concrete individual. According to Feinberg, the essence of human autonomy lies in ascribing significance to one's choices and desires, rather than to abstract rationality and autonomy, which are associated with the general concept of "human" but disconnected from the individual.

2 JOSEPH RAZ, THE MORALITY OF FREEDOM 369–70 (1986). According to Raz as well, an individual's capacity to live without constant fear is a central aspect of his ability to shape the course of his life, that is, his ability to have autonomous personhood. See *Id.* at 373–76.

this framework, it is important to consider Thomas Hobbes' concept of the "state of nature":

> Whatsoever therefore is consequent to a time of Warre, where every man is Enemy to every man; the same consequent to the time, wherein men live without other security, than what their own strength, and their own invention shall furnish them withal. In such condition, there is no place for Industry; because the fruit thereof is uncertain: and consequently no Culture of the Earth; no Navigation, nor use of the commodities that may be imported by Sea; no commodious Building; no Instruments of moving, and removing such things as require much force; no Knowledge of the face of the Earth; no account of Time; no Arts; no Letters; no Society; and which is worst of all, continuall feare, and danger of violent death; And the life of man, solitary, poore, nasty, brutish, and short.[3]

According to Hobbes, in a state where every person is allowed to kill anyone else, human life would lose its significance. There would be no humanity, no culture, and no creativity, and worst of all, individuals would be constantly engulfed in fear of others killing them. The problem is not merely one of constant warfare. Beyond the loss of life, fear itself significantly impairs human autonomy, hindering human development. In his book On Hobbes, Kavka mentions this fact:

> It is vitally important to recognize the rational element in Hobbes's account of death-avoidance, for this makes clear that self-preservation solely for its own sake, that is, mere survival, is not the guiding value of Hobbes's philosophy. Thus, Hobbes's view of the importance of survival does not commit him to ignoring quality of life consideration in favor of mere longevity. Further . . . it is the rational fear of death that plays a critical role in Hobbes's political philosophy. This fear is the source of both the greatest threat to humankind—the war of all against all.[4]

Even if we do not reach the extreme natural state described by Hobbes—a state of "war of all against all"—there still exists a great concern that without the prohibition against killing, some individuals might attempt to attack, harm, or kill others out of hatred, gain, survival, etc., which would engender fear. And even if people refrain from attacking each other, likely, they would still fear potential aggression. This is how Robert Nozick describes the state of society in the absence of laws against killing, assault, rape, and the like:

> A system that allowed assaults to take place . . . would lead to apprehensive people, afraid of assault, sudden attack, and harm . . . To avoid such general apprehension and fear, these acts are prohibited and made punishable.[5]

3 Thomas Hobbes, Leviathan 89 (Richard Tuck ed., Cambridge University Press 2003) (1651).

4 Gregory S. Kavka, Hobbesian Moral and Political Theory 81–82 (1999).

5 Robert Nozick, Anarchy, State, and Utopia 66 (1974).

2.2 A world without a prohibition against letting die

Regarding the second question, it appears that even without imposing a prohibition against letting die, individuals' lives could still be reasonably maintained. Even if it were not an ideal human existence, it would not lead to the extreme natural state described by Hobbes or to a state less severe than that, and individuals would not live in constant fear of being killed. Although they would need to be cautious of potential dangers, their exposure to risks would generally depend on their actions, and they could lead prudent lives to avoid unnecessary risks.

This distinction indicates that the underlying values of the two prohibitions are different. The prohibition against killing seeks to protect much more fundamental interests and values related to the human ability of individuals and society to lead reasonable lives than does the prohibition against letting die. It upholds individual autonomy and ensures a life free from persistent fear, unlike the prohibition against letting die. Although the prohibition against letting die may, in some instances, enhance individual autonomy by rescuing a person in danger, it does not constitute it.

The distinction between killing and letting die is only a particular example of the broader difference between doing and allowing harm. The proposed rationale, however, is relevant also to harm that are not a matter of life and death. For example, the prohibition against actively causing harm is more stringent than that against causing harm by omission because the former protects individual autonomy significantly more than the latter. Similarly, with regard to property, causing harm by an act damages the autonomy of individuals and society much more than causing harm by omission.

3. Differences between autonomy-based theory and other rationales

The proposed rationale differs significantly from those mentioned in the previous chapters in that it does not center around a causal distinction between acts and omissions because both can lead to harm. Furthermore, it differs from the rationale based on harm to the victim, which argues that in the case of killing, the victim's situation worsens whereas in letting die, it merely does not improve. According to the proposed rationale, in both cases, the victim's situation worsens. Finally, the proposed rationale contrasts with Kamm's entitlement rationale, which suggests that killing is more severe than letting die because killing as opposed to letting die deprives the victim of life that could have been preserved independently from the agent's aid. According to the proposed rationale, this distinction, if present, does not necessarily have a significant moral value. Instead, the focus of the proposed rationale is on the effect of the act or omission on the victim's autonomy. The prohibition against killing protects autonomy by offering an opportunity for individuals and society to live without fear, whereas the prohibition against letting die fosters, at most, social solidarity.

The autonomy-based theory also sets itself apart from the liberty rationale, according to which, the difference between the two prohibitions is based on the extent to which liberty is infringed. By contrast, the autonomy-based theory argues that the distinction between the two prohibitions is not merely about the degree of liberty infringement but about the divergent fundamental values that underpin each prohibition. Under the liberty rationale, if there were no difference in the level of infringement of liberty between the two prohibitions, there would be no distinction between them. Conversely, the autonomy-based theory suggests that even if there were no difference in the level of infringement of liberty, there would still be a significant distinction between the two scenarios because the two prohibitions safeguard different interests.

Furthermore, the concept of liberty in the liberty rationale differs from the notion of liberty that I refer to in the autonomy-based theory. According to the liberty rationale, the distinction is intended to protect an individual's ability to lead his regular life without the legislator's interference or a constant obligation to rescue others. Following this approach, if there were no differentiation between killing and letting die, the individual's liberty would be violated, as the absence of distinction would hinder people from pursuing their desires. But in my view, such an infringement on liberty does not violate an individual's dignity as a human being or undermine his inherent humanity. From my perspective, without the distinction between the prohibition against killing and letting die, it may have been difficult for individuals to live a regular life, but it would not have prevented them from living a meaningful one. There would still be specific situations where individuals could exercise their liberty, for example, when it is evident that there is no need to rescue others or when the individual is incapable of doing so. Moreover, even if the absence of distinction may have hindered individuals from living a regular life, it would still allow them to save the lives of others. The ability to save lives has significant implications because it provides individuals the opportunity to actualize their abilities in these situations.

The autonomy-based theory, however, focuses on individuals' ability to live a life free from fear and constant threat from other citizens. This is the primary liberty that the autonomy infringement theory seeks to protect; it is an essential one because any violation of it significantly degrades the individual's humanity and dignity. Without this primary liberty and the basic sense of security it affords, individuals would suffer severe infringement on their capacity to plan their lives and fulfill their aspirations, in other words, to be the authors of their own lives.

The means to safeguard these aspects of liberty is to impose a prohibition against killing. By contrast, without a prohibition against letting die, individuals could still lead reasonable lives with personal autonomy and a basic sense of security. Consequently, this prohibition carries less weight, and to convict the accused, a specific duty to act must be identified.

4. Rule utilitarianism and social contract theory in light of the autonomy-based theory

Within the framework of the autonomy-based theory, it may be argued that not every act of killing violates the interests protected by the prohibition against killing, as some killings may not violate our sense of security and autonomy. But even if a particular act of killing does not violate the interests protected by the prohibition, it would still be more severe than letting die because the severity of the act is measured in relation to the severity of the prohibition, and the severity of the prohibition itself is measured in relation to the significance of the interests it safeguards. My position is grounded both in rule utilitarianism theory and social contract theory, as illustrated in the following.

4.1 Rule utilitarianism

The theory of utilitarianism embraces two schools of thought: rule utilitarianism and act utilitarianism. Act utilitarianism defines an act as moral if it brings about the most beneficial result under the relevant circumstances. Any other result is considered immoral.[6] Rule utilitarianism defines an act as moral if it follows a set of rules that, if accepted by all (or almost all) of society, would result in the most beneficial outcome. An act that does not follow such a set of rules is considered immoral.[7]

The primary distinction between rule and act utilitarianism is that act utilitarianism measures the moral value of actions directly, whereas rule utilitarianism measures the moral value of actions in relation to a set of rules.[8] Act utilitarianism prohibits theft because stealing is less beneficial than not stealing; rule utilitarianism prohibits theft because it is contradictory to the rule "thou shalt not steal," and general acceptance of this rule would produce more beneficial results than if it were not accepted.

One of the reasons for adopting rule utilitarianism over act utilitarianism has to do with the fact that often act utilitarianism conflicts with our moral intuitions. I will provide two examples to illustrate this point:

1. Prima facie, act utilitarianism suggests that it would be permissible to kill an innocent person if that act leads to the best overall outcome among the available alternatives.[9] By contrast, rule utilitarianism argues that it is prohibited to kill an innocent person even if it would result in the best consequences because it contradicts the general rule that prohibits killing innocent people.[10]

6 J. S. Mill, Utilitarianism (Roger Crisp ed., Oxford University Press 1998) (1861). See also J. J. C. Smart & Bernard Williams, Utilitarianism: For and Against 9 (1973).

7 Brad Hooker, Ideal Code, Real World: A Rule-Consequentialist Theory of Morality 32 (2000).

8 Hence, some refer to act utilitarianism as "direct utilitarianism" and to rule utilitarianism as "indirect utilitarianism." See Brad Hooker, *Rule-Consequentialism*, 99 Mind 67 (1990) (hereinafter, Hooker 1990).

9 Philippa Foot, Morality, *Morality, Action and Outcome*, in Morality and Objectivity 23–25 (Ted Hondrich ed., 1985). Foot does not endorse utilitarianism and raises objections to our intuitions, primarily against act utilitarianism.

10 See Hooker 1990, *supra* note 8, at 69–70. Additionally, rule utilitarianism argues that a certain rule that prohibits killing except in cases where it would save a larger number of people would not be good overall because people would be unsettled by the fact that others could kill them in certain situations, causing them to act accordingly. Therefore, the rational rule is "do not kill the innocent" even if it saves a larger number of people.

2. Act utilitarianism can demand actions that are impossible for individuals to accomplish. For example, a person may be obligated to donate all his money to save people at risk of starvation because such an act would lead to the best consequences. But such a requirement contradicts our moral intuitions, which emphasize the importance of enabling individuals to exercise their abilities and use their resources. If someone were forced to donate all his money, he would be unable to fulfill that aspiration. Hooker argues that, in contrast to act utilitarianism, within the framework of rule utilitarianism, we do not isolate each specific case and analyze which action would result in the best outcome. Rule utilitarianism examines what would occur if everyone were to assist people in need of help. In a situation where everyone contributed to those in need, the requirement for financial contributions would likely be much less onerous.[11]

I argue that rule utilitarianism can provide a solution to the challenge presented by the fact that killing does not always result in loss of individual autonomy. Rule utilitarianism defines the ideal system of rules as one whose acceptance by society would be the most beneficial. But there appears to be a hierarchy even within this system. A rule that protects the basic interests of society carries more weight, and its violation produces a greater level of guilt than one that protects lesser interests. Because the prohibition against killing protects more fundamental interests, it is a more important and morally significant rule than the prohibition against letting die. These prohibitions must be assessed by considering the rule whose acceptance would prove most beneficial to society. Since the rule prohibiting killing is more stringent than the one against letting die, killing is considered to be more severe than letting die, regardless of the results of the act itself.

4.2 Social contract

According to social contract theory, an act is moral if people would agree to it in a hypothetical contract, and immoral if they would oppose it under such a contract.[12] The social contract theory embraces several schools of thought,[13] of which those of Hobbes and Rawls are dominant ones. The autonomy-based theory is consistent with both.

11 *Id.* at 72.

12 Ronald Dworkin criticized Rawls' social contract theory for relying on the hypothetical contract, which in practice is not a contract at all. See Ronald Dworkin, *The Original Position*, 40 U. Chi. L. Rev. 500 (1973).

13 See Will Kymlicka, *The Social Contract Tradition*, in A Companion to Ethics 186 (Peter Singer ed., 1993).

4.2.1 The Hobbesian social contract

A central source of the theory of social contract is Thomas Hobbes' book *Leviathan*,[14] where Hobbes refers, among others, to the moral norms that bind us, their origins, and their justifications.[15] According to the Hobbesian social contract, interpersonal moral obligations are conventions. The rationale behind these conventions is rooted in the willingness of individuals to contractually accept certain moral limitations upon themselves to maximize their personal benefit. According to Hobbes, the prohibition against harming another does not stem from natural law but from a social contract. Most proponents of the social contract theory point out that the social contract is a hypothetical one, whose purpose is to validate interpersonal moral obligations.[16]

According to Gauthier, Hobbesian social contract theory rests on three principal assumptions.[17] First, the world is devoid of moral facts; that is, there are no natural duties that require a person to perform or not to perform specific acts. Second, a person is a rational being as his actions are determined by his goals. Third, an individual's goals are rooted in self-interest, meaning that a person endeavors, above all else, to advance his interests and benefit himself. His primary aim is to safeguard his life, driven by both the fear of death and the desire to pursue his objectives.

The question arising from this theory is: If there are no natural duties that obligate us, and individual's goal is to promote his own interests, why do we restrain ourselves from doing certain things? To answer this question, Hobbes engaged in an intellectual experiment in which he asked how the world would look without a central government that required and prohibited certain acts. The absence of government is what Hobbes called the state of nature.[18] Hobbes claimed that the state of nature would lead to total war in which every man is an enemy to everyone else. In this state, people would be in constant competition, among other things, because of the limited resources of the world. Even if a person were willing to settle for his own share, he could not be certain that his fellows would make the same compromise. Therefore, everyone would live in constant fear of being killed, a condition that would lead to widespread killing as people would prefer to kill rather than be killed.

14 Hobbes, *supra* note 3.

15 In *Leviathan*, Hobbes dealt with the philosophical question of the source of the human obligation to obey the political authority, but through his exploration of the political question, Hobbes extends his focus to moral theory.

16 David Gauthier, *The Social Contract as Ideology*, 6 PHIL. & PUB. AFFS. 130, 135 (1977). Nevertheless, some argue that moral norms are the result of a contract between actual individuals. See, for instance, GILBERT HARMAN, EXPLAINING VALUE AND OTHER ESSAYS IN MORAL PHILOSOPHY 66–68 (2000). For an explanation of Hobbes's approach, see also JEAN HAMPTON, HOBBES AND THE SOCIAL CONTRACT TRADITION (1986).

17 David Gauthier, *Thomas Hobbes: Moral Theorist*, 76 J. PHIL. 547 (1979).

18 Hobbes, *supra* note 3, at 86–90.

The result would be war of all against all.[19] Thus, in the natural state, human life is precarious, wretched, and short. Because individuals are rational beings who seek their own well-being, they desire to escape this state. The means to achieve it is through a social contract where individuals restrain themselves from engaging in certain actions that could lead them back to the natural state. The condition of each person under the contract is superior to his condition in the natural state.

Considering that the rationale for the social contract is to rescue humans from the natural state, the first principle to be adopted is the prohibition against killing. Without this restriction, individuals would revert to the natural state, living lives filled with fear.[20] By contrast, the principle requiring the rescue of individuals may indeed be accepted as part of a hypothetical contract, but in a more limited way, and in any case, it carries less weight than the prohibition against killing. The reasoning behind this is that even without an obligation to rescue others, society can survive and life remains livable.

Harman also argued that the rationale distinguishing the prohibition against killing from the prohibition against letting die is based on a convention according to which there is an agreement between rich and poor, strong and weak, each member of these groups committing not to kill the other and to provide help in certain cases without requiring significant expenses or efforts. This convention is accepted because the prohibition against killing benefits everyone. By contrast, the prohibition against letting die benefits primarily the poor and the weak, as the rich and strong require no such assistance. The compromise is a compelling prohibition on killing and a limited prohibition on letting die: the rich and strong agreed to help in certain cases so that the poor and the weak would agree to the compelling prohibition on killing.[21]

My argument differs and does not rely on the existence of various groups in society with different powers; rather, it claims that even if everyone had equal power, it is still appropriate to make this distinction. Not only is the prohibition against killing more comprehensive than that against letting die, but it is also morally more stringent because it safeguards more fundamental interests.

19 *Id.* at 88–89.

20 Hobbes also noted that the fundamental principle is to pursue peace, and the principle derived from this is the prohibition against killing, provided that everyone accepts the principle. "From this fundamentall Law of Nature, by which men are commanded to endeavour Peace, is derived this second law; that a man be willing, when others are so too, as farre-forth as for peace and defence of himselfe he shall think it necessary, to lay down this right to all things; and be contented with so much liberty against other men, as he would allow other men against himselfe. For as long as every man holdeth this right, of doing anything he liketh; so long are all men in the condition of warre." *Id.* at 92.

21 Harman, *supra* note 16, at 69.

4.2.2 The Rawlsian social contract

In *A Theory of Justice*, Rawls presents a theory that purports to serve as a basis for the foundations of the national government. Rawls assumes that in each society there are shared and conflicting interests. Shared interests stem from the realization that cooperation is preferable to each individual acting alone. Conflicting interests arise because each individual is not indifferent to how rights and obligations are distributed between the parties.[22] For this reason, Rawls argues that it is necessary to create several principles to allow for the just distribution of rights and obligations among individuals as well as the proper distribution of resources.

Rawls uses the social contract to discover and justify the principles that serve the basic institutions of society.[23] These are the fundamental principles for the distribution of rights, obligations, and resources between members of society that free and rational people, concerned with furthering their interests, would accept in an initial position behind the veil of ignorance.[24] According to Rawls, this is not a real contract between particular people but rather an intellectual experiment designed to determine which principles would be accepted by people behind the veil of ignorance.[25] The fundamental idea behind the veil of ignorance is that individuals in this position do not know anything about their situation in society or their economic status. They are unaware of whether they are wise or foolish, poor or wealthy.[26] When no one knows their true position, absolute equality exists, and therefore, the laws formulated behind the veil of ignorance are fair.[27]

Rawls argues that behind the veil of ignorance, people would choose two basic principles: (1) each person has an equal right to the comprehensive basic liberties, and (2) social and economic inequalities can be allowed only if they benefit the least advantaged.[28]

Rawls maintains that the first principle takes precedence over the second, meaning that the government must not infringe on a person's basic liberties to improve his economic situation; this can be done only in favor of the basic liberties themselves.[29] When Rawls speaks of a person's basic liberties, he refers to political liberty (the right to vote and hold public office), freedom of speech and assembly, freedom of conscience and thought, and freedom of the person,

22 John Rawls, A Theory of Justice 4 (Rev. ed. 1999).
23 *Id.* at 10.
24 *Id.*
25 *Id.* at 11–14.
26 *Id.*
27 *Id.* at 17.
28 *Id.* at 53.
29 *Id.* at 53–54. For criticism, see H. L. A. Hart, *Rawls on Liberty and Its Priority*, 40 U. Chi. L. Rev. 534 (1973).

which includes freedom from psychological oppression, physical assault, and dismemberment.[30]

I propose that Rawls' idea that people behind the veil of ignorance would choose these principles, with priority granted to the first principle, has implications even for the distinction between killing and letting die. As noted, without the prohibition against killing, people's lives would be filled with fear, which impairs their autonomy. For our purposes, the key implication of this fact is that in a situation where there is no prohibition against killing, there is a general infringement on the comprehensive basic liberties that Rawls outlined: no freedom of voting, no freedom of speech, no freedom of thought, and clearly, no freedom from psychological coercion and physical attacks. Therefore, to preserve these liberties, people behind the veil of ignorance would choose to prohibit killing.

Nickel makes a similar argument:

> [C]reating an effective system of protections of security rights through the criminal law is one of the most important things that can be done to make possible the enjoyment of other liberty below. If those who would invade people's liberties and rights are unrestrained in their ability to threaten death, harm, violence, and loss of property, few if any liberties can be enjoyed. Security rights, like due process rights, are essential building blocks for a system of liberty.[31]

Yet the preservation of these liberties is not dependent on a rule obligating the rescue of others from danger. Such a rule has no bearing on political liberty, freedom of speech, freedom of thought, and freedom from psychological oppression and physical assault. I do not suggest that people in the original position behind the veil of ignorance would not agree to a rule requiring rescue in certain situations, but such a rule, even if accepted, would be much more limited and minor than the prohibition against killing. Rawls suggests that people in the original position would agree to a rule requiring rescue because it would improve people's quality of life even without the need for concrete assistance. According to Rawls, the real value in such a rule is not in the actual assistance but in the security that comes with knowing that such assistance would be made available.

> A sufficient ground for adopting this duty is its pervasive effect on the quality of everyday life. The public knowledge that we are living in a society in which we can depend upon others to come to our assistance in difficult circumstances is itself of great value . . . The primary value of

30 Rawls, *supra* note 22, at 53.
31 James W. Nickel, *Rethinking Rawls's Theory of Liberty and Rights,* 69 Chi.-Kent L. Rev. 763, 768 (1994).

> the principle is not measured by the help we receive but rather by the sense of confidence and trust in other men's good intentions and the knowledge that they are there if we need them.[32]

Rawls' argument regarding the duty to rescue can help us better understand the prohibition against killing. Just as people would accept the prohibition against letting die because it significantly affects their sense of security and everyday psychological state by the knowledge that they, too, would be saved if in danger, they would accept the prohibition against killing with even greater willingness. The knowledge that killing is prohibited would provide an even greater sense of security than the obligation to rescue and enormously improve their everyday psychological state.

Returning to the difficulty of different types of killings: some killings do not infringe on the protected interests of the prohibition, or perhaps not every case of killing is truly different from one of letting die. The response to this argument is clear: according to the theory of social contract, specific cases are not individually assessed; rather, we evaluate the severity of actions based on the general rule established within the framework of the social contract. A Hobbesian social contract is a hypothetical one that would be accepted in the state of nature, and a Rawlsian social contract is a hypothetical one accepted in the initial position behind the veil of ignorance. As demonstrated earlier, in both hypothetical social contracts, the fundamental accepted general rule is the prohibition against killing, not the duty to rescue because the interests protected by the former are broader and more significant.

In sum, the proposed rationale may be understood not only as a moral one but also as a legal one. As noted, it can be regarded as a moral rationale based on the theories of rule utilitarianism and social contract. However, even if we disagree on them, it remains appropriate to differentiate between killing and letting die from a legal perspective based on these theories. For example, a supporter of Kantian moral theory may cite the individual's intention and argue that although there may not be a moral distinction between killing and letting die with the same intentions, from a legal standpoint, it makes sense to make this distinction because the goal of criminal law is to maintain social order and safeguard individuals' autonomy.[33]

5. The definition derived from the autonomy-based theory

Based upon the preceding discussion, it is clear that the definitions of killing and letting die should align with the autonomy-based theory: killing must

32 Rawls, *supra* note 22, at 297–98.

33 See Andrew Ashworth, Principles of Criminal Law 25–28 (2006). Regarding rule utilitarianism, Brandt explicitly argued that this distinction can be made. See R. B. Brandt, *Conscience (Rule) Utilitarianism and the Criminal Law*, 14 Law & Phil. 65, 66 (1995).

be defined in a way that, by prohibiting it, allows for a life free from fear that protects autonomy for all members of society and letting die in a way that embraces the values of assistance, contributing to the expansion of personal autonomy.

To establish a fundamental sense of security without fear, the prohibition against killing must prevent intrusion into the individual's protected space. Intrusion into another individual's life is caused primarily by creating a risk or removing a shield that belongs to the individual. Therefore, the definition of killing is sometimes intertwined with the issue of ownership, specifically, who owns the shield that was removed. The main idea is to create a safe space, an inviolable zone, secure from intrusion. If a person's death results from such an intrusion, it is classified as a killing. In such cases, it would not be necessary to identify a specific legal duty to act to convict the agent. But if a person dies not as a consequence of an intrusion into his protected space, the case is categorized as letting die.

Regarding these definitions, it should be noted that some cases involve bodily movements that do not categorized as killing because they did not breach a protected space. Conversely, there are cases that do not involve bodily movement that are still categorized as killing because they involve such a breach.

Ownership of the shield should not be viewed as a matter of personal property rights. The removal of a shield belonging to the victim should not be classified as killing due to the loss of personal property. Rather, what matters is that individuals protect themselves primarily through their bodies and their property, making the removal of a shield belonging to the victim infringe the fundamental interests underlying the prohibition against killing.[34]

5.1 *The implications of the ownership of the shield*

5.1.1 *Who owns the shield: the agent or the victim?*

A fundamental principle is that when the perpetrator creates a risk, it leads to categorizing the act as killing. For example, when A drowned B, resulting in his death, A created the risk, and there was a direct infringement of B's protected space by physically harming his body. Therefore, A's act is categorized

34 The property context I propose does not rest on the view of property as a form of libertarian sovereignty, where private property is preserved to maximize an individual's negative liberty, seen as a prerequisite for self-development. The autonomy-based theory I propose is not built on the value of property as "personality," that is, the notion that certain resources of an individual are part of his "self." The property I refer to is distinct and serves as a barrier against intrusion into the individual's protected sphere. This defense is primarily required not against governmental tyranny but against other individuals. In my understanding, in their protected sphere, individuals can live without fear, ensuring a reasonable degree of security to sustain life.

as killing.[35] Conversely, when A observed B drowning and did not provide assistance (even if a causal connection to B's death existed), A did not create the risk of drowning; therefore, there was no infringement of B's protected space, and as a result, A's conduct is categorized as letting die.

Here are two examples that clarify my position on the removal of the shield and the relevance of its ownership.

1. **Mid-ocean escape 1:** B is about to drown in the middle of the ocean when he sees A in his boat, observing him. B swims toward A's boat to be rescued. A is unwilling to save B and steers his boat toward the shore. As a result, B drowns.[36]
2. **Motion 1**: C shoots at A. A is wearing body armor or is inside a vehicle and would not have been harmed by the bullet, but A moves, causing the bullet to hit and kill B.

I claim that neither case should be categorized as killing but rather as letting die. In both scenarios, A removed the shield belonging to himself, not to the victim. In Mid-ocean escape 1, A moved his own boat, which effectively acted as a shield against B's drowning. In Motion 1, A moved his body or his car, which served as a shield against C's bullet.[37] We can see the moral implications if we slightly modify the cases:

3. **Mid-ocean escape 2:** A stands on B's boat and steers it toward the shore. As a result, B drowns.
4. **Motion 2:** A seizes B and places him between himself and C, causing C's bullet to hit B.

These two cases should be categorized as killing, not as letting die because A removed the shield that belonged to the victim. The crucial difference between cases 1/2 and 3/4 lies in the ownership of the shield: in 1 and 2 the shield belongs to the agent, whereas in 3 and 4 it belongs to the victim.

The distinction between removing a shield belonging to the agent and one belonging to the victim is not technical but substantive. When the agent removes a shield belonging to himself, it is not perceived as an intrusion into the victim's protected space, but when he removes a shield belonging to the victim, it constitutes such an intrusion. The interference in this space violates

35 There may be situations where the creation of risk is not directly carried out on the human body, for example, planting a bomb that causes the deaths of people. However, even in these cases as well, there is a direct intrusion into the protected sphere of the individual.

36 Another example is Death by hypothermia 1, which was presented as a critique of the liberty rationale.

37 I do not argue that this is an act of killing, but A should be acquitted based on some defense or another. My argument is that this case falls within the scope of cases where A did not save B but let him die. In this case, A can be convicted only if a legal duty to act exists.

the norm that safeguards individual autonomy; therefore, we condemn it more severely.[38]

In some cases, an agent may not be guilty of manslaughter even if he removed a shield resulting in the victim's death because of the absence of legal causation. In these situations, although the removal of the shield may have been a necessary condition for the outcome, the perpetrator is not liable for manslaughter because of the remoteness of the act from the harm. For example, if A steals money intended for buying medicines and life-saving equipment for a hospital, and as a result, patients die for lack of medication and equipment, A may not be guilty of manslaughter because of the absence of legal causation. The distinction between removing a shield belonging to the victim and removing one belonging to the agent, as noted, is applicable only when factual and legal causation exists.

5.1.2 The shield belongs to a third party or to no one

What is the legal outcome when the shield does not belong to either the agent or the victim but to a third party or to no one? In this situation, is the removal of the shield classified as killing or as letting die? In other words, do we need a duty to act to convict the agent?

In the case of the shield belonging to a third party, we must differentiate between a situation when the third party granted the right of use to the victim and one in which it did not. In the first situation, we can perceive the shield as belonging to the victim; therefore, this case will be categorized as killing. Thus, if a hospital connects B to a life support machine and A disconnects the machine, it is categorized as killing because A removed a shield that was granted to B by the hospital. By contrast, if the agent

38 In the theory I propose, the significance of property is rooted in the notion that individuals' resources, together with their bodies, form a safeguarded realm. This enables a person to lead a reasonably secure life, achieving a minimum level of security. Consequently, distinguishing between resources that delineate an individual's protected sphere and those that do not would be a logical step. According to this distinction, there may be cases in which the agent removed a shield that belonged to him, but we would categorize the case as killing rather than letting die, for example, where B jumps off the roof of a building, aware that A's net is stretched at the bottom and can save him. If A removes the net and B dies, although the net is A's resource, we may not require a duty to act to convict A. Not every resource belonging to an agent is a resource that defines his protected space. In this situation, it may be argued that the net does not define the protected space of A, and therefore, its removal is categorized as killing. By contrast, a person's home defines his protected space, so if A closed his door and B died of exposure as a result, the case would be classified as letting die, requiring a duty to act to convict A. It may be argued that within the framework of a hypothetical social contract, to ensure life without fear, we determine the conditions under which certain resources constitute a protected space for the individual. Some resources, like a person's home, always constitute a protected space, and others do so only in certain cases.

removes a shield belonging to a third party that did not grant the right of use to the victim, the situation is more ambiguous. For example, what would be the legal outcome if A stands on a boat belonging to C and steers it toward the shore, resulting in B's death? The answer appears to depend on the need of the agent for the shield. The greater the agent's need for the shield, the less likely we are to view his behavior as killing, and vice versa. In situations where the victim's need for the shield is greater than the agent's, the victim possesses a "need right" over the shield.[39] In such cases, removing the shield constitutes an intrusion into the protected space of the victim. If both the victim and the agent have a significant need for the shield, they both possess a "need right" over it, and neither party has a stronger right over the shield; therefore, the right of use is equally given to both. In this case, there is no intrusion into the protected space of the victim; as the right is equally given to both parties, there is no protected space from the outset.[40]

The scenario in which the shield does not belong to anyone is more complex. Consider a case where an agent pilots away an ownerless boat instead of allowing the drowning victim to climb into it. Although the answer here may also rely on each party's need for the shield, our legal and moral intuition may lead us to a different conclusion. Consider the following scenario:

Death from disease: B faces a life-threatening disease that can be cured by a costly medical procedure. B discovers a treasure hidden outside his house that can finance the procedure, bringing him much delight. A also learns about the treasure and quickly digs it up, using it for his own needs. Consequently, B is unable to afford the procedure and dies.

In this scenario, both parties have an equal right to the treasure, B having the greater need. Still, A's act should be categorized as letting die. To convict A of manslaughter or murder, we would need to identify a duty to act—a specific obligation requiring A to rescue B, whereas if B had been the owner of the treasure, A's act would be categorized as killing, and he could be guilty of manslaughter or murder, irrespective of a duty to act.

Thus, we can distinguish between situations where the shield belongs to a third party and cases where it is ownerless. When the shield belongs to a third party, categorizing the act depends on the "need right" of the agent and the victim. When the shield does not belong to anyone, the categorization is independent of the "need right."

39 The term "need right" originates in Draper's article. See Kai Draper, *Rights and the Doctrine of Doing and Allowing*, 33 Phil. & Pub. Affs. 253, 271 (2005). Draper uses this concept to argue that even when the shield belongs to the agent, moving the shield could be regarded as killing if the victim's need surpasses the agent's.

40 Compare: Draper, *Id.* at 274.

Kamm[41] and McMahan[42] also defined killing and letting die in cases of shield removal, tied to the property ownership of the shield, but there is a crucial distinction between the rationales underlying their definition. According to Kamm, the difference between killing and letting die lies in an individual's right over his body and resources. Every person has such a right but does not possess the same right over another person's body and resources.

According to McMahan, when A removes a shield that he initially placed, we do not consider him as the one who created the threat. Therefore, his causal connection to the outcome is weaker than when A removes a shield placed by someone else. In the latter case, we view A as the one who created the threat that led to the harm; thus, his causal connection to the outcome is more direct.

According to the autonomy-based theory, the property ownership aspect stems from the need to establish a protected space for individuals, safeguarding them from fear and harm, while preserving their autonomy. Consequently, according to this theory, A drowning B is more severe than A failing to rescue B because drowning involves a violation of B's protected space, infringing on the norm that protects human autonomy. In letting die, there is no intrusion into the individual's protected space and no violation of the norm that protects human autonomy. The emphasis here is not the violation of property rights but rather the creation of a protected space, where life can be lived with reasonable autonomy and without fear.

5.1.3 The separation of Siamese twins: act or omission

This position finds support even in an English legal precedent dealing with the separation of Siamese twins. Jodie and Mary were born as Siamese twins. Each had a brain, heart, kidneys, hands, legs, and other organs, but Mary's heart and kidneys received their blood and oxygen supply from Jodie's body. If Mary had been born alone, she would not have survived.

The parents and the court faced the following medical situation: If no surgery to separate the twins was performed, both of them would die within a few months because Jodie's heart could not sustain the burden. If the twins were

41 F. M. Kamm, Morality, Mortality: Rights, Duties, and Status (Volume 2) 28–29 (1996).

42 Jeff McMahan, The Ethics of Killing: Problems at the Margins of Life 381 (2002); For another position that establishes the distinction between acts and omissions and between killing and letting die based on property rights, see also Draper, *supra* note 39, at 269–70. This is also the explicit position of Judith Jarvis Thomson. See Judith Jarvis Thomson, *Physician-Assisted Suicide: Two Moral Arguments*, 109 Ethics 497, 503–04 (1999). According to Thomson, if A provides protection to B through his efforts or resources, the categorization of the removal as letting die applies only if A was not obligated to provide that protection. If A was obligated to provide the protection to B, the removal of the protection is categorized as killing.

separated, Jodie would continue to live, but Mary would die immediately. The parents of the twins could not agree to the surgery since they could not decide to kill one twin to save the other.

During the legal proceedings, the question arose whether performing the surgery would be permissible or whether it would amount to murdering Mary. The English court considered, among others, the distinction between acts and omissions, that is, whether the separation of the twins would be classified as an act or an omission. Some argued that the separation of the twins was similar to turning off a life-support machine (as Jodie provided blood and oxygen to Mary), and according to the Bland legal precedent,[43] turning off life support is considered an omission, not an act. The court did not accept this analogy because to separate the twins, it would not be sufficient to treat Jodie's organs, but it would be necessary to invade Mary's body. Therefore, it was impossible to classify the behavior as an omission, and it had to be regarded as an act.

> I set out earlier (I realize with embarrassment a lot earlier) how this operation would be performed. The first step is to take the scalpel and cut the skin. If it is theoretically possible to cut precisely down the mid-line separating two individual bodies, surgically it is not feasible. Then the doctors have to ascertain which of the organs belong to each child. That is impossible to do without invading Mary's body in the course of that exploration. There follow further acts of separation culminating in the clamping and then severing of the artery. Whether or not the final step is taken within Jodie's body so that Jodie's aorta and not Mary's aorta is assaulted, it seems to me to be utterly fanciful to classify this invasive treatment as an omission in contra-distinction to an act.[44]

6. The duty requirement in omissions

The autonomy-based theory offers an alternative rationale to the duty requirement in cases of omission. According to this rationale, the duty requirement does not aim to resolve the infringement on the individual's liberty or the absence of a direct causal link in omissions. Rather, the duty to act addresses the moral vulnerability inherent in omissions compared to actions, manifested in the disparity between fundamental values underlying prohibitions against killing and letting die. As noted, killing violates the norm that enables us to live without constant fear and constitutes our autonomy, whereas letting die does not.

In certain cases, however, an individual's autonomy can be significantly compromised if he knows he will not receive assistance in given situations.

43 See Airedale NHS Trust v. Bland, [1993] A.C. 789. Regarding this case, see RICHARD CARD, CARD, CROSS & JONES, CRIMINAL LAW 42–44 (2012).

44 See Re A (Children) (Conjoined Twins: Surgical Separation) [2000] 4 All ER 961, 1003.

First, in some instances, becoming entangled in a dangerous situation is not the individual's fault, as in the case of illness or a fire caused by weather conditions. Second, the infringement of autonomy can also occur when an individual refrains from taking necessary actions out of fear of not receiving aid when needed. Consequently, society imposes certain duties and allocates resources to certain agents whose role is to protect members of the community in hazardous situations that may cause harm. These agents include physicians who attend to emergencies, rescuers in the aftermath of accidents, parents who look after their children, and so on. These roles are essential for providing the stability and security that enable individuals and society as a whole to exercise their autonomy.

If we were to abolish the duty to rescue and assist in specific cases, including duties imposed on police officers, physicians, parents, or contractual obligations, it would substantially harm the autonomy of both individuals and society. Therefore, the duty to act in these cases is intended, among others, to safeguard our autonomy. At times, the gravity of the failure to fulfill this duty is akin to that of the harm caused by killing.

Based on the foregoing, I propose to regard the obligations concerning harm caused to individuals on a spectrum. The least stringent obligation is to rescue a stranger unrelated to us by roles or contractual obligations. The next level involves rescuing someone with whom we share a contractual relationship or have a duty imposed on us by virtue of our roles. The most significant obligation is the prohibition against killing.

The level of severity is gauged by the harm caused to the individual and society as a whole in the absence of these obligations. From a social contract perspective, the question that arises is which laws would people willingly accept in a hypothetical contract. An individual who constantly faces the threat of being killed lives in perpetual fear, losing his capacity for autonomous action, and societal progress becomes impossible. But even individuals who cannot rely on others for aid based on their role or obligation experience limited personal growth: although they may not live in constant fear of death, their ability to flourish and thrive is impeded because progress and growth require taking certain risks, which, in turn, necessitate cooperation between individuals. Hence, within the framework of the social contract, laws that prohibit killing and mandate rescue based on roles and contracts have greater significance than duties to rescue that exist between two strangers unrelated by role or contract.

From the standpoint of rule utilitarianism, the focus is on identifying the rule that, if followed by all or most individuals, leads to the most favorable outcomes. Based on the aforementioned considerations, abiding by the rule that prohibits killing produces better results than adhering to the rule that forbids letting die, even in cases involving contractual obligations or duties arising from an agent's role. Moreover, when such duties exist, adhering to the rule prohibiting letting die produces better results than when it is applied to two unrelated strangers without any other binding obligation between them.

Not all duties may be explained in the way presented earlier, and it is reasonable to assume that other moral foundations exist for certain duties. But the rationale presented earlier provides an edifying perspective on some of the mentioned duties.

7. Possible criticisms against the autonomy-based theory: exploring limitations and challenges

The proposed rationale assumes that people would fear harm or attacks if there were no prohibition against killing, leading to defensiveness and harm to individual autonomy. But this assumption may not be valid. A counterargument may claim that human nature is inherently good and most people would not attempt to harm or kill others so that even without the prohibition against killing, people may not be fearful to the point that substantially affects their autonomy. In response to this criticism, it can be addressed that while we may not reach the extreme natural state described by Hobbes, a more moderate approach still acknowledges that some individuals may attempt to harm or attack others, resulting in significant apprehension. Furthermore, people may fear potential attacks of such nature even in the absence of attempts to harm them.

Moreover, even if there is a dispute about human nature and what would happen without the prohibition against killing, it is reasonable for the legislature to adopt a cautious approach, given that it is possible that without the prohibition against killing individuals may attempt to harm or kill each other. Given the potential risks, it would not be prudent or sensible for the legislature to adopt a sanguine view of human nature and assume that nothing would happen if killing is not prohibited. Therefore, even if it is not clear what would occur in practice without a prohibition against killing, it is advisable to adopt a strict standpoint, recognizing the possibility that individuals may attempt to harm or kill each other for various reasons.

Another potential critique of the autonomy-based theory argues that according to it, the prohibition against letting die aims to protect, among others, the physical lives of individuals. If so, why not convict of homicide every person who could have prevented death but failed to do so? After all, the failure to rescue in such cases may harm the protected value of a person's life, even if it does not compromise the sense of security of the entire society.

This criticism should also be dismissed. I do not argue that the liberty rationale described earlier is rejected and irrelevant to the distinction between acts and omissions in criminal law; rather, it is not the only rationale, and it needs to be integrated with the autonomy-based theory. On the one hand, we want individuals to live without fear, and on the other, we want them to be able to live their lives without having to rescue others all the time; it is necessary to strike a balance between these considerations. When the purpose of the prohibition is to allow individuals to live without fear and with a basic sense of security, the liberty consideration, as expressed in the liberty rationale, carries less weight. Therefore, even if the prohibition against killing infringes on liberty, it is still valid because it seeks to enable individuals to live their daily lives without fear. By contrast, when the prohibition is not intended to allow individuals to live without fear, the liberty consideration becomes more significant. Because the prohibition against letting die does not seek to enable individuals to live without fear given that individuals can still live reasonable lives with a basic sense of security even without this prohibition, there is no obligation to rescue in every situation because such a requirement would cause a substantial infringement of liberty.

A somewhat different perspective leads to the same conclusion. On the one hand, the prohibition against killing seeks to protect the possibility of living without fear, and on the other, it does not significantly infringe on human liberty. Therefore, it should be applied categorically. By contrast, the prohibition against letting die does not aim to allow individuals to live without fear, and its enforcement would substantially interfere with liberty, so it should not be applied categorically. The liberty consideration, as expressed in the liberty rationale, is relevant only because even without the prohibition, individuals can still live without fear. Without the crucial distinction between the prohibition that seeks to protect basic human security (prohibition against killing) and the prohibition that does not seek to protect basic human security (prohibition against letting die), the liberty consideration alone would not have been beneficial.

8. Addressing criticism of alternative theories

I briefly address some criticism of alternative theories and show why the proposed autonomy-based theory remains unrefuted by these challenges. I argued earlier that the liberty rationale is more relevant to offenses where the required mental element is negligence or recklessness. In such offenses, without the duty requirement in omissions, individuals would be held liable whenever they failed to provide aid to someone in need. These scenarios can be many because they require only a subjective or objective awareness of potential harm and the capability to prevent it. Conviction for such offenses would significantly violate one's liberty. But this concern is less applicable to offenses requiring a specific mental state, such as intent, because, in these offenses, a person cannot be convicted unless he had the requisite intent for the prohibited result. But because criminal law does not differentiate between acts and omissions based on mental state, the liberty rationale alone cannot justify this distinction.

By contrast, the autonomy-based theory remains unchallenged in this regard. Its distinction between acts and omissions does not rest on the difficulty of adhering to a general prohibition against letting die vs. the prohibition against killing. Rather, it is based on the understanding that the prohibition against killing safeguards broader and more fundamental interests than the prohibition against letting die. This distinction applies to all mental states: negligence, recklessness, and intent.

I presented a critique of the causation theory using two scenarios: Death by hypothermia 1, where B seeks shelter from hypothermia by entering A's home, but A locks the door and denies B entry; and Death by hypothermia 2, where B wants to enter his own home, but A locks the door and prevents him from entering. I argued against the causation theory, pointing out that from a causality perspective, it is challenging to distinguish between the two scenarios because A's actions are identical in both. The only difference is that in the former, the shield belongs to A, and in the latter, to B.

According to the autonomy-based theory, it is possible to explain the distinction between the two scenarios. This theory is based on the premise that even in classical cases of letting die, there is a causal link between the agent's behavior and the victim's death, yet a significant difference remains between the prohibitions against killing and against letting die. The prohibition against killing allows for a life of security without fear, which is not the case with the prohibition against letting die. To enable a life of security, a protected space must be established for an individual where others are forbidden from intruding. This protected space is based primarily on the individual's body and resources, which enable him to protect himself.

Therefore, the distinction between Death by hypothermia 1 and 2 becomes evident. In the former, A did not enter B's protected space because it was A's own home, whereas in the latter, A intruded on B's protected space and shut him out. Therefore, Death by hypothermia 1 is categorized as letting die and Death by hypothermia 2 as killing. The two cases are morally dissimilar, and it is appropriate for them to be legally distinguished as well.

Even the criticism of Kamm's theory regarding the Swimming case can be reconciled with the autonomy-based theory. Briefly, in this case, B is about to drown but attempts to save himself by grabbing A's leg. This grip does not burden A. However, to break free from the grip, A shoots B, causing his death.

Under Kamm's theory, this case may not appear more severe than a typical case of letting die because B loses a life that could have been saved only with A's help. Nevertheless, it appears that morally, the case is not different from a regular case of killing. According to the autonomy-based theory, the prohibition against killing forbids intrusion into an individual's protected space because it constitutes the person's autonomy. In the Swimming case, when A shoots B, he intrudes into B's protected space and violates the norm that constitutes the person's autonomy, regardless of whether or not B loses a life that practically could have been preserved only with the aid of A.

Part II

The judicial stance and the implications of various rationales for practical questions regarding the act vs. omission distinction

Part II

The judicial stance and the implications of various rationales for practical questions regarding the act vs. omission distinction

5 The judicial standpoint regarding the definition of acts and omissions

1. Introduction

In the first part of this chapter, I discuss the lack of uniformity in the American judicial position regarding the definition of acts and omissions. Some court rulings have aligned the definition of acts and omissions with the bodily movement test, whereas others have not restricted the definition to this criterion. According to court rulings that adhere to the bodily movement test, any situation in which there is no bodily movement, such as staying in place, requires the identification of a duty to act. According to court rulings that do not adhere to the bodily movement test, scenarios lacking bodily movement can still be categorized as acts from a legal perspective and situations involving bodily movement as omissions.

A productive way of examining the American judicial position in this matter is by analyzing court decisions that addressed the question of whether an accused can be convicted of aiding and abetting based strictly on his presence at the scene of the crime. The question is whether inactive presence can be categorized as an act from a legal perspective. The scrutiny of such court decisions requires caution, however, because, on occasion, the accused may be present at the time of the crime but his conviction may not be due exclusively to his presence but to some form of active involvement in the criminal act, demonstrating that conviction hinges on the act itself, not merely presence at the scene.

In the second part of the chapter, I describe the lack of uniformity in defining acts and omissions in the rulings of the Supreme Court of Israel.

In the concluding section of the chapter, I present two models of absence of movement, based on the perspective that does not tie the definition of acts and omissions to the bodily movement test. The first model deals with situations in which an absence of movement enables harm to occur. The second model addresses risk-creating absence of movement, where the lack of movement itself leads to the harm rather than merely enabling it.

DOI: 10.4324/9781003380405-8

2. The American judicial standpoint

2.1 Court rulings aligned to the bodily movement test

(1) In the Pace case,[1] the defendant was driving in a car and his friend was one of the passengers. At some point, he picked up a hitchhiker. During the ride, the friend pulled out a knife and robbed the hitchhiker. The defendant neither said nor did anything in the course of the journey. The prosecution accused him of aiding and abetting the robbery. The court found him not guilty:

> The main question presented in the facts at bar is what evidence beyond the mere presence of a person at the scene of a crime is sufficient to sustain a connection as an accessory before the fact? This court has previously stated that negative acquiescence is not enough to constitute a person guilty of aiding and abetting the commission of a crime . . . Consequently, this court has always looked for affirmative conduct either in the form of acts or words from which reasonable inferences of a common design or purpose to effect the commission of a crime might be drawn.[2]

(2) In the Walden case,[3] a mother was tried for aiding and abetting a serious injury[4] by failing to prevent the father from beating their one-year-old child with a belt. She argued that she could not be held liable for aiding since she did not actively participate. The court ruled that if the mother had no duty to prevent the father's actions, she couldn't be convicted of aiding and abetting because she did not commit any act, even if her silence may have encouraged the defendant to commit the offense. In this case, however, such a duty existed, leading to her conviction for aiding and abetting by omission. Thus, this court supported the bodily movement test as a principle for distinguishing between acts and omissions.[5]

(3) Another case that reflects this position is Dixson.[6] The defendant was accused of assisting another person (the second defendant) in tampering

1 Pace v. State, 224 N.E.2d 312 (1967).
2 *Id.* at 213.
3 State v. Walden, 293 S.E.2d 780 (1982).
4 N.C. Gen. Stat. 14–32(b).
5 "Further, we find our holding today to be consistent with our prior cases regarding the law of aiding and abetting. It remains the law that one may not be found to be an aider and abettor, and thus guilty as a principal, solely because he is present when a crime is committed . . . It will still be necessary, in order to have that effect, that it be shown that the defendant said or did something showing his consent to the criminal purpose and contribution to its execution . . . But we hold that the failure of a parent who is present to take all steps reasonably possible to protect the parent's child from an attack by another person constitutes an act of omission by the parent showing the parent's consent and contribution to the crime being committed." Walden, *supra* note 3, at 786–87.
6 State v. Dixson, 546 S.W.3d 615 (2018).

with the vehicle by removing the tires without permission. A police officer, who received a report about the removal of tires from a silver Dodge Magnum, arrived at the scene and saw the two defendants standing next to the car with two missing tires. Behind the car was a black Dodge Magnum with two tires matching those of the silver Dodge Magnum. The defendant and his accomplice did not flee or do anything. It was later revealed that the black car belonged to the second defendant's girlfriend, and he admitted to removing the tires without permission. The prosecution claimed that the defendant assisted in removing the tires from the car. The trial court found the defendant guilty of aiding in the removal of the tires from the car based on his presence at the scene. On appeal, however, the court acquitted him and argued that mere presence alone cannot be considered assistance to commit a crime and cannot be the sole evidence of the defendant's active involvement in the offense.

> To support Defendant's accomplice liability for that crime, the State was required to prove beyond a reasonable doubt that Defendant affirmatively participated in committing it. Any affirmative act, even mere encouragement, is enough . . . While mere encouragement is enough, mere presence at the scene of a crime is not enough to show affirmative participation . . . Presence at the scene can give rise to an inference of affirmative participation only when combined with other circumstances connecting the defendant to the crime: namely, his association with the others involved in the crime before, during and after the offense and his conduct before and after the offense, such as his flight from the scene or his attempts to conceal crime.[7]

2.2 Court rulings not aligned to the bodily movement test

(1) The Parker case[8] revolves around an incident where three men demanded the victim to drive them to a party in his car. At some point, the three started brutally beating the victim. Even after he pretended to be unconscious, they continued to beat him all over his body until they believed he was dead. When they released their grip on him and the car slowed down, he managed to free himself from the car and escaped. The accused, Parker, denied any involvement in the attack and claimed that he merely sat in the car and did not participate. The court made the following determination:

> It has been established that a person may aid or abet without actively participating in the over act. If the proof shows that a person is present at the commission of a crime without disapproving or opposing it, it is competent for the jury to consider this conduct in connection with other

7 *Id.* at 619.
8 State v. Parker, 164 N.W.2d 633 (1969).

> circumstances and thereby reach the conclusion that he assented to the commission of the crime, lent to it his approval, and was thereby aiding and abetting its commission. Certainly, mere presence on the part of each would be enough if it is intended to and does aid the primary actors.[9]

This court ruling suggests that even the absence of physical movement may be considered an act from a legal perspective, and therefore, there is no need to establish a duty to act.

(2) A similar point arises from the Goodwin case,[10] which involved the defendant and another person named Taylor traveling together in the defendant's car. At some point, Taylor kidnapped a young woman and forced her into the car. During the ride, the defendant sat in the passenger seat next to the driver and drank beer. Eventually, they all went to the defendant's apartment, where Taylor raped the young woman and the defendant did nothing. The defendant was convicted of aiding and abetting the kidnapping and rape.[11] During the trial, the defendant argued that he should not be convicted since he did nothing, and no duty was imposed on him to prevent the crime. The court ruled:

> Mere presence at the scene of a crime is insufficient to make a person criminally responsible . . . Nevertheless, presence can be enough to prove complicity if the presence is intended to, and does, aid the primary actor . . . "Presence is thus equated to aiding and abetting when it is shown that it designedly encourages the perpetrator, or facilitates the unlawful deed. . ." Moreover, "the circumstances under which the defendant is present . . . may be such as to warrant the jury inferring beyond a reasonable doubt that he sought thereby to make the crime succeed. . ."[12]

(3) In the Swanson case,[13] the court deliberated on a situation where a four-year-old girl was sexually abused twice by her mother's partner. In both instances, he inserted his finger into the child's genital area while the mother was sitting on the edge of the bed and watched but took no other action. The State of California brought her to trial for aiding and abetting the offense of a lewd or lascivious act on a child under the age of 14.[14] The court convicted her, determining that her presence constituted an act and not a mere omission.

> However, the magistrate could reasonably determine that the defendant did "act" during each incident, by standing over the bed and watching as

9 *Id.* at 641.

10 State v. Goodwin, 395 A.2d 1234 (1978).

11 N.H. Rev. Stat. Ann. §626:8 and §633:1; N.H. Rev. Stat. Ann. §626:8 and §632 A:2 (Supp. 1977).

12 Goodwin, *supra* note 10, at 1236.

13 People v. Swanson-Birabent, 114 Cal. App. 4th 733 (2003).

14 Cal. Penal Code § 288(a).

> Umble molested the victim. Defendant argues that this was not an "act," citing the rule that, ordinarily, mere presence at the scene of a crime and the failure to take steps to prevent a crime are insufficient to establish aiding and abetting liability . . . However, in this case defendant was not merely present. Her presence served an important purpose: it encouraged the victim to comply with Umble rather than resist. Defendant's presence also encouraged Umble to continue molesting the victim.[15]

This ruling, in which the definition of an act and an omission is not strictly bound by the bodily movement test, has been reflected in recent court rulings.

(4) In the Delgado case,[16] the court examined the involvement of the defendant in the murder of two individuals. The defendant was associated with a gang seeking revenge against another gang that harmed one of their members. He was present in the house where the revenge plot was planned, and although he desired revenge, he remained silent. The court did indeed acquit him of aiding and abetting the murder, noting that, generally, mere presence at the time of the offense is not considered assistance. However, the court emphasized that this rule is not absolute, and when the mere presence encourages the principal offender to commit the crime, the presence itself can be considered an act of assistance.

> In Garguilo, for example, we considered whether a defendant's mere presence at the scene of a crime could render him liable for aiding and abetting that crime . . . Generally, we said, the answer is no, because accomplice liability requires a defendant to "do something to forward the crime." . . . We recognized, however, that in some cases, a defendant's presence may advance the commission of the crime: an example would be "the attendance of a 250-pound bruiser at a shakedown as a companion to the extortionist, or the maintenance at the scene of crime of someone useful as a lookout." . . . We therefore drew a distinction between those cases in which a defendant's presence "help[s]" or "positively encourage[s]" the commission of a crime and those cases in which a defendant's presence merely marks him as "a companion" to the actual perpetrator of the crime, observing that the former, but not the latter, can serve as a basis for accomplice liability.[17]

(5) Finally, in the Etters case,[18] the defendant, Etters, met with his friends Bobby Morton and Sierra Gomez. Morton proposed robbing drugs from a person named Matthew Trammell. When Trammell and his spouse arrived, Morton

15 Swanson-Birabent, *supra* note 13, at 744.
16 United States v. Delgado, 972 F.3d 63 (2020).
17 *Id.* at 75.
18 State v. Etters, 2021 N.C. App. LEXIS 109 (2021).

threatened Trammell with a rifle and demanded the drugs. After a struggle with Morton, Trammell managed to escape, leaving money behind in his car. Morton took the money, and all three fled the scene. The defendant was charged with aiding robbery with a dangerous weapon and argued that he could not be convicted since he did not actively participate in the incident. The court determined that in the context of close friends, mere presence can constitute aiding and abetting if it encourages the perpetrator to complete the offense.

> Importantly, a defendant's "communication of intent to aid" does not have to be express; it may be "inferred from his actions and from his relation to the actual perpetrator." . . . This principle led to what is known as the "friend exception" to the mere presence rule: "when the bystander is a friend of the perpetrator, and knows that his presence will be regarded by the perpetrator as an encouragement and protection, presence alone may be regarded as an encouragement."[19]

These rulings indicate that there are cases where the absence of bodily movement is considered an act rather than an omission from a legal perspective; therefore, the defendant can be convicted even without identifying a duty to act. The rationale behind this is that the mere presence assisted and encouraged the principal offender in committing the offense.

3. The position of the Israeli Court regarding acts vs. omissions

3.1 Court rulings aligned with the bodily movement test

(1) In John Doe v. State of Israel,[20] the court dealt with allegations of sexual assault perpetrated by the accused against a minor. The accused contended that certain sexual acts, for which he was convicted, occurred with the complainant initiating physical contact without resistance from him. He argued that his role was passive, suggesting that his behavior should be categorized as an omission rather than an act.

The court rejected the defendant's argument because an act could be identified in the case in which he actively participated with the victim and derived pleasure from it. Despite the bodily movement not being significant, there was still an expenditure of physical energy, categorizing it as an act rather than an omission. As a result, there was no need to identify a duty to act in order to convict the defendant. The ruling reflects a clear stance on the definition of acts and omissions. An act involves the expenditure of energy whereas an omission does not.

19 *Id.* at 5; see also State v. Holland, 234 N.C. 354, 358 (1951).
20 CA 7832/04 John Doe v. State of Israel (2006) Nevo Legal Database (Isr.).

(2) The ruling in the Weitzman case reflects the same position.[21] In this ruling, the court addressed a situation in which a police officer was killed in a hit-and-run accident after the driver failed to obey the officer's order to stop. Inside the car were four individuals: the driver, Shlomi, Orna, and Keren. All three passengers were convicted of aiding the offense of abandonment after an accident. Shlomi was convicted of active assistance because he shouted "Drive on!" after the accident. Orna and Keren, who merely looked at the driver and remained silent without taking any further action, were convicted of passive assistance. The court noted that although Orna and Keren's silence encouraged and reinforced the driver's intent to leave the scene, it should not be considered an act but rather an omission that requires the identification of a duty to act, as they did not physically move their bodies.

3.2 Court ruling not aligned with the bodily movement test

In the Margolin case,[22] the Supreme Court dealt with actions taken against patients in a psychiatric hospital. The patients suffered from various conditions, mainly severe autism and moderate to severe intellectual disability. The treatment aimed to teach them to attend to their basic needs, such as sleeping, eating, and more. As part of the treatment, items were tied to their backs to prevent them from wandering around; they were prohibited from speaking for long hours every day; punishments were imposed, including isolation, denying them showers and brushing their teeth, and assigning them excessive tasks; medication was withheld from patients suffering from seizures, under the assumption that they were merely "acting out"; and their clothes were torn when they showed signs of stress, with the intention to cause suffering and humiliation to prompt behavioral change.

The defendants were prosecuted for the offense of cruelty to an incompetent person under Section 368(c) of the Israeli Penal Law. The head nurse of the department, who issued instructions to carry out these actions, and the department manager, who was aware of the actions but did nothing, were brought to trial. The department manager argued that he should not be convicted for cruelty to an incompetent person because he did nothing. The court rejected his claim and determined that he was aware of the cruel actions and did nothing to prevent them. His silence not only allowed harm to occur but also served as encouragement, support, and endorsement of the abusive actions taking place in the department. Therefore, his silence was not a mere omission but an "eloquent silence," signifying an act rather than an omission because it implied positive affirmation of the treatment methods employed, considering them legitimate and desirable.

21 CA 3626/01 Weitzman v. State of Israel (2002) Nevo Legal Database (Isr.).
22 CA 7704/13 Margolin v. State of Israel (2015) Nevo Legal Database (Isr.).

4. The rationales underlying the divergent rulings

Although not explicitly stated, it may be suggested that the core dispute between judges who adhere to the bodily movement test and those who do not is rooted in the various rationales underlying the distinction between acts and omissions.

Judges who adhered to the bodily movement test relied on one of two possible rationales. The causation rationale posits that an act has the potential to cause a change in the world and therefore, can lead to harm, whereas an omission does not create any change in the world and thus cannot cause harm. Consequently, an act involves bodily movement whereas an omission does not.[23] The liberty rationale supports the bodily movement test and states that imposing a requirement to avoid an act defined as bodily movement infringes on a person's liberty to a lesser degree than actively mandating a particular action.[24]

Judges who did not adhere to the bodily movement test arguably based their position on Fletcher's causation rationale, which posits that there is no substantial causal distinction between bodily movement and a lack thereof.[25] This contradicts Moore's view, according to which bodily movement leads to change and potential harm whereas absence of bodily movement does not.[26] According to Fletcher's rationale, there may be cases that do not involve bodily movement but should still be considered as acts from legal perspective, such as standing guard at the king's palace, a psychologist's silence during treatment, or participating in a boycott.[27] In my opinion, court rulings that perceive mere presence as assistance contend that, in certain instances, for example, when the defendant's presence encouraged the primary perpetrator to commit the offense, the absence of bodily movement creates a threat that leads to the harm. Therefore, from a legal perspective, these cases are regarded as acts rather than omissions eliminating the need to identify a legal duty to act for conviction.

The position of the judges who did not apply the bodily movement test aligns also with the autonomy-based theory that I proposed and examined earlier. According to this rationale, without a prohibition against killing, individuals would live in constant fear of being killed, undermining their ability to lead a reasonable life with a basic level of autonomy. Moreover, the prohibition against killing would extend to preventing the creation of threats that lead to fatal outcomes, forbidding the removal of safeguards belonging to the victim because such actions breach the individual's protected sphere, leading to a

23 See Chapter 2 Section 3.3.1.
24 See Chapter 2 Section 2.1.2.1.
25 See Chapter 2, Section 3.4.2.1.
26 See Chapter 2, Section 4.3.
27 *Supra* note 25.

constant fear.[28] As I argued in Chapter 4, the creation of threats and inflicting harm do not necessarily require bodily movement but can also result from staying put or remaining silent.

Although not all the previously mentioned cases involve life-threatening offenses, the autonomy-based theory is applicable to instances where harm does not result in death. Therefore, in certain situations where staying put or remaining silent resulted in harm and encouraged the primary perpetrator to commit the offense, it is possible to convict for aiding or even for the main offense even without identifying a duty to act because in these scenarios, the person's protected sphere has been violated.[29]

5. Two models of absence of bodily movement

Two models of absence of bodily movement can be derived from the court rulings that do not apply the bodily movement test: enabling the pre-existing risk to materialize and creating the risk that caused the harm.[30]

Enabling a pre-existing risk to materialize refers to situations where the lack of bodily movement did not prevent the risk but neither did it create it in the first place. The absence of bodily movement can be referred to as "enabling inaction." In these cases, the threat already exists, and the agent did not prevent the risk from coming to pass. A classic example of such a scenario is when an agent fails to prevent another person from drowning. In this case, the risk of drowning exists independently of the potential rescuer, whose presence did not create the risk. These cases represent omissions that require identifying a duty to act for conviction.

Creating the risk that caused harm refers to situations where the absence of bodily movement itself created the risk that led to the harm. This absence of bodily movement can be termed "creative inaction." In these instances, remaining silent or staying put not only allowed the risk to become reality but created it. It may be argued that in such cases, the absence of bodily movement is equivalent to an act because, from the point of view of culpability, there is no real distinction between causing harm by an act or by silence. Therefore, in cases resembling these examples, no duty to act is required for conviction.

In the Swanson case described earlier,[31] the mere presence of the mother by the bedside while her partner was committing a sexual offense against her daughter, with full awareness of the situation, encouraged him to continue his actions. This is not a situation where the mother merely allowed her partner to commit the act by inaction; rather, her inaction heightened the risk by

28 See Chapter 4 Section 5.

29 See Chapter 4 Section 2.

30 See Roni Rosenberg, *Two Models of "Absence of Movement" in Criminal Jurisprudence*, 12 OHIO ST. J. CRIM. L. 195, 205–10 (2014).

31 See Swanson-Birabent, *supra* note 13.

encouraging her partner in his act. Therefore, this conduct was classified as an act rather than an omission. This situation is not different from a scenario where the mother verbally encouraged her partner to commit the offense.

Another illustrative case is when B extended his hand to A, and A, fully aware, refused to extend his hand back, insulting B.[32] In this case, A made no bodily movement, but the refusal to shake hands created the risk and not just brought a pre-existing risk to pass. Therefore, there is no substantial difference between this case and a situation where A verbally insulted B, a conduct that is classified as an act rather than an omission.

From a different perspective, another example of harm caused by an absence of bodily movement was mentioned earlier:[33]

Silent threat: A and B are sitting together near C. B threatens C, claiming A intends to harm C's family. A, a known criminal and aware that C will take the threat seriously, remains silent and continues sitting alongside B and C.

In this situation, A's continued presence does not merely bring the pre-existing threat to pass but is an integral part of the threat itself. Therefore, this is classified as an act and not as an omission.

This position aligns with the opinion of Fletcher, who argues that the act requirement in criminal law should not be treated as a metaphysical abstraction separated from its context. Human conduct invariably serves as a form of expression or meaningful communication between individuals. Therefore, the interpretation of the terms "act" and "omission" should not be confined to a strictly biological or physical understanding and should not be inherently linked to the bodily movement test. In certain scenarios, the absence of bodily movement does not automatically entail a duty requirement because the conduct may still be categorized as an act rather than an omission.[34]

Anthony Duff's perspective aligns closely with Fletcher's. In his explanation of the act requirement in criminal law, Duff rejects Moore's position that an act is a bodily movement caused by volition. Duff argues that this approach interprets the act requirement as a natural, asocial phenomenon that, in its essence, interacts only with the material world in which we physically move and which can causally affect through our movement. This perspective holds that an act, being a physical movement, can impact the world and is thus pertinent to criminal law. Conversely, the absence of an act does not influence the world and is irrelevant to criminal law.[35] Duff maintains that criminal law is concerned with the broader relationship between individuals and the world. We must perceive and interpret actions as social phenomena deeply intertwined with the social fabric of our existence.[36] Thus, at times, even the

32 James Rachels, *Killing and Starving to Death*, 54 PHIL. 159, 166 (1979).

33 Chapter 2, section 2.1.2.3.

34 Chapter 2, Section 3.4.2.2.

35 R. A. DUFF, ANSWERING FOR CRIME – RESPONSIBILITY AND LIABILITY IN THE CRIMINAL LAW 99–100 (2007).

36 *Id.* at 100.

absence of bodily movement can be a form of "doing" because our influence on the world is also tied to social norms.[37] According to Duff, this perspective implies that failing to stand when the Queen enters can be seen as insulting her. If insults were prohibited in certain circumstances, the argument against prohibiting insults in the absence of physical movement would not hold because there is no fundamental distinction between insulting by action or inaction. In both cases, they represent forms of "doing."[38]

The autonomy-based theory also resists imposing a rigid definition of acts and omissions based on the bodily movement test. Under this theory as well, the physical definition of the term "act" is not essential. The fundamental question is whether there is intervention in the protected space of the individual. Intervention may exist even when a person remains silent and makes no bodily movements; conversely, there may be situations when no intervention occurs despite the individual making bodily movements. In these cases, a duty to act is necessary for conviction.

37 *Id.* at 97.

38 *Id.* at 98. See also A. P. Simester, *Why Omissions Are Special*, 1 Legal Theory 311, 313 (1995). ("Many non-movements constitute things done; consider, for example, sitting for a portrait or hunger-striking.")

6 Types of duties that can serve as a basis for criminal liability in omissions

1. Introduction

Following the exposition of the diverse rationales for distinguishing between acts and omissions in criminal law, I now examine the duties that can serve as a basis for criminal liability in omissions.[1] Does every duty established by law have the potential to lead to criminal liability in cases of indirect omissions such as homicide offences, or only particular duties qualify for this purpose? I find a significant correlation exists between this inquiry and the various rationales presented earlier. In this chapter, I analyze three distinct approaches regarding the issue at hand.

The expansive approach contends that every duty can form the basis for criminal liability in omissions.

The restrictive approach argues that only certain duties can be considered as a source of criminal liability in omissions. According to this view, specific duties must arise from the connection between the agent and the source of the threat, the victim, or the agent's role.

The intermediate approach posits that not every duty can necessarily serve as a basis for criminal liability in omissions, but it does not set rigid requirements for particular duties that can do so. The central question under this approach is whether the duty gave rise to an expectation that it would be fulfilled. If the answer is affirmative, the duty can provide a basis for criminal liability in the relevant offense; if it is negative, the duty cannot serve as a basis for criminal liability in that offense.

I conclude the chapter by analyzing the position of American courts on this issue.

2. Presenting the problem

If an individual has committed a direct omission offense, he can be convicted of it and punished according to what is specified in the offense. Now, suppose

1 We must distinguish here between two questions: (1) whether duties that are not found in criminal law can serve as a basis for criminal liability in omissions in result or conduct offenses and (2) which types of duty can provide a foundation for liability in omissions—whether they stem from criminal or civil law.

DOI: 10.4324/9781003380405-9

that the same individual's omission resulted in a harmful consequence, forming the basis for a result offense. If the punishment for the result offense is more severe than that for the direct omission offense, a claim may arise that the individual should be prosecuted for the result crime and penalized according to the punishment provided therein, considering that the source of the duty for the result offense lies in the direct omission offense. The following examples illustrate the problem:[2]

(1) A cinema owner is on vacation. A visitor at the cinema informs the owner that the smoke detector is malfunctioning. Despite being aware and foreseeing the possibility that his omission might cause death if a fire were to break out during a screening, the owner takes no action and proceeds with his vacation. The next day, during a show, a fire breaks out and, because of the malfunctioning smoke detector, a person dies. In the jurisdiction where this occurs, wood structures are common, and there is an offense mandating the installation of smoke detectors, with strict adherence to their proper functioning. Violation of this offense carries a maximum penalty of one year of imprisonment. Should the cinema owner be charged with a result crime for causing death, based on the direct omission offense as a duty to act?

(2) In a certain country, the Good Samaritan law imposes a duty to provide aid to anyone who becomes aware of an individual in immediate and serious danger to life, bodily integrity, or health due to a sudden event. If the person can provide aid to the individual in danger without endangering others, failure to act constitutes a punishable offense. Suppose that A is aware of the offense and foresees the possibility that his failure to act may cause death or serious injury, and tragically, this outcome occurs. Should A be charged with the result crime for causing death or serious injury based on the direct omission offense, with the Good Samaritan law being the source of the duty to act?

(3) In a certain country, there is an offense that imposes a duty on anyone who becomes aware of an individual planning to commit a crime to take reasonable action to prevent it. Suppose a scenario in which a bystander knows that his friend is about to commit murder and he can prevent it by notifying the police but fails to do so. As a result, a person is killed. Can the bystander be prosecuted for a result crime of murder or manslaughter based on the direct omission offense of failure to prevent a crime as the source of the duty to act?[3]

2 Compare: Yitzhak Kugler, *Criminal Omissions – part 2,* 20 BAR-ILAN L. REV. 379, 380–81 (2004).

3 Regarding this offense, see Miriam Gur-Aryh, *A Failure to Prevent a Crime – Should it be Criminal?* 20 CRIM. JUST. ETHICS 3 (2001). See also Fla. Stat. Ann. § 794.027; Mass. Gen. Laws Ann. c. 268 § 40; Gen Laws RI §§ 11-37-3.1, 11-37-3.3; Haw Rev. Stat. Ann. § 663-1.6; §§ 138–39 of the German Criminal Code, 1975; §§ 135–36 of the Netherlands Criminal Code, as amended in 1952; §139 of the Norwegian Criminal Code, as amended in 1961; C. 16 § 19 of the Finnish Criminal Code, as amended in 1983; § 26 of the Greenland Criminal Code, 1954. In Israeli law, the duty is defined under § 262 of the Penal Law (1977).

2.1 *The expansive approach*

According to this approach, every legal duty and direct omission offense can serve as a basis for criminal liability under the relevant result offenses, including general duties derived from the Good Samaritan law or the offense of failure to prevent a crime. This position aligns with the rationale that distinguishes between acts and omissions based on considerations of liberty. According to this rationale, the duty requirement in the case of omissions originates in the need to allow individuals the liberty to conduct their lives without interference from the legal system. In cases involving a direct omission offense, the legislature decided that the consideration of liberty is overridden when the situation falls within the realm of a particular omission and the citizen is obligated to act. Therefore, if the relevant outcome obtains, one can be convicted for the result offense. For example, any individual who causes another's death, whether through an act or omission, with criminal intent, is liable under the applicable homicide offense. In cases of omission, a duty to act is required. If this duty arises from a consideration of liberty, and such considerations become irrelevant as determined by the legislature (through duties imposed by the legislator), then one can be convicted of a homicide offense.[4]

Ashworth, who also supports the liberty rationale for distinguishing between acts and omissions in criminal law,[5] argues that there is no impediment to prosecuting someone for murder, even if he violated the Good Samaritan law or the offense of failure to prevent a crime, provided that the relevant mental element for the offense is proven.[6] This position aligns also with the Model Penal Code, which states in section 2.01.(3)(b) that the conviction for crimes committed by omission is contingent on the duty to act being "imposed by law."[7]

4 Kugler, *supra* note 2, at 383–84; C. M. V. CLARKSON & H. M. KEATING, CRIMINAL LAW: TEXT AND MATERIALS 111 (1998).

5 ANDREW ASHWORTH, PRINCIPLES OF CRIMINAL LAW 46, 110 (2006).

6 Andrew Ashworth, *The Scope of Criminal Liability for Omissions*, 105 LAW. Q. REV. 424, 457 (1989). Ashworth notes that a problem may arise in proving the causal connection between the omission and the required result in an offense. For example, it is not clear whether a causal connection can be proven between the police officer's lack of intervention and the victim's death. For our purposes, however, it is clear that this is a secondary question, as the primary issue is whether one can theoretically be convicted if he committed an offense such as non-prevention of a crime. Ashworth's answer is affirmative. He also argues that it is possible to convict for murder or manslaughter even in cases where a contractual obligation was breached and as a result a person died. But he differentiates between two types of obligations: those aimed at protecting a person's body, where breaching the obligation can result in criminal liability for murder or manslaughter, and those not aimed at physical safeguarding, where a breach cannot lead to such convictions. (For instance, A has a duty to assist B by visiting her home to cook for her. A fails to meet this obligation. Meanwhile, B suffers a heart attack and subsequently dies. Indeed, if A had fulfilled his duty, B would not have died, as he would have taken him to the hospital. Nonetheless, A will not be convicted of the manslaughter offense.) *Id.* at 455.

7 Model Penal Code § 2.01.(3)(b) (Official Draft and Explanatory Notes, 1985).

This approach also maintains that the duty to act can arise from civil law, not only criminal law.[8] The rationale is clear: when the law establishes that a duty to act exists, even if it stems from civil law, it demonstrates that the consideration of liberty is overridden by other factors; therefore, one may be held liable for the relevant outcome offense.

The position supporting that every direct omission can serve as a basis for imposing criminal liability in a relevant result offense aligns also with Feinberg's position, who argued that there is no moral distinction between an act that caused harm and an omission that caused the same harm. The need for identifying a duty to act in omissions arises from the coordination problem. Feinberg pointed out that without the duty requirement in omissions, there would be a significant waste of resources, as many people attempting to save a few people without the need for it. Moreover, it would create a problem of fairness since not all citizens would fulfill this duty. The duty requirement in omissions helps resolve the coordination and fairness challenges.[9]

From this perspective, it is possible to convict an individual for the relevant homicide offense (based on the perpetrator's mental state) if he failed to fulfill the duties outlined in the Good Samaritan law because the duty to act is clearly specified for a particular group of individuals and situations, eliminating all coordination issues. Moreover, when there is a duty to act, whether it arises from a general obligation under the Good Samaritan law or from a specific duty based on the relationship between the defendant and the victim or the source of the danger, the legislature has already determined that the consideration of coordination is irrelevant or overridden, and therefore, there is no reason not to convict for the relevant homicide offense.[10]

Robinson also contends that, in principle, there is no obstacle to using any duty to act prescribed by law to convict in homicide or bodily harm offenses. He argues, however, that it may be appropriate to distinguish between different types of duties. With respect to the Good Samaritan law, it appears that the legislature had in mind situations where someone's life was in immediate peril and the person could face fatal consequences if not assisted; therefore, the failure to provide help would entail the prescribed punishment. By contrast, an offense that imposes a duty on parents to care for their young children includes many situations, even when the children are not in life-threatening danger. In these cases, where no harm is caused, the parent would be convicted of a direct omission offense according to the prescribed sanction. But if

8 See, for example, Commonwealth v. Levesque, 436 Mass. 443, 449 (2002); People v. Heitzman 886 P. 2d 1229, 1234 (1994) ("When a criminal statute does not set forth a legal duty to act by its express terms, liability for a failure to act must be premised on the existence of a duty found elsewhere . . . A criminal statute may thus incorporate a duty imposed by another criminal or civil statute"); Paul H. Robinson, Criminal Law 195–96 (1997).

9 For a discussion about Feinberg's stance, see Chapter 3, Section 4.

10 See Joel Feinberg, Harm to Others: The Moral Limits of the Criminal Law 171 (1984).

physical harm or death is caused, the duty to act specified in the direct omission offense may serve as a basis for conviction in the relevant result offense.[11]

2.2 The restrictive approach

In contrast to the expansive approach, the restrictive one argues that not every duty or every direct omission offense can serve as a basis for conviction in a relevant result offense. For example, some claim that if a person fails to perform the actions required by the Good Samaritan law and, as a result, someone dies, he cannot be convicted of manslaughter even if the necessary mental element is present. Similarly, if someone neglects his duty to take reasonable measures to prevent a crime and, as a result, a person dies, he cannot be charged with causing the death. According to this approach, liability for the result should be attributed only to those who have a unique connection to the harm, either by special connection to the source of the harm or to the victim, not to those who have a general duty to assist as a result of their random encounter with the dangerous situation.[12]

Thus, a father can be charged with manslaughter if he fails to prevent his child from running onto the road because in this case, the father has a unique connection to the victim. Similarly, a person who has a contractual obligation to care for a child can be charged with causing death if the child dies because of his omission. This liability stems from the duty arising from the role the defendant undertook or the relationship he has with the victim.

The justification for this restrictive approach stems from the moral rationale that distinguishes between acts and omissions in criminal law. According to this perspective, the distinction relies on the causation rationale, as elaborated earlier, stating that an act can directly cause harm whereas an omission cannot, or if it can, only indirectly. To bridge the moral gap between acts and omissions, it is necessary to identify a duty to act based on a solid moral foundation, such as the relationship between the defendant and the victim, between the defendant and the source of the danger, or by virtue of a particular role.[13] Punishing for manslaughter by omission when the duty to act arises from a general duty and not from the fundamental connection between the defendant and the victim or the source of the danger is unfair toward the person who failed to act.

11 Robinson, *supra* note 8, at 198–99.

12 Wayne R. LaFave, criminal law 410–16 (2017); David Ormerod & Karl Laird, Smith and Hogan's Criminal Law 88 (2015); Jacobo Dopico Gomez-Aller, *Criminal Omissions: A Europian Perspective*, 11 New Crim. L. Rev. 419, 421 (2008). Mordechai Kremnitzer & Re'em Segev, *Omission in Criminal Law*, in Tamir Book 197, 218–19 (Yosef Tamir & Ora Hirsh eds., 1999). Compare: Ken Levy, *Killing, Letting Die, and the Case for Mildly Punishing Bad Samaritanism*, 44 Ga. L. Rev. 610 (2010).

13 Elazar Weinryb, *Omissions and Responsibility*, 30 Am. Phil. Q. 1, 16–17 (1980); Kremnitzer & Segev, *supra* note 12, at 218–19.

The position maintaining that a general duty to act cannot be used to convict in result offenses, such as injury or homicide by omission, can also be based on the argument that an act causing harm worsens the victim's condition, whereas an omission does not improve it but neither does it worsen it. From this perspective, only a significant duty to act arising from the relationship between the defendant and the victim or between the defendant and the source of the danger can bridge the moral gap between acts and omissions as opposed to a general duty to act.[14]

This is also the position of German law, which stipulates that not every legal duty to act meets the duty requirement in cases of omissions. To convict someone of a result offense based on an omission, the legal duty must stem from a significant moral obligation. Therefore, under German law, the violation of a duty to assist a stranger cannot be used as a basis for imposing liability in result offenses.[15]

The restrictive approach also advocates the idea that a non-criminal legal duty to act can serve as grounds for imposing criminal liability in cases of result offense omissions.[16] The point of contention between the restrictive and expansive stances lies in whether the duty should be derived from a specific relationship between the accused and the victim or the source of danger, or whether any duty to act, irrespective of the relationship, can be used as a basis for conviction.[17]

Based on this, an intriguing aspect comes to light concerning the two stances mentioned earlier. If the duty requirement in omissions arises from the necessity to bridge the moral gap between causing harm by act or by omission, as in the causation and the harm to the victim rationales, only a "strong" duty stemming from a unique connection to the harm can form a basis for conviction in the relevant result offense. This is because only strong duties that arise from a particular relationship between the accused and the victim, the source of danger, or a role-based obligation can bridge the moral gap between an act and an omission.

By contrast, if the duty to act does not arise from the necessity to bridge the moral gap between causing harm by act and by omission because there is no intrinsic moral difference between the two, every duty can serve as a basis for conviction in result offenses. For example, according to the liberty

14 Michael S. Moore, Act and Crime: The Philosophy of Action and Its Implications for Criminal Law 54–57 (1993). For the analysis of Moore approach see Chapter 2, Section 4.3.

15 "Omission as commission. (1) Whoever fails to prevent a harm which is part of the constituent elements of a crime may be punished under this Code only if he was under a legal duty to prevent the harm, and if his failure to act was equivalent to an affirmative act for purposes of establishing the statutorily defined constituent elements of the crime." The translation is from Volume 28 of The American Series Foreign Penal Codes 13.

16 See *supra* note 8.

17 See for example, Levesque, *supra* note 8.

and the coordination problem rationales, the duty requirement in omissions does not stem from the fact that causing harm by an act is intrinsically more severe than causing harm by an omission. Rather, it stems from the fact that the prohibition against an act interferes less with human liberty than does the prohibition against an omission, or that the prohibition against an act does not create a coordination problem, unlike the prohibition against an omission. According to these rationales, when a duty to act exists (even a "weak" one), the legislature has shown that the consideration of liberty or of the coordination problem is not relevant or overridden, and therefore, convicting in the relevant result offense is not problematic.

2.3 *The intermediary approach*

2.3.1 *Causation as deviating from social expectations and reasonable norm*

According to Fletcher Hart and Honoré, who contended that an omission can also be the primary cause of an offense when it deviates from accepted norms and societal routines,[18] it may be argued that not every duty establishes a routine or an accepted norm, and not every duty creates an expectation. For instance, a father who neglects to feed his child deviates from accepted norms and reasonable expectations. However, a person who refrains from rescuing a stranger is not typically seen as violating reasonable expectations, and thus there is no causal link between his inaction and the victim's death. This approach is an intermediary one. On the one hand, it does not dictate that any violation of duty is sufficient for convicting someone in a result offense in cases of an omission. On the other hand, it does not necessarily require that only certain omissions serve as a basis for conviction in the relevant result offense. The response to the question whether a given duty can serve as a basis for conviction in a result offense depends on the circumstances. If it is a duty that creates an expectation, the duty can be a basis for a conviction in a relevant result offense because the failure to fulfill it caused the result. But if it is a duty that has not yet generated an expectation for action, the failure to fulfill it has not caused the result.[19]

According to this approach, the duty arising from the Good Samaritan law may not serve as a basis for conviction of result offenses in certain situations or times. This is because the duty may not have created the required expectation; therefore, the omission of that duty cannot be considered a cause of the harm. In other situations, however, it may be a valid basis for conviction if it creates the essential expectation that identifies the perpetrator as being a primary cause of the harm.

18 See the analysis of these positions in Chapter 2, Section 3.4.

19 George P. Fletcher, Basic Concepts of Criminal Law 70 (1998).

In other words, the capacity of a particular duty to form the basis for a conviction in result offenses may vary over time. Moreover, the same duty might not ground a conviction in some contexts, while it could in others. For example, one could argue that if A witnesses B injured in an accident and fails to rescue him, A's inaction is not typically viewed as causing B's death, given the relatively low expectation of intervention. Conversely, if A observes a baby drowning in a pool and does not save him, despite an easy opportunity to do so, A's omission is regarded as causing the baby's death, because of the strong expectation to act in such a scenario.

2.3.2 The autonomy-based theory

In Chapter 4, I argued that the distinction between killing and letting die arises from the divergent interests underlying the prohibition against killing and those underlying the prohibition against letting die. I argued that the prohibition against killing seeks to enable a life free from fear without the need for constantly defending oneself, which is the condition for individual autonomy, whereas the prohibition against letting die does not aim to achieve the same goal.[20]

Given this rationale, it is possible to identify reasons why certain duties can serve as valid basis for conviction in relevant result offenses like homicide, in cases of omissions. Some duties, if not fulfilled, could impair an individual's autonomy. Regarding such duties, the state appoints certain societal "agents" tasked with providing protection to members of society in hazardous situations that may cause harm. These agents' role is to provide stability and security to individuals: a physician attending to emergencies, a lifeguard preventing drowning, a police officer ensuring safety, parents watching over their children, and others. These roles are crucial to ensure social stability and security, enabling individuals to reasonably exercise their autonomy. By contrast, an individual's autonomy does not appear to have been significantly impaired if the Good Samaritan law had not been enacted because even without this law, the individual could lead a reasonably secure life without fear.

The central idea is as follows: duties to act that can serve as a basis for conviction in result offenses are those that effectively safeguard an individual's autonomy by providing stability and security to society. Duties that cannot serve as a basis for criminal liability in result offenses are those that do not significantly protect an individual's autonomy so that even without these duties, the individual could still lead a reasonably fulfilling life.

This approach is also an intermediary one because according to it, duties to act that can serve as a basis for criminal liability are not limited to those arising from the connection to the source of danger or the victim. It does not adhere to a closed list of duties. According to it, although the Good Samaritan

20 See Chapter 4, Section 2.

law may not serve as a basis for convicting in cases of homicide or injury, the "failure to prevent a crime" offense may serve as a basis for conviction in the relevant offense.

Why is this? The offense of "failure to prevent a crime" pertains to situations where the norm that sustains autonomy is at risk, as it involves cases where a crime such as murder, homicide, rape, or similar is about to be committed. A bystander can prevent the occurrence of the crime and uphold the norm of safeguarding autonomy. In certain challenging circumstances, it may be possible to convict someone for homicide by omission.

Additionally, the possibility of using the offense of "failure to prevent a crime" as a basis for criminal liability in the relevant offense may be time-sensitive. For example, during a period of increasing violence and when law enforcement is unable to fulfill its role effectively, the concern for violent attacks and the need for citizens' assistance in preventing such violence becomes more important. This fear of violence may significantly impair individual autonomy, making it justifiable to use this offense as a source of a duty to act in the relevant offense during that period.

2.4 The civil sources of legal duty: two challenges

We saw earlier that a duty to act can be recognized in both criminal and civil law. But two challenges may emerge. First, is it suitable to apply obligations originating in civil law for convicting someone in a criminal case? One may argue that a duty to act derived only from civil law may not be sufficiently strong to justify imposing criminal liability on an individual. Second, a crucial consideration is whether using a duty to act from civil law is compatible with the principle of legality. The potential complication lies in the fact that, typically, an individual's mistake regarding the existence or extent of his duty is not a valid defense because ignorance of the law is generally not accepted as an excuse. But the principle of legality is, in part, meant to ensure that citizens can reasonably be expected to know the laws they must abide by before facing sanctions. Is it reasonable to expect citizens to be aware of every duty specified in civil law, and does it make sense to require them to connect between duties arising from civil and criminal law?

Regarding the first point, I argue that the mere absence of certain duties in criminal law, which are present in civil law, does not necessarily indicate their unsuitability for inclusion in criminal law. It may be argued that the absence of a specific duty in criminal law is a deliberate legislative choice, intended to avoid classifying every violation of that duty as a criminal offense, particularly when there may be no concrete harm caused. If harm has been caused, however, the duty to act outlined in civil law could serve as a foundation for conviction under criminal law.

For example, suppose there is a duty in civil law to install lighting in a certain shopping area to prevent harm to people and that a shop owner fails to provide lighting for an entire store. In criminal law, this might not be considered an offense if no harm has yet occurred, but if someone falls and dies because of the lack of lighting, the shop owner could be charged with manslaughter.

Although I believe that a civil duty can serve as a basis for a conviction in a result crime, it is important to ensure that the duty is designed to prevent the particular harm for which criminal liability is being established. For example, if the duty of providing lighting was not intended to prevent harm to others, it would not be appropriate to use it as a basis for convicting someone of manslaughter.

According to the position of Hart and Honoré, mentioned earlier, it may be argued that an obligation to act, which is present in civil law, can serve as a basis for conviction in a criminal offense only if the civil law obligation created an expectation for the citizen to act. Thus, if he violated it, his breach would be considered a primary cause of the prohibited harm.

Regarding the second question, I think that an individual should face conviction based on a civil law duty only if he was aware of the existence of the duty or at least had a reasonable opportunity to become aware of it.[21]

3. Sources of legal duty to act in American law

The sources of legal duty to act in American law are diverse and varied. They are based on the special relationship between the accused and the victim, the relationship between the accused and the source of danger, contractual obligations, voluntary assumption of responsibility, or specific roles that impose a duty to assist another person in danger.[22]

3.1 Duty based on a relationship between the accused and the victim

Common law imposes duties to act that are rooted in close relationships between the accused and the victim.[23] For example, parents have an obligation to assist their young children,[24] step-parents are required to care for their child

21 See Robinson, *supra* note 8, at 196–97.

22 For the sources of the legal duty to act in the UK, see A. P. Simester, J. R. Spencer, F. stark, G. R. Sullivan & G. J. Virgo, Simester and sullivan's Criminal Law – Theory and Doctrine 77–82 (2019). Compare: Smith and Hogan's Criminal Law, *supra* note 12, at 78–82.

23 Today, there are many laws in various countries that explicitly establish duties to act based on special relationships.

24 People v. Valdez 2022 IL App (1st) 181463, 145; People v. Pollock 202 Il 2d. 189, 215–16 (2002) "In sum, we conclude that a parent may not sit idly by while another person abuses her child. Parents are required to intercede on their child's behalf and, if they fail to act, they risk being held responsible for the other person's criminal conduct. By failing to act, the parent may be deemed to have implicitly sanctioned the criminal behavior and, therefore, may be held accountable for the abusive conduct." See also Degren v. State, 722 A. 2d 887 (Md. 1999).

in certain situations and provide adequate medical care,[25] spouses have a duty to assist each other under specific circumstances,[26] and employers are obligated to maintain a safe workplace for their employees.[27] If someone violates a duty based on such a relationship, they may be held liable for the harm caused to the victim as a result of that violation.

Thus, a mother can be held liable for causing harm to a child by omission if she left her child with her partner, knowing that he had a history of abusing the child.[28] A parent may be convicted of manslaughter if he failed to provide proper medical care for his young child, resulting in the child's death.[29]

In the Myers case, a stepfather was convicted for murder of a two-year-old child for failing to feed him, provide water, and heat the room. Although it may not be a strict obligation of a non-biological parent to care for the health and well-being of a child, it becomes an exception if the individual perceives himself as a parent to the child and voluntarily assumes responsibility through words or actions to care for him.[30]

In the Bleimeyer case, a stepmother was convicted of causing physical harm to her child by failing to fulfill her duty to feed the child, care for the child's health, and provide proper medical treatment for the child. The child suffered from chronic malnutrition, resulting in significant developmental delays and organ failure. The duty to act arose from the stepmother's voluntary assumption of responsibility for the child's physical and mental well-being through her actions.[31]

In American law, contrary to the parental duty toward their minor child, there is generally no legal obligation imposed on individuals to provide assistance or medical care to their parents. But when it is evident that the individual voluntarily assumed the duty to act based on a contractual relationship,

25 People v. Myers, 2022 IL App (4th) 200592-U; see also State v. Sherman, 266 S.W. 3d 395 (Tenn 2008).

26 State v. Mally (1961) 139 Mont. 599, 366 P. 2d 868.

27 Beckwitt v. State, 477 Md. 398 (2022); see also: State v. Far West Water & Sewer Inc., 224 Ariz 173 (2010).

28 Faulkner v. State 2023 Tex. App. Lexis 1473, 6–7. See also, *supra* note 24.

29 People v. Burden 72 Cal. App. 3d 603 (1977); People v. Borom, 2013 Mich. App. LEXIS 2186, 12 (2013); United States v. Scott, 954 F. 3d 74, 81 (2020).

30 Myers, *supra* note 25; see also Commonwealth v. Barlow-Tucker 493 Mass. 197 (2024), which determined that it is possible to convict for manslaughter those responsible for a foster child who failed to seek the medical care he needed.

31 Bleimeyer v. State, 616 S.W. 3d (2021). (The defendant, married the biological father of the child, ensured that the child had a specific place to sleep. The child referred to her as "Mom," and during medical examinations, the defendant was present and responded to the doctor's questions, demonstrating a better understanding of the child's medical history than the father. All these circumstances proved that she took upon herself the duty to care for the child's nutrition and medical needs.) State v. Miranda, 245 Conn. 209 (Conn. 1998) (A boyfriend who considered himself the victim's stepfather had assumed the duty of care for the child).

he may be held criminally liable for causing harm or death to his parent if it is proven that he violated this duty.[32]

The duty to act to prevent foreseeable harm also extends to a spouse. In one case, a person whose wife suffered from heart and kidney disease, and broke both her hands in a fall, was convicted of involuntary manslaughter for failing to seek medical help in time.[33] In another case, however, a wife who had both epilepsy and diabetes chose to stop taking her insulin, relying on her faith that God would heal her. The state contended that the husband, by not providing insulin to his wife or seeking medical aid, failed to fulfill his legal duty of care. Consequently, he was indicted for criminally negligent homicide under N.Y. Penal Law § 125.10. The court, acknowledging the husband's legal duty, nevertheless ruled that he was not criminally liable in this situation, because his wife, a competent adult, had made a deliberate choice to eschew medical help.[34]

At least in some jurisdictions, the duty to act is not limited to married spouses but extends also to partners who have close and other family relationships.[35] A duty toward a partner, however, appears to differ in scope from that toward a child. If an injured partner declines to accept assistance, such refusal may relieve the agent from the duty to act, as opposed to the duty of parents toward their young child.

Special relationships between the accused and the victim can also arise from employment relationships. In the Beckwitt case, the accused, who was the victim's employer, was convicted of involuntary manslaughter for failing to provide appropriate working conditions. The accused, who feared a nuclear war with North Korea, employed the victim to dig tunnels under his home. The victim was forced to reside in the basement and tunnels, where the electrical system was faulty, and he had no reasonable means of communication with the accused, who did not possess a cellular phone. On September 10, 2017, a fire broke out in the basement, resulting in the victim's death. It was determined that the employer had a duty to ensure a safe workplace, and in this case, the accused failed to fulfill it.[36]

3.2 *Duty based on a relationship between the accused and the source of danger*

In many US states, there are laws that impose a duty to act based on the relationship between the accused and the source of danger. For example, in many

32 Peterson v. State, 765 So. 2d 861 (2000). Compare: Smith and Hogan's Criminal Law, *supra* note 12, at 78 ("Presumably children above the age of responsibility owe a corresponding duty to their parents").

33 Mally, *supra* note 26.

34 People v. Robbins 83 A.D. 2d 271, 274–75 (1981); see also Commonwealth v. Konz, 498 Pa. 639 (1982).

35 State Ex Rel. Kuntz v. Montana Thirteenth Judicial Dist. Court, 298 Mont. 196, 2000 MT 22, 18–19 (2000).

36 Beckwitt, *supra* note 27.

jurisdictions, there is a law that requires a driver involved in an accident to stop and provide assistance to others if there is reason to believe they have been injured as a result of the accident.[37]

It is clear that if a driver fails to stop, he may be charged with a hit-and-run offense, but if someone is harmed or killed as a result of not providing assistance, he may be held criminally responsible for the injury or death. In Spain, Italy, and Austria, however, an individual who was negligently involved in an accident but did not stop to provide assistance would not be convicted of manslaughter due to failure to provide aid, but rather for the hit-and-run offense, which is less severe.[38]

A duty to act can also arise from owning a dangerous object or being responsible for it. For example, if someone leaves a firearm unattended and a child plays with it, resulting in injury, that person may be criminally liable not only for leaving the firearm unattended but also for causing harm through omission. The duty to act in this scenario is based on the legal requirement not to leave firearms unattended. Dog owners have a similar duty. If a person is bitten by a dog, the owner may be held criminally responsible for the resulting harm.[39]

In the Davidson case, the defendant was convicted of second-degree murder[40] after her Rottweilers killed an 11-year-old child. The court determined that she had a duty to ensure her dogs would not pose a danger to people, a duty that she breached. The court held that her breach was manifested in several ways: failing to properly train the dogs despite their aggressive nature, ignoring expert advice on proper training methods and choosing not to socialize her dogs, neglecting to address the issue of the dogs escaping on numerous occasions, and overlooking the aggressive behavior her dogs displayed toward neighbors and their children.[41]

A duty to act is also imposed in certain situations on a host toward the individuals visiting his premises. For example, if people die as a result of a fire and the property owner failed to fulfill his legal obligation to provide escape routes, he may be held criminally responsible not only for the direct omission in failing to create escape routes but also for involuntary manslaughter.[42] In these situations, however, the duty to act is not always

37 LaFave, *supra* note 12, at 413; State v. Shepherd, 357 P. 3d 598 (2015).

38 Gomez-Aller, *supra* note 12, at 422.

39 *Id.* at 420.

40 Kan. Stat. Ann. § 21–3402(b) (Supp. 1998).

41 State v. Davidson, 267 Kan. 667, 683 (1999). See also Turnipseed v. State, 186 Ga. App. 278 (1988); Berry v. Superior Court, 256 Cal. Rptr. 344 (1989); Freeman v. State, 969 So. 2d. 473 (2007) (Defendant's six pit bulls escaped confinement in his home and killed an elderly neighbor. The defendant was convicted of manslaughter, in violation of § 782.07(1), Fla. Stat. (2003)).

42 Commonwealth v. Welansky, 316 Mass. 383 (1944).

comparable in scope to the duties arising from roles or relationships between the accused and the victim. For example, in the Murray case, the accused was charged with negligent homicide for failing to seek medical help in time, despite noticing that a person who was traveling with him in the same car had taken a large amount of drugs, which ultimately led to the passenger's death. The court acquitted the accused of this offense and determined that although there is a legal duty imposed on the driver toward the passenger, it is not extended to providing medical treatment but confined to safety-related aspects of the car.[43]

3.3 Duty based on the creation of a risk

Another duty that relates to the relationship between the accused and the source of danger is based on the creation of the risk by the accused. If A puts B at risk, he is obligated to prevent harm if the danger was created intentionally or through negligence. For example, if A digs a hole in an area with pedestrian traffic, posing a risk of falling into the hole, A is required to prevent the potential harm.[44]

In the Voss case, the defendant was found guilty of involuntary manslaughter for supplying drugs to the victim and advising him on what would be an appropriate dosage. When he realized that the victim consumed an excessive amount, the defendant left the scene without checking on him or seeking help. It was established that in this circumstance, when the defendant created or heightened the risk, he had an obligation to provide assistance and call for help.[45] Similarly, in the Levesque case, the court ruled that the defendants, who resided in a vacant warehouse and caused a fire as a result of an accident, were obligated to promptly inform the fire authorities. They failed to do so, and as a consequence, six firefighters died while attempting to extinguish the spreading fire. The court ruled that the defendants could be charged with involuntary manslaughter.[46]

43 People v. Murray, 84 N.Y.S. 3d 314 (2018).

44 United States v. Hatatley, 130 F.3d 1399 (10th Cir. 1997). For further elaboration on this matter, see Larry Alexander, *Duties to Act Triggered by Creation of the Peril: Easy Cases, Puzzling Cases, and Complex Culpability*, in The Ethics and Law of Omissions 180 (Dana Kay Nelkin & Samuel C. Rickless eds., 2017); see also R v Miller [1983] 2 AC 161; R v Evans, [2009] 1 WLR 1999. By contrast, in Spain, drivers and passengers are required to remove from the road an object that has fallen from their vehicle. If they fail to do so and an accident occurs as a result, they are not convicted of causing the harm but only of failing to remove the object. Thus, in some cases, even if a person created the risk that led to the harm, he is not convicted of causing the harm but of not acting to prevent it. See Gomez-Aller, *supra* note 12, at 427–28.

45 State v. Voss, 488 S.W. 3d 97, 113 (2016).

46 Levesque, *supra* note 8, at 450; also see Commonwealth v. Doyle, 2006 Mass. Super. Lexis 198. In that case, the defendant was charged with child endangerment for creating a risk of

Yet, within the framework of the duty arising from creating the risk, there is a question about what the law dictates when a person unintentionally and without culpability places another in danger. If A digs a pit in a location with no human traffic, does he have an obligation to prevent potential harm? In the Sanford case, it was ruled that if there was no intention or negligence in creating the risk, the person who created it is not obligated to rescue the victim. In this case, the defendant accidentally caught her mother's finger, causing her to lose her balance and fall down the stairs. The court ruled that because the risk was not created intentionally or negligently, the defendant was not required to help.[47] By contrast, the Kuntz case demonstrates that even when the risk was created unintentionally and without negligence, there is still an obligation to act to save the victim.[48]

Another question arises regarding the creation of risk as a result of self-defense. If A defended himself against an attack by B and shot B, is he obligated to seek appropriate medical treatment for B after the shooting, or is his legal status at this point similar to that of any other stranger in most jurisdictions, who is not under a duty to rescue? According to the Sanford case mentioned, it appears that a person acting in self-defense is not under a duty to act. If in a regular case, unrelated to self-defense, there is no duty to act, it is clear that if he acted justifiably in self-defense, there is no duty to act. However, consistent with the Kuntz case, if a person acts in self-defense, he is obligated to rescue the victim after it becomes clear to him that there is no danger on the part of the victim.[49]

3.4 Duty based on the agent's role

In certain situations, the legislature imposes an obligation to act on individuals because of their official position. For example, prison officers have a duty to

---

sexual abuse to a child by engaging in sexual relations in a child's room, knowing that there was a person in the same apartment with a history of committing sexual offenses against children. It was ruled that even if the creation of the risk was negligent, the accused still had the duty to prevent the risk. Regarding this point, see Miller, *supra* note 44. (D, a trespasser, fell asleep while smoking a cigarette, which led to his mattress catching fire. Upon waking up and discovering the smoldering mattress, he failed to take any measures to extinguish the fire, resulting in the entire house going up in flames. D was convicted of arson contrary to s. 1(1) and (3) of the Criminal Damage Act 1971 because of his role in starting the fire, which imposed a legal duty to act.) Compare: Fagan v. Metropolitan Police Commissioner [1969] 1QB 439 (DC). See discussion on this issue: Simester and Sullivan's Criminal Law, *supra* note 22, at 80–81; Smith and Hogan's Criminal Law, *supra* note 12, at 76–77. MICHAEL J. ALLEN, CRIMINAL LAW 46–47 (2017).

47 People v. Sanford, 2004 NYLJ LEXIS 1943 (2004). In this case, the court ruled that no duty to act arose, among others, because the victim rejected assistance; Compare: People v. Galatro 153 Misc. 2d 54 (1992).

48 Kuntz, *supra* note 35.

49 *Id.* See also JOSHUA DRESSLER, UNDERSTANDING CRIMINAL LAW 105 (2022).

provide medical treatment to the inmates under their care. Failure to fulfill this duty could lead to criminal liability for causing harm.[50] Similarly, police officers and firefighters may be subject to duties based on their roles.[51]

3.5 *Duty based on contract*

The duty to act can be based also on a contractual obligation.[52] For example, a lifeguard employed by the municipality to watch over swimmers is obligated to assist a person in danger and take active measures to prevent harm or death. If the lifeguard fails to act when he sees someone drowning, resulting in the person's death, he may be held criminally responsible for manslaughter.

In the Benton case, the defendant, a train watchman, failed to operate the red flash and signal lights designed to warn the public about an approaching train. This failure led to a collision between a train and the victim's vehicle, resulting in the victim's death. The defendant was subsequently indicted and convicted of involuntary manslaughter. The court ruled that his legal duty to act stemmed from his employment contract.[53]

Contractual duty to act is also imposed on physicians in relation to their patients, and it applies only to the patients in their care. In criminal law, a death resulting from a physician's neglect to provide care is treated as though it were caused by a direct action.[54] In the US, however, some courts ruled that the duty to act extends beyond contractual relationships, applying even in the absence of a contract between the physician and patient.[55] Yet this duty is not absolute. In cases where a patient is terminally ill, the obligation is not to ensure the patient's survival at all costs but rather to make reasonable efforts

50 State v. Kanavy 416Md 1, 4 A. 3d 391 (2010).

51 Weinryb, *supra* note 13, at 15–16.

52 For further elaboration on using a contract as a basis for conviction in cases involving omissions, see Roni Rosenberg, *The Contract: Between Contract Law and Criminal Jurisprudence*, 26 St. Thomas. L. Rev. 444 (2014); Geoffrey Mead, *Contracting into Crime: A Theory of Criminal Omissions*, 11 Oxford J. Legal Stud. 147, 152–58 (1991).

53 State v. Benton, 38 Del. 1, 18 (1936). Another example is reflected in R v Pittwood (1902) 19 TLR 37 (A gatekeeper at a railway crossing forgot to close the gate, resulting in a haycart being struck by a train while crossing the line. As a result, one of the riders died). According to these cases, a contract may establish an obligation to assist individuals, even those who are not party to the contract but are likely to be injured by its non-performance.

54 Simester and Sullivan's Criminal Law, *supra* note 22, at 79.

55 See Stanley v. McCarver, 208 Ariz. 219, 221 (2004) ("The requirement of a formalized relationship between the parties has been quietly eroding in several jurisdictions"). See also Diggs v. Arizona Cardiologist, Ltd. 198 Ariz. 198, 201 (2000) ("Although an express contractual physician-patient relationship clearly gives rise to a duty to the patient, the absence of such a relationship does not necessarily exclude a duty to the patient"). Although these rulings dealt with civil law, it seems that the obligation to act in relation to criminal law, which pertains to physician-patient relationships, also includes situations where there was no contract between the parties.

to sustain life using appropriate medical practices, provided that these efforts serve the patient's best interests.[56]

A babysitter's assignment is another example of a duty arising from a contractual obligation, the breach of which could lead to manslaughter charges. For example, in the Wong case, a couple undertook to care for a three-month-old baby. Two weeks later, the baby died, and the police investigation revealed the cause of death to be "shaken baby syndrome." The Wongs claimed they did not shake the baby but the court determined that even if it is proven that they did not shake the baby, they could still be convicted for manslaughter because they had a contractual duty to supervise the infant, and this duty was breached.[57]

On occasion, there is a duty to act even when the contract is not explicit but rather implied, and it can be inferred from the defendant's behavior that he took responsibility for the victim. For example, in the Davis case[58] the defendant's mother died of pneumonia, freezing to death, and a chronic state of starvation. The mother was incapable of tending to her personal needs, and the defendant informed multiple individuals of her responsibility for her mother's care. Additionally, the defendant served as her mother's authorized representative for both food stamps and social security benefits. The court ruled that the defendant had a legal duty to care for her mother and that her receipt of her mother's benefits proved the existence of an implied contract.[59] The court convicted the defendant of involuntary manslaughter for her breach of this implied contract, ultimately resulting in her mother's death.

3.6 Duty based on voluntary assumption of responsibility

The duty to act can arise from various circumstances, beyond pre-existing relationships or contractual obligations. It can also arise when an individual voluntarily assumes the responsibility to care for or protect someone who is unable to care for himself. For example, if A observes B burning inside a house and starts to rescue him, A is obligated to continue providing assistance until B is safely rescued, as long as such conduct does not endanger A's life. Similarly, if A assumes responsibility for a minor or an incapacitated person, A cannot simply cease providing assistance without a valid reason.[60]

56 See Dressler, *supra* note 49, at 108.

57 People v. Wong, 182 A.D. 2d 98, 108 (1992); see also People v. Zemek, 93 Cal. App. 5th 313 (2023) (In this case, the court of appeal affirmed the conviction of Zemek for first degree murder under Cal Pen. Code, § 187 (a) as it was proven that the she had a contractual obligation to care for a woman who was known to be at risk of drug use, and she breached this duty); Smith and Hogan's Criminal Law, *supra* note 12, at 80.

58 Davis v. Commonwealth, 335 S.E. 2d 375 (1985).

59 *Id.* at 378.

60 Sickel v. State, 363 P. 3d 115 (Alaska App. 2015); People v. Oliver, 210 Cal. App. 3d 138 (Ct. App. 1989); Flippo v. State, 258 Ark. 233 (1975) (One of the defendants shot a person

In the Proo case, for example, the defendant was convicted for injury to a child by omission by failing to provide adequate nutrition and to seek medical treatment. The defendant was convicted after it was proven that she acted as a caretaker for the child and assumed responsibility for his care without an explicit contract.[61]

In the Burris case a 70-year-old man who suffered from dementia and severe health issues, including an inability to move independently, tragically died. His wife, who lived with him alone, assumed responsibility to take care of him and rejected any assistance from family members or home health services. As the sole caregiver, she was responsible for meeting his needs.[62] She failed, however, to fulfill her duties. She left him on the floor for days after he fell, inadequately fed him, and neglected to buy his medications. Her mistreatment led to his death. Due to her omissions, the court convicted her of mistreating a dependent adult and second-degree murder.[63]

3.7 Between contract and assuming responsibility

What is the fundamental difference between an obligation arising from a contract and from assuming responsibility for a potential victim? In both cases, there is a particular type of commitment assumed by the individual toward the potential victim rather than a duty explicitly mandated by legislation. Two approaches can be identified in American jurisprudence. According to the first approach, there is a distinction between the duty arising from assuming responsibility and from a contractual obligation. When the duty arises from assuming responsibility, it exists if the agent increases or intensifies the risk to the victim by secluding the victim so that others are unaware of his deteriorating condition.[64] By contrast, when the duty arises from a contract, the duty

---

during a hunting expedition, believing he was a deer. The defendants, a father and a son, told the victim's father that they would call an ambulance, but they only did so after they returned home and hid their rifles. The court convicted them of involuntary manslaughter after ruling that they had a duty to call for help when they assumed this duty and caused the victim's father not to seek help himself.)

61 Proo v. State, 587 SW. 3d 789 (2019). See also Deleon v. State, 2006 Tex. App. LEXIS 5270. The court convicted the accused, who was the victim's grandmother, for the offense of injury to a child through omission after ruling that the duty to feed the child and provide medical care had been imposed upon her by her assumption of care, custody, and control. In this case, the evidence included a phone conversation between the accused and the child's mother, in which she explicitly undertook to care for the child. Additionally, the accused prevented others from taking the child for medical treatment, interfered with a person who tried to feed the child, and determined when the child could be visited. This behavior proved that she took responsibility for the child.

62 State v. Burris, 63 Kan. App. 2d. 250, 258–63 (2023).

63 *Id.* at 263–65. Kan. Stat. Ann. § 21-5417(a)(3) (2016); Kan. Stat. Ann. § 21-5403(a)(2) (2022).

64 State v. Gargus, 462 S.W. 3d 417, 422 (2013); see also Jones v. United States, 308 F.2d 307, 309 (1962); Flippo, *supra* note 60; Oliver, *supra* note 60, at 147.

to act exists whether the victim is secluded or not. According to the second approach, there is no distinction between a duty arising from a contractual obligation and from assuming responsibility, as both impose an obligation to act, whether the victim is isolated or not.

In my opinion, the difference between the two approaches is in the underlying reason that dictates the duty to act. According to the first approach, the duty to act, arising from voluntarily assuming responsibility, is derived from the increased risk to the victim resulting from taking on that responsibility. Therefore, the obligation to act arises only when the victim is secluded and the risk has been intensified as a result of that seclusion. By contrast, the duty arising from a contract emanates directly from the contractual commitment; therefore, the obligation remains, regardless of whether the victim is secluded or not.

According to the second approach, when the duty to act arises from the voluntary assumption of responsibility, the act of assuming responsibility for the victim creates a close relation between the parties, from which the duty arises for the individual to continue aiding the victim. Therefore, according to this perspective, the duty remains in force irrespective of whether the victim is secluded or not.[65]

An illustration of these two approaches can be observed in the Gargus case.[66] The victim, an 81-year-old woman who suffered from diabetes, was unable to walk and was confined to her bed. The appellant, her daughter, in this case, quit her job as a nurse to take care of her mother but she failed to provide proper treatment for her bedsores or to ensure that the victim received proper nutrition and hydration. At a certain point, the victim was hospitalized, and it was determined that her leg needed to be amputated because of severe gangrene. The victim died in March 2010 from the bedsores and gangrene in her left foot. The appellant was charged with the offense of elder abuse in the first degree, primarily because of her failure to provide proper medical treatment for her mother. The court concluded that the defendant had a legal duty to act, as she voluntarily assumed the responsibility for her mother's care and secluded her in a way that prevented others from rendering aid.[67]

The court noted further that according to an additional position in the American jurisprudence, a duty to act arises when a defendant voluntarily assumes responsibility for someone who is unable to care for himself, and it remains in force whether the victim is secluded or not. Therefore, in this case, it was irrelevant whether the appellant secluded her mother and prevented others from providing aid.[68]

65 Rosenberg, *supra* note 52, at 451–52.

66 Gargus, *supra* note 64, at 418–21.

67 *Id.* at 422. ("When a defendant volunteers to assist an ailing victim, thus preventing or hindering others from providing assistance, the defendant is considered to have secluded the helpless victim, creating a duty to then provide aid.")

68 *Id.* at 423. See also State v. Shroat, 415 S.W. 3d 123 (2013).

7 Differences in the level of punishment between acts and omissions

1. Introduction

The various rationales that distinguish between acts and omissions not only influence which duties can serve as a basis for conviction in indirect omission offenses but also pertain to whether there should be a distinction in the level of punishment between causing harm through action and by omission, even when a specific duty to act has been breached.

Prima facie, the answer hinges on whether the distinction between an act and an omission is based on a moral or legal rationale. If it is based on a legal rationale, there should be no disparity in punishment levels because the duty to act resolves the legal distinction, effectively bridging the gap between acts and omissions. Conversely, if the distinction is based on the difference in moral culpability between causing harm by action vs. omission, although the imposed duty to act may allow for conviction in a result crime, there should still be a disparity in punishment levels between the two scenarios. It is important to recognize, however, that moral rationales, such as the liberty rationale, which do not focus on the agent's culpability, may also argue for equalizing the punishment levels for acts and omissions.

Given this distinction, three main approaches can be discerned regarding the level of punishment for omissions. At one end is the approach that maintains that when a duty to act is identified, there should be no difference in the level of punishment between acts and omissions. At the other end is the approach according to which even when a duty to act is identified, there should still be a distinction in the level of punishment between acts and omissions. Between these two approaches, is the position that some omissions should be penalized as severely as acts whereas others should be subject to less severe punishment.

2. Presenting the problem

Consider a scenario where a firefighter refrains from providing aid to a person trapped inside a burning house. It is generally acknowledged that such a case falls under the category of duties that can form the basis for criminal liability

DOI: 10.4324/9781003380405-10

in result crimes, particularly in causing death. Should the punishment be less severe for an omission that resulted in death than for an action that led to the same outcome, or should they be equally treated?

3. The position that equates the level of punishment

3.1 The coordination problem rationale

As noted, according to Feinberg, the distinction between an act and an omission does not stem from moral considerations but rather from a legal rationale of coordination. Therefore, there should be no difference in the level of punishment between an act and an omission when there is a duty to act. Feinberg argued that if we were to impose a duty on every individual to prevent harm, it would result in a significant waste of resources and create issues of fairness. The duty to act resolves the coordination problem between individuals. Therefore, if a person violates a particular duty to act and causes harm, the punishment should be the same as in cases where an act caused harm, as there is no distinction between the two cases.[1]

As noted, Feinberg argues that there is no moral difference between an individual who fails to fulfill his duty under the Good Samaritan law, leading to someone's death, and one who kills another person. If we apply the same standard to cases involving duties between strangers, it becomes evident that the approach should also apply to duties arising from a professional role or a close relationship, like that between a parent and child or a rescuer and a drowning person.

The position outlined here, associated with Feinberg, can serve as a model for other viewpoints that consider the distinction between act and omission in criminal law to be founded on a legal rather than a moral rationale. According to this view, once the duty to act is identified, there is no difference between causation by an act or an omission, and therefore, there should be no distinction in the levels of punishment.

3.2 The liberty rationale

A similar perspective emerges from the liberty rationale discussed earlier. The underlying reason for imposing a duty to act in relation to omissions is to afford individuals the liberty to lead their ordinary lives without undue interference from the legal system. When a legal duty to act exists, it indicates that the law has deemed the consideration of liberty as either irrelevant or overridden, thereby obligating individuals to act. As a result, if the prohibited harm occurs, it becomes possible to convict for the resulting crime. It may

1 See Joel Feinberg, Harm to Others: The Moral Limits of the Criminal Law 169–71 (1984).

be argued that if the sole consideration is the liberty aspect, the punishment should remain the same, because once the liberty consideration is overridden, there is an inherent equivalence between causation by act or omission. This appears to be Ashworth's position:

> A general principle in criminal law should be that omissions liability should be possible if a duty is established, because in those circumstances there is no fundamental moral distinction between failing to perform an act with foreseen bad consequences and performing the act with identical foreseen bad consequences.[2]

4. The position that distinguishes between the levels of punishment

4.1 The causation rationale

Moore, who bases the legal distinction on a sharp causal differentiation between an act and an omission, argues that since an omission can never cause a particular result, a distinction should be made in the severity of punishment imposed for acts and omissions. According to this perspective, because an omission cannot worsen the situation of the victim, it is always considered to cause lower culpability than an act that directly causes harm and worsens the situation of the victim.

> There is also another legality worry about the present criminalization of certain omissions, which stems from the metaphysical fact that an omission to save, even when a death ensues, is not a killing . . . Not only are omissions to save not killings, but acts that are killing are the more serious moral wrong, even when saving is obligatory . . . Such status would attach lesser penalties to omission to save than to active killing, a lesser punishment juries and judges now typically give anyway but without statutory guidance or authorization.[3]

Thus, when a person drives recklessly, causing a car accident that results in serious injuries to another driver, the legal system is likely to impose a significant punishment, such as substantial imprisonment, considering the direct causation of harm. But when a person witnesses a car accident and fails to call for help or aid the victim, the omission indirectly contributes to the harm. In such instances, the legal system may impose a less severe punishment, taking into account the absence of direct causation in omission.

2 Andrew Ashworth, *The Scope of Criminal Liability for Omissions*, 105 Law Q. Rev. 424, 458 (1989).

3 Michael Moore, *More on Act and Crime*, 142 U. Pa. L. Rev. 1742, 1794–95 (1994).

According to Moore's standpoint, it is also possible to distinguish between the level of punishment for theft by act and by omission. Under the Model Penal Code § 223,[4] theft by act occurs, for example, by taking an item without the owner's permission. Theft can also occur by omission, such as by failing to return lost or misdelivered property. It may be argued that although both cases could be subject to theft charges, the punishment should vary because theft by act implies aggravating the victim's situation, whereas failure to return the item does not worsen the victim's circumstances but rather leaves the victim's condition as it is.

4.2 The entitlement rationale

The distinction in the severity of punishment between acts and omissions is also reflected in Kamm's viewpoint. As noted, Kamm contends that an act resulting in harm carries a higher moral culpability than an omission leading to an equivalent harm because in an act, the victim loses life or property that could have been preserved independently from the agent's aid, whereas in an omission, the victim loses life or property that could have been preserved only with the agent's assistance. Therefore, killing is morally more reprehensible than letting die. Kamm argues that this moral distinction is applicable even where the agent had a duty to act.

> Within the class of aiding behaviors which we compare with negative duties not to interfere, there are (1) acts that we decide we have no duty to perform, (2) acts that we decide we have a duty to perform even without a contractual obligation, and (3) acts that we decide we have a duty to perform due to contractual obligations . . . the claim that negative duties are stricter than positive duties need not be merely the claim that there are no comparable positive duties. It may also be that the duties in categories (2) and (3) are not as stringent, even though the presence of a duty implies that we are not fully entitled relative to another to what we have independently of her, and may be subject to a claim for efforts on her behalf. Although we are not entitled to keep from her what we have independently of her, it may be that denying her our efforts is less bad than interfering with what she has independently of us.[5]

Considering the moral distinction between an act that causes harm and an omission that leads to identical harm, even in the case of a significant duty to act (such as the parents' duty to save their child), the level of punishment should be influenced by whether the harm resulted from an act or an omission, even if certain duties were not fulfilled.

4 Model Penal Code § 223 (Official Draft an Explanatory Notes, 1985).

5 F. M. Kamm, *Action, Omission, and the Stringency of Duties*, 142 U. Pa. L. Rev. 1493, 1496–97 (1994).

5. The intermediary approach

5.1 The causation rationale of Honoré

As noted, Honoré's position relies on a causal analysis, which is different from Moore's perspective. According to Honoré, when a concrete duty to act exists, and it creates an expectation of action, if an individual failing to act results in harm, his omission can be considered a primary cause of the harm. According to this perception, in some cases, there should be no distinction in the level of punishment between acts and omissions because even when a person violates a particular duty to act, creating an expectation, he causes harm similar to that caused by an act. According to Honoré, a father who neglects to feed his child should be subject to the same severity of punishment as one who actively kills the child.

> If the distinct duties theory is right, positive acts are on a level, or nearly on a level, with omissions in contexts where the person concerned—the agent as he may be called—is under a distinct duty like that of parent to child. It then makes little or no difference whether the agent breaks his duty by a positive act or an omission. Beating and starving one's child are equally culpable when the harm to the child is equal (say, comparable suffering culminating in death).[6]

Nevertheless, Honoré distinguishes between different types of omissions: some warrant the same level of punishment as acts but others call for an approach to punishment different from that applied to acts.

> On the distinct duty theory, distinct duties are stronger than the background duties we owe to everyone and take priority over them. Moreover, distinct duties can have varying strengths among themselves. Though both the parent and the householder have distinct duties, a parent's duty to a child may be stronger than a householder's to a visitor. It may have a higher priority and require more of the person subject to it.[7]

According to Honoré, although duties can serve as a basis for liability in result crimes in cases of omission, the punishment for breaching each duty may differ. For example, if a father fails in his duty to feed his child, resulting in the child's death, it is appropriate for the punishment to be the same as if the father had outright killed the child. By contrast, the breach of duty by a landowner for harm caused to those on his property should not entail the same punishment as an act, as the moral duty of a father toward his child is greater than that of a landowner toward those visiting his property.

6 Tony Honoré, Responsibility and Fault 44 (1999).
7 *Id.*

The theory proposed by Honoré regarding causality can be tied to his position on punishment. As noted, according to Honoré, a causal connection is measured by the degree of expectation that society has from an agent to perform a given act in certain circumstances and the routine that emerges as a result of it.

It can be reasonably argued that causal connection exists along a spectrum. The causal link is measured by the depth of the established routine resulting from societal expectation for the agent to undertake a certain action. The stronger the routine established by the expectation, the closer the causal connection resulting from the omission. Conversely, if the expectation results in a weaker and less established routine, the causal link becomes weaker as well.

Thus, a deeper explanation can be provided for the distinction between the duty of a parent toward his child and that of a landowner toward visitors on his property. Because society has a substantial expectation that the parent care for his child, and the routine resulting from this expectation is well-established, the moral duty of a parent toward his child is significant and the causal link between the parent's inaction and the harm caused to the child is tight. By contrast, a societal expectation that a landowner assist those visiting his property is less substantial. Therefore, the routine concerning the duty of a landowner toward visitors to his property is less firmly established, leading to a weaker causal link between the landowner's inaction and the ensuing harm.

According to Honoré's theory, a different explanation concerns the need to distinguish the level of punishment between theft by act and by omission. The obligation not to take someone else's property is deeply ingrained in societal and moral norms, leading to a strong commitment by individuals not to steal from others. By contrast, the expectation that individuals should return lost property they found or a misdelivered item is weaker than the expectation not to take someone else's property without their permission. Because the causal link is also weaker in the latter case, it is necessary to differentiate the level of punishment between the two types of theft.

5.2 The dominance rationale

The dominance rationale also lends support to differentiating in the severity of punishment between causing harm by an act and by an omission. According to this rationale, an omission is recognized as a mitigating factor, justifying the exercise of judicial discretion to distinguish between acts and omissions, resulting in a practical reduction in the penalty for omissions.[8] Even under this rationale, however, some omissions merit the same punishment as acts. Advocates of this viewpoint propose a distinction between routine omissions, where intervention is necessary to restore a disrupted social order, and

8 Mordechai Kremnitzer & Re'em Segev, *Omission in Criminal Law*, in TAMIR BOOK 197, 205–06 (Yosef Tamir & Ora Hirsh eds., 1999).

scenarios where the duty to act is aimed at ensuring the proper functioning of a certain aspect of life. Without fulfilling this duty, the activity itself cannot be sustained, such as safeguarding human life or operating the trains. When omission involves a breach of duty of the latter kind, its social implication resembles those of active engagement.[9]

Thus, parents starving their child or railway workers failing to change train tracks could lead to a punishment similar to that imposed for an act. Conversely, in a scenario where someone fails to rescue a drowning person, the punishment for the rescuer should be less severe than that for a person who caused harm by an act.

5.3 *The autonomy-based theory*

According to the autonomy-based theory proposed earlier, it is necessary to differentiate between the levels of punishment imposed for acts and omissions, at least concerning certain duties. Causing death by an act is more severe than causing death by an omission because of the underlying interests that support the prohibition against killing, as opposed to the interests underlying the prohibition against letting die. Beyond the physical preservation of life, the prohibition against killing enables individuals to lead reasonable lives without constant fear of unjustified death, constituting and promoting both individual and social autonomy. This is different from the prohibition against letting someone die, which does not seek to protect an individual's ability to live without fear.[10]

Yet certain rules impose obligations that, if not fulfilled, can severely undermine both individual and social autonomy. A society without cooperation cannot develop and advance.[11] Still, violating such a duty is not commensurate with violating the prohibition against killing because even in the absence of specific duties, individuals would not live in constant fear. Therefore, the level of punishment for killing should be higher than the level of punishment for letting die even when violating a particular duty to act.

At the same time, according to this rationale, violating certain duties may warrant a punishment approaching the severity of that imposed for killing. An example of such a duty is the obligation of a parent to feed his child. Failure to fulfill this duty can have profound implications for society because the well-being of the next generation depends on parental care. In a society where everyone neglects such responsibilities, the fabric of the community is at risk, leading to a moral consequence akin to causing death by an act. The duty to provide nourishment to one's child is not merely an isolated personal obligation. It is intrinsically tied to the preservation and continuity of society itself.

9 *Id.*
10 For a discussion of the autonomy-based rationale, see Chapter 4.
11 See Chapter 4, Section 6.

Distinguishing the level of punishment between killing and letting die even when there is a duty to act is also applicable to property-related offenses like theft, as mentioned earlier. Although both theft by act and by omission cause harm to the property owner, it is important to consider the underlying interests in the two offenses.[12] In addition to protecting an individual's property, the prohibition against theft by act also provides him with a sense of security, allowing him to live without constant fear of being robbed. It offers a safeguard against potential losses and peace of mind. By contrast, the prohibition against theft by omission does not address the interest of living without constant fear of theft and fails to provide the same sense of security and protection that the prohibition against theft by act does.

12 There are at least four ways to commit theft through omission: (1) finding lost property and neglecting to return it to its owner even when it would be easy to do so, (2) not returning property to its owner after receiving it by mistaken delivery, (3) failing to make a required financial disposition of funds received, and (4) committing theft by deception by failing to disclose information required by law. In contemporary Anglo-American theft law, there is a tendency to impose uniform penalties for all four variations of theft by omission, treating them on a par with commissive theft. This tendency is influenced by the Model Penal Code. See Model Penal Code § 223.3(3); § 223.3(4); § 223.5 and § 223.8. Stuart P. Green, *Theft by Omission* in ESSAYS IN CRIMINAL LAW IN HONOUR OF SIR GERALD GORDON 158 (James Chalmers, Fiona Leverick & Lindsay Farmer eds., 2010).

8 Distinguishing between result and conduct crimes

1. Introduction

In this chapter, I distinguish between result and conduct crimes concerning the need to identify a duty to act in omission cases.[1] I argue that considering most of the rationales presented in the previous chapters for distinguishing between acts and omissions, the need to identify a duty to act in omissions arises mainly in relation to result rather than conduct crimes. Yet I do not argue that the duty requirement in omission is unnecessary in every conduct offense but rather that it is more limited in conduct offenses.

After analyzing the distinction between result and conduct crimes, I apply this insight to certain sexual offenses classified as conduct crimes and argue that, given the rationales that distinguish between acts and omissions, there may not be a need to identify a duty to act in these offenses when they occur by omission. I do not argue that this is necessarily the current situation in American jurisprudence, where the distinction between acts and omissions exists in relation to both result and conduct crimes. I contend that from a desirable legal standpoint, the duty requirement is better suited to result than to conduct crimes.

2. The difficulty of convicting in cases of omissions in conduct crimes

In several conduct offenses, there is a fundamental challenge when it comes to addressing omissions because often they do not fit conceptually within the definition of the offense. In result offenses, an individual may be considered the main perpetrator of the offense even if he only failed to prevent the prohibited outcome defined in the offense, because the emphasis is on preventing the prohibited outcome itself rather than how the prohibited outcome

1 I do not refer here to simple omissions that are also conduct crimes. I address conduct crimes that can be committed both by act and by omission. Furthermore, for the purposes of this chapter, I assume, for the sake of clarity, that the definition of acts and omissions is based on the bodily movement test.

DOI: 10.4324/9781003380405-11

came to pass. By contrast, in conduct offenses, it is usually necessary to carry out a certain behavior to be deemed the primary perpetrator of the offense. Consequently, often, it is challenging to interpret omission-based behavior using the language of the offense.[2] For example, an individual who did not prevent a death may be charged as the primary perpetrator of a manslaughter offense, whereas one who did not prevent a rape would not be charged as the primary perpetrator of the offense but rather as an accomplice of the primary perpetrator.[3]

Nonetheless, if we resolve the conceptual and interpretational challenges and establish that inaction can indeed fulfill the conduct element of the relevant conduct offense, another question emerges: should we have to identify a duty to act in these cases to convict the perpetrator? I am not persuaded that such a duty requirement is necessary, at least not for all conduct offenses. To illustrate the question, consider the following scenario: A is sitting in a doctor's waiting room with his legs stretched in front of him. Suddenly, B is running toward him. A knows that B cannot see his legs and will trip over him if he does not move them. A is capable of moving his legs but chooses not to do so. As a result, B stumbles and falls.[4] Let us assume that this scenario can be classified as battery.[5] Do we need to identify a duty to act to convict A for battery? The answer depends on the rationales we apply to distinguish between acts and omissions, as discussed earlier.

2.1 *The liberty rationale*

According to the liberty rationale, the distinction between acts and omissions in result offenses is based on the effect on the individual's liberty, owing to two cumulative conditions: First, in the prohibition of an act, the citizen is required only to refrain from performing that act but is free to engage in an endless array of others. But when a person is obligated to perform a certain act to prevent a particular harm, he is limited to executing only that act, at which

2 Compare A. P. Simester, J. R. Spencer, F. Stark, G. R. Sullivan & G. J. Virgo, Simester and Sullivan's Criminal Law – Theory and Doctrine 82–84 (2019).

3 In the case of complicity by omission in a conduct offense, I agree that a duty to act should be identified for conviction.

4 See David Ormerod & Karl Laird, Smith and Hogan's Criminal Law 713 (2015); Glanville Williams, *What Should the Code Do about Omissions*, 7 Legal Stud. 92, 116 (1987). Williams does not classify this case as an omission but rather as an act.

5 At least in several US states, battery is a conduct and not a result offense because all that is required is the use of force or violence against another person. See, for example, Cal Pen Code § 242 ("A battery is any willful and unlawful use of force or violence upon the person of another"). See also People v. Shockly 58 Cal. 4th 400, 404 (2013) ("It has long been established that 'the least touching' may constitute battery. In other words, force against the person is enough; it need not be violent or severe, it need not cause bodily harm or even pain, and it need not leave a mark. Witkin & Epstein, Cal. Criminal Law (4th ed. 2012) Crimes Against the Person, § 13, p. 804").

point, his ability to engage in other actions is curtailed. Second, the need to prevent harm in general and death in particular is an ongoing necessity that continually renews itself.[6]

In contrast to result crimes, in cases of direct omission offenses, it appears that there is no significant limitation imposed on the individual's liberty, despite the requirement to perform a given act that prevents the person from engaging in other activities. This is because this need does not continually renew itself.[7] For example, an offense that requires one to submit an income tax report twice a year to the tax authorities does not significantly impinge on one's personal liberty, and the definition of the offense already narrows the instances when an individual is obligated to abandon his activities.[8]

Another example is the offense that requires a driver involved in an accident to stop and provide reasonable assistance to others who may be injured. This offense does not significantly violate a person's liberty because the number of times an individual is compelled to provide reasonable assistance in such a situation is minimal.[9] Quite likely, most individuals will not encounter a situation of this type even once in their lifetime. Therefore, this offense does not pose a serious obstacle to leading a regular life.

Similarly, omissions incorporated within the scope of conduct offenses do not substantially curtail human liberty either. These cases usually involve individuals generating the circumstances that fall within the definition of the offense and retaining the ability to determine their frequency, which is generally low and places an insignificant limitation on liberty.

The earlier example of the offense of battery further illustrates this idea. Does it encroach upon an individual's liberty to be obligated to move his legs out of the way? Certainly not.[10] In cases of omissions in result offenses, however, the harm to the protected interest often arises not directly from the

6 See the discussion regarding the liberty rationale in Chapter 2, Section 2.1.

7 Yitzhak Kugler, *Criminal Omissions*, 20 Bar-Ilan L. Rev. 201, 216 (2003).

8 *Id.* 218–19.

9 See, for example, Cal Veh Code § 20001 & 20003. People v. Mace 198 Cal. App. 4th 875 (2011). See also People v. Dimacali 32 Cal. App. 5th 822 (2019) which relates to Cal Veh Code § 20002, subd. (a); 23 V.S.A. § 1128; Va. Code. Ann § 46.2–894. Regarding this section, see Pollard v. Commonwealth 2022 Va. App. Lexis 462 (2022).

10 The distinction I make between conduct and result offenses may be challenged as follows: in the previous example of battery, consider a scenario where the victim falls and sustains an injury. As this is a result offense, a duty to act is needed to convict the defendant because it involves an omission. But why is there a duty requirement when an injury occurs, whereas in the case of conduct offenses, like battery, there is no duty requirement to convict? I believe this question may be answered. It can be argued that, according to the liberty rationale, if we were to convict someone in a situation resembling this for causing injury by omission, it would not inflict serious harm on his liberty. But because criminal liability for causing injury by omission generally demands a duty to act owing to the significant infringement on liberty, it would be inappropriate to differentiate between cases necessitating a duty to act and those not requiring one in relation to this offense. Such a distinction would undermine the principle of legality and result in ambiguity.

individual who omits the action but rather from another party. Therefore, the frequency of occasions requiring action may be greater. An individual cannot determine when another person will require rescue because the circumstances are not under his control and may occur frequently.[11]

Some argue that the problem of liberty in omissions arises strictly from the fact the individual can perform only one action at a time, which deprives him of all other possible actions.[12] If we accept this argument, it makes sense to distinguish between acts and omissions in conduct offenses as well. This position, however, faces robust criticism because the infringement of liberty is not significant if the likelihood of recurrence is low, and it depends on the nature of the duty. For example, if a person enjoys smoking and the law prohibits this activity, it could be a severe infringement on his liberty, even if he is allowed to perform various other actions. Conversely, a one-time requirement for a person to assist a police officer does not significantly limit his liberty.[13]

2.2 *The causation rationale*

If the rationale that distinguishes between acts and omissions is based on causality, meaning that the need for a specific duty to act in omissions arises from the fact that no causal relationship exists in omissions, in conduct offenses, this rationale is entirely irrelevant because a causal link is not one of the elements defining the offense. Therefore, when an omission conceptually falls within the scope of a conduct offense, it may be punishable even without a duty to act.[14]

2.3 *Minimizing the number of defendants rationale*

If the rationale stems from the difficulty of pinpointing a particular offender in the case of an omission, the issue does not exist in several conduct offenses, where it is generally clear who omitted. The problem usually arises in result offenses, where many people could have intervened to prevent the prohibited result that defines in the offense but chose not to.[15]

11 Another example is the offense of desertion. Consider a soldier on leave who fails to return to his unit, a case conceptually classified as desertion. Would it be an infringement on liberty if the soldier were compelled to return to his unit? The frequency of desertion cases depends entirely on the individual involved. If he is obligated to return, there is no concern that the need to do so will recur if he does not repeat the act. By contrast, in the case of result offenses, such as those involving death or harm, liberty is infringed because the situation can always recur regardless of the potential rescuer. Therefore, according to this perspective, a distinction between acts and omissions in conduct offenses is not necessarily required.

12 P. J. Fitzgerald, *Acting and Refraining*, 37 Analysis 133–39 (1967).

13 George P. Fletcher, *Moral Irrelevance of Bodily Movements*, 142 U. Pa. L. Rev. 1445, 1451 (1994).

14 For a discussion of the causation rationale in relation to the distinction between acts and omissions, see Chapter 2, Section 3.

15 See Chapter 3, Section 5.

2.4 *The coordination problem rationale*

If the rationale is based on the coordination problem, the issue usually does not arise in conduct offenses. As noted, the coordination problem arises because of efficiency and fairness concerns. The efficiency problem is rooted in the fear that many resources will be wasted, with many people spending their time helping few others. The fairness problem arises when some people help while others do not. These problems do not appear to exist in conduct offenses because the offense is committed by a particular individual who has the ability to prevent it. There appears to be no problem of efficiency or fairness.[16] We can analyze this in relation to the earlier example of the battery offense, where A stretched out his legs when nobody was near him. When B approached, A chose not to move his legs, despite being aware that B would likely fall as a result. I believe that it is possible to convict A even without pinpointing a concrete legal obligation requiring him to move his legs. In this instance, convicting an individual without a particular duty to act would not create a coordination problem with other citizens because the scope of the battery offense is limited to those directly performing the behavior in question, in this case, specifically A.[17]

2.5 *The autonomy-based theory*

According to the autonomy-based theory, where the omission falls within the scope of the prohibited conduct (in conduct offenses), there may not be a significant difference in moral blameworthiness, and therefore, the duty to act in omissions may not be required. In such cases, the omission could imply intervention in the protected sphere of the individual. Therefore, it is likely that even under the autonomy-based theory, there should not be a rigid distinction between acts and omissions concerning conduct offenses, especially in offenses aimed at preventing physical harm to individuals.[18]

In conclusion, the preceding discussion showed that the duty requirement may have greater relevance in result than in conduct offenses. This does not mean that there can be no instances in conduct offenses where the duty requirement in omissions is necessary. Each conduct offense must be examined individually to determine whether there is a need for a duty to act in cases of omission, taking into consideration the various rationales.

3. Sexual offenses as an illustration

In the following I examine a few sexual offenses that are conduct offenses to illustrate my position.

16 See Chapter 3, Section 4.

17 Regarding an individual who did not prevent the assault, it is clear that a duty to act is required to convict him, but as a secondary party and not as a primary perpetrator.

18 For a discussion of the autonomy-based theory, see Chapter 4.

3.1 Indecent assault against a minor

In John Doe v. State of Israel,[19] the court dealt with allegations of indecent assault perpetrated by the accused against a minor. The accused contended that certain indecent acts, for which he was convicted, occurred with the complainant initiating the physical contact (such as touching his body) without resistance on his part. He argued that his role was passive, suggesting that his behavior should be categorized as an omission rather than an act, and therefore, he should not be convicted for the offensive conduct.[20] The Court examined this argument and concluded that it was not an omission but an act because the defendant actively engaged in these indecent acts and derived pleasure from them.

The question is whether such an examination was necessary. Let us assume the defendant did not actively engage in these acts, yet the case is still conceptually classified as indecent assault. Should we require a duty to act to convict him of this offense? What infringement on liberty exists here based on the liberty rationale? All that is required from the defendant is to stop the minor's actions involving him. The requirement is both easy to do and infrequent. It applies only to the given situation or similar ones that may arise in connection with the defendant, but the number of such cases is not high. In contrast to situations that form the basis for result offenses, which can occur independently of the defendant and frequently, situations in conduct offenses such as the case at hand are not many, and their infringement on liberty is minimal. Therefore, it is not clear that it is appropriate to distinguish between acts and omissions in offenses of this type, and it is questionable that it was necessary to identify a duty to act to convict the defendant.

Nor is there a need to identify a duty to act from the perspective of the causation rationale, according to which the duty to act is intended to bridge the moral gap between the act that caused harm and a failure to prevent it. As this case involves a conduct offense and there is no need to prove a causal connection, there is no need either to identify duty to act to convict the offender.

3.2 Indecent exposure

Another illustration of my approach is the offense of "indecency with a child by exposure," defined under Tex. Penal Code § 21.11(a)(2).[21] The elements of this offense are as follows: (1) the child is in the protected age group (below 17) and not married to the accused, (2) the child is present, (3) the accused

19 CA 7832/04 John Doe v. State of Israel (2006) Nevo Legal Database (Isr.); In many US states there is a specific offense regarding indecent assault against a minor. See, for example, 18 Pa. C.S. § 3126 (a)(7). Commonwealth v. Graves 276 A. 3d 217 (2022).

20 For an analysis of the indecent assault offense in the US, see, for example, Commonwealth v. Fisher, 782 A.2d. 992 (2001) (regarding 18 Pa. C.S.A. § 3126(a)(7)).

21 Tex. Penal Code Ann. § 21.11(a)(2) (West 2003).

intends to arouse or gratify someone's sexual desire, (4) the accused knows that a child is present, and (5) the accused exposes his anus or genitals.[22] According to the interpretation of the courts, this is a clear conduct offense because it does not require a resulting harm, and unlike the offense of indecent assault, it does not require a victim at all. The primary focus of the offense lies in the act of exposure and the mental element. Let us assume that A exposes himself in front of a window in his home when no one is outside, with the intent to arouse or gratify his sexual desire. At this point, A has not committed the offense of "indecency with a child by exposure" because there is no one present outside. Let us assume further that at a later point, a 12-year-old child arrives and sits on a bench facing A's window. If A remains motionless and continues to stand naked in front of the window, under the current legal situation he can be convicted only if a duty to act can be identified requiring him to leave the area or get dressed. In my opinion, however, A could be convicted even without a specific legal duty to act, considering the rationales that distinguish between acts and omissions in criminal law.

Under the liberty rationale, would there be an infringement on liberty if we require someone to leave a room? Clearly not. Additionally, such situations are rare and entirely under the control of the individual, minimizing the infringement of liberty. Thus, holding someone criminally liable for indecent exposure does not necessarily limit his freedom, even without a specific duty to act.

Similarly, if we consider the causation rationale, which states that an act causes harm whereas an omission does not, there is no need in this case to prove a particular harm or a concrete victim. Therefore, prima facie, there may not be a need to distinguish between an act and an omission, and we could convict without a specific duty to act.

The same argument can be applied to the coordination problem proposed by Feinberg. Even if we were to convict in this situation without a duty to act, it would not cause a coordination problem between people because in offenses of this type, only the person who undressed committed the crime, unlike in a result offense. Therefore, imposing responsibility in this case, even without a specific duty to leave the room or get dressed, would not result in inefficiency.[23]

3.3 Rape

Consider a situation where the offense of rape by omission is applicable, as in a case where initial consent was given for sexual intercourse, but the woman

22 Yanes v. State, 149 S.W. 3d 708 (2004).

23 Those who refrained from stopping the exposure are not the principal wrongdoers but rather can be convicted for aiding and abetting as a secondary party. For the purpose of holding them accountable, I agree that it is necessary to identify a legal duty to act.

withdraws her consent during the act.[24] Let us assume that after her withdrawal of consent, the defendant refrains from all physical action, and conceptually, the act of intercourse could have continued without any physical act on the part of the defendant. Is it necessary to establish a duty for the defendant to stop the intercourse to convict him? In my opinion, it is not.

According to the liberty rationale in the case at hand, there is no significant infringement of the individual's liberty because situations of this type are rare. Therefore, there is no need to establish a duty to act in these cases. This conclusion applies to other rationales as well. For example, the causation rationale does not seem relevant here because we are dealing with a conduct rather than a result offense. Similarly, according to the autonomy-based theory, a violation of the individual's protected sphere can occur even in a situation where there is no physical movement.

In sum, in cases like the ones examined in this chapter, it is not necessary to establish a duty to act. The different rationales support this conclusion.

24 Compare: Kaitamaki [1985] AC 147, 151 [PC]; Sexual Offences Act 2003, §79(2); Simester & Sullivan's Criminal Law, *supra* note 2, at 80–81; Regarding the legal situation in the US concerning the rape offense, see Joshua Dressler, Understanding Criminal Law, Chap. 33 (2022).

9 Distinguishing between active and passive euthanasia

1. Introduction

In this final chapter, I discuss the distinction between active euthanasia, which is categorically prohibited in most countries, and passive euthanasia, which is permitted under certain conditions. I argue that the majority of rationales proposed for distinguishing between acts and omissions in criminal law are not applicable to the distinction between active and passive euthanasia. Therefore, even if there is a general distinction between acts and omissions in criminal law, and in particular between killing and letting die, it does not necessarily lead to a distinction between active and passive euthanasia. If passive euthanasia is permissible under certain circumstances, active euthanasia should also be permitted under the same circumstances.[1]

2. Definitions and classifications of euthanasia

The term "euthanasia" is derived from two Greek words: "eu," meaning good, and "thanatos," meaning death, signifying "good death."[2] Euthanasia refers to the intentional act of bringing about the death of a terminally ill patient to alleviate his suffering for his own benefit. Consequently, euthanasia encompasses two essential components: (1) the deliberate killing of the patient and (2) the act is intended for the benefit of a terminally ill patient in severe pain.[3]

Euthanasia is divided into two main types: active and passive. Active euthanasia entails causing the death of a patient by direct action, such as the

1 The approach I adopt in this chapter diverges from that of other writers in the field who argued that because of the absence of a moral distinction between killing and letting die in typical cases, there should be no differentiation between active and passive forms of euthanasia. For discussions on the skeptical viewpoints about the distinction between acts and omissions and between killing and letting die, see Chapter 1. My perspective in this chapter is different because, in my opinion, even if a distinction exists between killing and letting die in criminal law, it may not be pertinent to the two types of mercy killing.

2 Helga Kuhse, *Euthanasia*, in A Companion to Ethics 294 (Peter Singer ed., 1993).

3 *Id.*

DOI: 10.4324/9781003380405-12

injection of a lethal drug. Passive euthanasia involves allowing the patient to die by withholding medication or life-supporting devices.[4]

In the gray area between these two types of euthanasia, there is also the concept of physician-assisted suicide for terminally ill patients. This typically involves a physician prescribing a lethal medication for the patient, who then takes it, causing his own death. The crucial difference between active euthanasia and physician-assisted suicide is that in the former, the physician directly causes the patient's death whereas in the latter, the patient takes the lethal medication and causes his own death.[5]

There are also situations where a physician must decide whether to disconnect a patient from life-support devices. In such cases, some categorize the act as passive euthanasia, where the patient's death results from a terminal illness caused independently of the physician's intervention. By contrast, active euthanasia involves the physician's direct administration of lethal medication, which becomes the immediate cause of death.[6] But positions differ, and some consider the act of disconnecting a patient from life-support devices as active euthanasia because the physician's action directly contributes to the patient's death.[7]

Paralleling the distinction between active and passive euthanasia, there is another relevant categorization of the types of euthanasia: voluntary,

4 Heather Draper & Anne Slowther, *Euthanasia*, 3 Clinical Ethics 113–15 (2008); Jeff McMahan, The Ethics of Killing: Problems at the Margins of Life 457 (2002). Not everyone agrees with this definition. For a discussion on this definition, see: E. Garrard & S. Wilkinson, *Passive Euthanasia*, 31 J. Med. Ethics 64–68 (2005).

5 Andriy Danyliv & Ciaran O'Neill, *Attitudes Towards Legalising Physician Provided Euthanasia in Britain: The Role of Religion Over Time*, 128 Soc. Sci. & Med. 52 (2015); Regarding physician-assisted suicide and its relation to the Fourteenth Amendment, see Wash v. Glucksberg, 521 U.S. 702 (1997). In this *case*, the United States Supreme Court held that Washington State ban on physician-assisted suicide, Wash. Rev. Code § 9A.36.060(1) (1994), did not violate the Fourteenth Amendment to the United States Constitution. See also Kligler v. Attorney General, 491 Mass. 38, 40–41 (2022). (In this case, the court concluded that the Massachusetts Declaration of Rights does not protect physician-assisted suicide from manslaughter conviction). Compare: Baxter v. State, 354 Mont. 234 (2009). (terminally ill patient's consent to physician-assisted suicide constitutes statutory defense to charge of homicide).

6 See Airedale NHS Trust v. Bland, [1993] A.C. 789; Barber v. Superior Court, 147 Cal. App. 3d 1006 (Ct. App. 1983); McMahan, *supra* note 4, at 459; David Shaw, *The Body as Unwarranted Life Support: A New Perspective on Euthanasia*, 33 J. Med. Ethics 519 (2007); Reinhard Merkel, *Killing or Letting Die? Proposal of a (Somewhat) New Answer to a Perennial Question*, 42 J. Med. Ethics 353 (2016). Nathan Emerich & Bert Gordijn, *Beyond the Equivalence Thesis: How to Think about the Ethics of Withdrawing and Withholding Life Saving Medical Treatment*, 40 Theoretical Med. & Bioethics 21, 26–27 (2019); James Cameron, Julian Savulescu & Dominic Wilkinson, *Is Withdrawing Treatment Really More Problematic Than Withholding Treatment?* 47 J. Med. Ethics 722, 724 (2022).

7 Emerich & Gordijn, *supra* note 6, at 34–38; Compare: Andrew McGee & Robert Truog, *Withholding and Withdrawing Life-Sustaining Treatment and the Relevance of the Killing Versus Letting Die Distinction*, 19 Am. J. Bioethics. 34–36 (2019). See also discussion regarding this issue: David Ormerod & Karl Laird, Smith and Hogan's Criminal Law 84–88 (2015).

non-voluntary, and involuntary.[8] Voluntary euthanasia refers to the act of mercy killing carried out by A at the request of B to alleviate B's suffering. Non-voluntary euthanasia entails mercy killing by A when B is unable to express his desire for death, such as in the case of a terminally ill infant or an incapacitated individual unable to communicate his wish to die following an accident or illness. Last, involuntary euthanasia denotes the act by A causing B's death although B is in a condition where he could request euthanasia but chooses not to do so.[9]

As noted, both active and passive euthanasia can fall into one of these categories. In this chapter, I address the distinction between active and passive voluntary euthanasia, which occurs after the terminally ill patient expresses a desire to end his life.

3. The legal situation in the world—in a nutshell

In most countries, active euthanasia is strictly prohibited, and passive euthanasia is allowed under certain conditions.[10] For example, in some US states, patients may be disconnected from respirators or not given life-prolonging medications under certain circumstances.[11] However, in most US states, both active euthanasia and physician-assisted suicide are prohibited, although there are exceptions in Oregon, California, Colorado, Hawaii, Maine, and a few other states where physician-assisted suicide is permitted.[12]

In England, both active euthanasia and physician-assisted suicide are prohibited.[13] In Switzerland, active euthanasia is forbidden, but physician-assisted suicide is permitted for terminally ill patients who request it.[14] In the Netherlands and Belgium, active euthanasia is permitted in certain cases.

8 McMahan, *supra* note 4, at 457; see also Penney Lewis, *The Empirical Slippery Slope—from Voluntary to Non-Voluntary Euthanasia*, J. L. MED. & ETHICS 197 (2007).

9 *Id.*

10 Danyliv & O'Neill, *supra* note 5, at 52–53.

11 E. Gedge, M. Giacomini & D. Cook, *Withholding and Withdrawing Life Support in Critical Care Setting: Ethical Issues Concerning Consent*, 33 J. MED. ETHICS 215–16 (2007).

12 See Kligler, *supra* note 5, at 41("Physician-assisted suicide has been legalized in ten States and the District of Columbia"); Raphael Cohen-Almagor, *The Right to Die with Dignity: An Argument in Ethics and Law*, 2 HEALTH L. & POL'Y 2–3 (2008); Joseph G. Barsness, Casey R. Regnier, C. Christopher Hook & Paul S. Mueller, *U.S. Medical and Surgical Society Position Statements on Physician-Assisted Suicide and Euthanasia: A Review*, 11 BMC MED. ETHICS 111 (2020); Cal. Health & Safety Code §443.1 et seq.; Colo. Rev. Stat. §§ 25-48-101 et seq.; D.C. Code §§ 7-661.01 et seq.; Haw. Rev. Stat. §§ 327L-1-2 et seq.; Me. Rev. Stat. tit. 22, § 2140; N.J. Stat. Ann. §§ 26:16-1 et seq.; N.M. Stat. Ann. §§ 24-7c-1 et seq.; Or. Rev. Stat. §§ 127.800 et seq.; Vt. Stat. Ann. tit. 18, §§ 5281 et seq.; Wash. Rev. Code §§ 70.245.010 et seq.

13 Cohen-Almagor, *supra* note 12, at 3–4.

14 *Id.* at 4; Samia A. Hurst & Alex Mauron, *Assisted Suicide and Euthanasia in Switzerland: Allowing a Role for Non-Physicians*, 326 BRIT. MED. J. 271 (2003).

In Canada, until 2016, active euthanasia and physician-assisted suicide were prohibited. In a landmark case, in 1993, Sue Rodrigez, who suffered from ALS, requested assistance to end his life and brought the matter before the Supreme Court of Canada. The majority decision of the Supreme Court was to disallow the procedure.[15] In 2016, the Medical Assistance in Dying law was enacted, allowing both procedures.[16] According to government estimates, there were 4,438 deaths by euthanasia (active and physician-assisted suicide) in Canada, in 2018 and 5,444 in 2019. From the enactment of the new legislation until 2020, euthanasia deaths amounted to 2% of all deaths in Canada, while in the Netherlands and Belgium, euthanasia deaths accounted for approximately 5% of all deaths.[17]

4. The distinction between acts and omissions in criminal law and its implications on euthanasia

The central question of this chapter is why in most countries a distinction is made between active euthanasia, which is categorically prohibited, and passive euthanasia, which is allowed under certain conditions. One of the main rationales for this distinction is based on differentiating between killing and letting die. Active euthanasia is classified as "killing"; therefore, it is strictly forbidden, whereas passive euthanasia is classified as "letting die," and permissible under certain circumstances.[18]

In the following, I examine whether the rationales presented earlier regarding the distinction between acts and omissions in criminal law are relevant to the distinction between active and passive euthanasia. In this examination, I consider both the position that death is intrinsically bad, including by euthanasia, and that in cases of euthanasia, death is perceived as a favorable outcome.

4.1 The liberty rationale

A fundamental argument for distinguishing between acts and omissions in criminal law is based on the liberty rationale that focuses on the importance of the duty requirement in omissions as a means to safeguard human liberty.[19] When used as the basis for distinguishing between acts and omissions, the liberty rationale also has implications for cases involving euthanasia. When a terminally ill patient requests to die, the physician does not raise the liberty

15 Rodrigez v. British Columbia (Attorney General) [1993] S.C.J. N.O. 94.

16 Leoni Herx, Margaret Cottle & John Scott, *The "Normalization" of Euthanasia in Canada: The Cautionary Tale Continues*, 66 World Med. J. 28 (2020).

17 *Id.* at 29.

18 John Griffiths, Alex Bood & Helen Weyers, Euthanasia and Law in the Netherlands 158–59 (1998).

19 See the discussion in Chapter 2 Section 2.1.2.

argument because he is not arguing that connecting the patient to life support equipment would infringe on his liberty. Therefore, the differentiation between administering lethal medication to the patient and not connecting him to life support devices in the context of a duty to act is not relevant. Furthermore, within the physician-patient relationship, especially in these unique situations, the liberty argument is not applicable because of the special nature of the relationship and the infrequent occurrence of such cases that only minimally limit the physician's liberty. Thus, the law should not regard the liberty consideration as a valid reason for exempting the physician from the duty to act; therefore, the liberty rationale is not relevant for differentiating between active and passive euthanasia.

This means that the argument for allowing passive euthanasia is based on other considerations, such as an individual's autonomy to choose how to die or the dignity of a terminally ill patient in severe pain.[20] Based on the autonomy consideration, a person has the right to decide how to live and die as long as it does not harm others.[21] The state should not protect the right to life when the individual to whom this right applies does not seek such protection.[22] Under this approach, the role of the state should be limited to creating conditions where all citizens can exercise their autonomy. These conditions include the freedom to die when faced with a terminal illness and the ability to seek assistance in exercising this right.[23]

Given that the liberty consideration is irrelevant to differentiating between types of euthanasia and the rationale for permitting passive euthanasia is based on autonomy or human dignity, the same rationale may seem applicable to active euthanasia as well. If a patient's autonomous consideration allows a physician not to intervene and thus hasten his death, why should the autonomy consideration not allow the physician, at the patient's request, to actively end his life? The same question applies to the dignity consideration. If human dignity is a significant factor in allowing passive euthanasia, why should this rationale not allow actively ending the patient's life, considering that the distinction between acts and omissions, according to the liberty approach, is not causal?

Another justification for permitting passive euthanasia concerns the physician's duty to act in the patient's best interest.[24] According to this rationale, the physician is obligated to alleviate the patient's suffering, even if it entails his death, as in this situation, the patient's death is considered a good outcome. Death is defined as good because the patient himself has defined it as such for

20 Griffiths, Bood & Weyers, *supra* note 18, at 168–69.
21 Cohen Almagor, *supra* note 12, at 2–3.
22 Griffiths, Bood & Weyers, *supra* note 18, at 169.
23 *Id.*
24 *Id.* at 172–74.

putting an end to his suffering. However, even under this argument, there should be no distinction between active and passive euthanasia. If it is permissible not to prolong the patient's life because death is considered good, would it not be more ethical to actively hasten death?

4.2 The agent as a means rationale

Another rationale proposed to distinguish between acts and omissions in criminal law is based on the deontological principle that individuals should not be treated merely as a means to an end.[25] According to this rationale, when an act is prohibited, the agent is not reduced to a mere instrument, unlike when an omission is prohibited. Thus, prohibiting an act of killing does not entail making the agent a means to save the victim's life because compliance with this prohibition does not require the agent to take any specific action, and he remains free to choose any course of action he desires.

By contrast, when a prohibition against letting die is enacted, the law compels the agent to use his body to rescue the victim, effectively treating the agent as an instrument. This rationale suggests that the duty to act sets forth a concrete list of cases in which the law deems it appropriate to use the agent as a means to prevent harm, and such instances are expected to be infrequent.[26]

In my opinion, even this rationale falls short of explaining the distinction between active and passive euthanasia. Prima facie, when we consider death as intrinsically bad even in the case of euthanasia, it becomes challenging to argue that as part of the physician-patient relationship, the law would not impose a duty on the physician to preserve life. The argument that this duty would reduce the physician to a mere instrument seems weak, given the physician's role and the usual obligation to act in close relationships. Therefore, there appears to be no fundamental difference between active and passive euthanasia in this regard.

The justification for permitting passive euthanasia in certain cases, as noted, lies elsewhere, specifically, in respect for the patient's autonomy to decide how to end his life or preserve his dignity. But these justifications apply equally to both passive and active euthanasia.

The lack of distinction between active and passive euthanasia is reinforced by the fact that in such instances, death is considered a desirable and favorable outcome, given the patient's request to end his suffering. If in cases of passive euthanasia, the physician is not obligated to intervene and prolong the patient's life because death is considered desirable, why should we not consider allowing active euthanasia to accelerate the process and end the suffering sooner?

25 See discussion in Chapter 2, Section 2.2.
26 *Id.*

4.3 *The autonomy-based theory*

The autonomy-based theory also fails to justify the distinction between active and passive euthanasia. According to this rationale, the prohibition against killing is more stringent because it protects broader and more significant values than the prohibition against letting die.[27] The argument relies on the premise that without the prohibition against killing, individuals would constantly live in fear and anxiety of being killed. By contrast, without the prohibition against letting die, an individual's life would still be reasonably secure.[28]

However, the arguments of the autonomy-based theory are relevant only for common scenarios of mortality where the individual has expressed no intention to end his life. In cases of voluntary euthanasia, this distinction becomes irrelevant because even if there were no prohibition against voluntary active euthanasia, no individual would live in constant fear and anxiety of being killed at any moment.

This argument holds regardless of whether we perceive the death in this situation as intrinsically good or bad.

4.4 *The coordination problem rationale*

The legal rationales for distinguishing between acts and omissions also fail to support the distinction between active and passive euthanasia. For example, according to the coordination problem rationale proposed by Feinberg, there is no moral distinction between acts and omissions because both can cause harm. The duty requirement in omissions, according to Feinberg, arises from the problem of coordination, which could have existed without the distinction.[29]

In the case of passive euthanasia, the absence of a duty to act with regard to the physician does not stem from an issue of coordination because only the physician has the capacity and the means to prolong the life of the patient under his care. Therefore, the argument not to impose a duty on the physician arises from other reasons mentioned earlier, which are relevant to both active euthanasia and passive euthanasia.

4.5 *The causation rationale*

In contrast to the previously discussed rationales, alternative moral justifications can provide insight into distinguishing between active and passive euthanasia. According to the causation rationale, actions have the potential to directly cause specific outcomes whereas omissions either lack the capacity

27 See discussion in Chapter 4, Section 2.
28 *Id.*
29 See discussion in Chapter 3, Section 4.

to cause outcomes or do so indirectly.[30] Within this framework, assuming that death is intrinsically bad, even in scenarios involving euthanasia, we can explain the contrast between active and passive euthanasia. The law may hold that passive euthanasia carries a relatively lighter weight because of the absence of a direct causal link between a physician's passive conduct and the patient's death. Given the central aspects of patient autonomy and human dignity, it may not be appropriate to obligate physicians to actively extend the patient's life.

Conversely, when dealing with active euthanasia, a causal connection exists between the physician's action and the patient's death. In these cases, considerations of autonomy and human dignity are overridden by the obligation not to bring about an individual's death, even when the individual is a terminally ill patient.

At the same time, it may be argued, as noted, that death in the case of a terminally ill patient is not intrinsically bad, but intrinsically good because it ends the patient's suffering at his request. Therefore, there is no reason to distinguish between active and passive euthanasia. Moreover, if there is a significant moral distinction between killing and letting die in situations where death is an unfavorable result, then in cases where death leads to a desired outcome, as in euthanasia, killing ought to be considered more favorable than letting die because the act of killing achieves the desired outcome sooner than letting die.[31]

4.6 The entitlement rationale

Another rationale that could explain the distinction between active and passive euthanasia is Kamm's entitlement rationale.[32] According to Kamm, in cases of killing, the victim loses a life that could have been preserved independently from the agent's assistance, whereas in cases of letting die, the victim loses a life that could have been preserved only with the agent's aid. According to Kamm, there is moral significance to the essential component that the victim loses a life that could have been preserved exclusively with the agent's assistance because every individual, in relation to another individual, is entitled only to what he possesses independently of the other person. He is not entitled to things that can be his only with another person's assistance.[33] Therefore, when the agent allows the victim to die, the victim loses a life that is possible only with the assistance and efforts to which the victim is not entitled, in other words, the victim loses a continuation of life to which he is not entitled. By

30 See discussion in Chapter 2, Section 3.3.

31 Compare: McMahan, *supra* note 4, at 461; James Rachels, *More Impertinent Distinctions and a Defense of Active Euthanasia*, in KILLING AND LETTING DIE 139, 151–52 (Bonnie Steinbock & Alastair Norcross eds., 1994); see also Holly Smith Goldman, *Killing, Letting Die, and Euthanasia*, 40 ANALYSIS 224 (1980).

32 See the discussion in Chapter 2, Section 4.2.

33 *Id.*

contrast, in most cases of killing, the victim loses a life to which he is entitled because he could have continued to live autonomously were it not for the agent's intervention.[34]

At first glance, one may argue that it is easier to permit passive euthanasia because the victim loses a life that could have been preserved only through the physician's aid, whereas in active euthanasia, the patient loses a life that could have continued independently from physician's aid. But in the context of physician-patient relations, it may be argued that the patient is entitled to the assistance and intervention of the attending physician and healthcare facility. Therefore, if the patient does not receive life-prolonging treatment, he loses a life to which he is entitled. In other words, the permission of passive euthanasia is not based on the claim that the patient is not entitled to the assistance and efforts of the attending physician. If the patient had desired such intervention, the physician would be obligated to provide care within the scope of his medical responsibilities.

Therefore, the rationale for permitting passive euthanasia rests on different considerations, such as the principle of autonomy manifested in the explicit wish of the patient not to prolong his life and to end his suffering. But if this is the basis for permitting passive euthanasia, then it also applies to active euthanasia because in both cases, the patient explicitly relinquishes his right to life. In both scenarios, the patient loses a life to which he is entitled, and in both scenarios, he explicitly waives this entitlement so that euthanasia should be permissible in both cases.

The argument I presented about the entitlement rationale remains highly relevant, particularly if we assume that death is intrinsically good in cases of euthanasia. If we allow passive euthanasia because of the perceived goodness of death, which ends the suffering of the patient at his request, there is no reason not to also permit active euthanasia as well.

34 *Id.*

Summary and future outlook

The distinction between acts and omissions is deeply rooted in criminal law and ordinary morality. Nevertheless, extensive debates and controversies have arisen regarding both the validity of the distinction and the main rationale behind it. In the realm of morality, some question the very existence of a distinction between acts and omissions. According to this skeptical viewpoint, all other conditions being equal (intentions, outcomes, and efforts to prevent harm), there is no distinction between an act that caused harm and an omission that led to the same harm. In the realm of criminal law, although it seems that there is no dispute about the need for such a distinction, a profound disagreement persists concerning the rationale underlying it. I don't think there is another legal distinction in criminal law that elicits such extensive controversy.

As I showed throughout the book, the various rationales underpinning the distinction lead to diverse positions on a range of practical questions, such as the following: Which duties can serve as a basis for conviction in the relevant omission offense? What is the definition of an act and an omission that arises from the relevant rationale? Should the punishment for an act that caused harm differ from punishment for an omission that led to the same harm, even when there is a legal duty to act?

The complexity of the issue surrounding the distinction between acts and omissions extends to questions that greatly concern our society, such as whether it is appropriate, legally and morally, to distinguish between active euthanasia, which is categorically prohibited in most countries, and passive euthanasia, which is permitted in most countries in certain circumstances. Is the distinction between acts and omissions in criminal law relevant to distinguishing between these two types of mercy killings?

From a bird's-eye view, there is a deeper and more strategic question: what is the significance of having such diverse viewpoints regarding the distinction between acts and omissions? It is possible to argue that the many viewpoints about it attest to the fact that the distinction itself is flawed. I believe that the distinction is valid and that each of these viewpoints reveals a portion of the truth about the essence of the distinction. The profound debate surrounding the act-omission distinction suggests that it is not merely a moral or legal

DOI: 10.4324/9781003380405-13

question rooted in reason, but rather it concerns matters arising from deep human emotions. How do we treat the indifference of an individual who did not prevent the death of another although he could have done so? How do we, as a society, deem it appropriate to treat such an individual? And in a broader sense, the dilemma of whether to act or refrain from acting, even in matters unrelated to morality or criminal law, is a question we all confront daily. To do or not to do, that is the question.

Last and looking to the future, the moral and legal distinction between an act and an omission is a substantial matter that will yet present many challenges. Technological advancement as well as cultural and ethical shifts in matters of life and death may prompt significant inquiries regarding this distinction. From a technological standpoint, as robotics, automation, and artificial intelligence continue to advance, questions may arise about the distinction between acts and omissions. One ready example is the development of autonomous vehicles that operate without human intervention. When such a vehicle is involved in an accident, should criminal liability be imposed, and if so, would the criminal responsibility be attributed to an act or an omission?

Social, cultural, ethical, and technological shifts can also affect the issue of mercy killings. As briefly demonstrated earlier, changes have taken place in recent years in some countries, including the US and Canada. As the equilibrium between individual freedom and human dignity on the one hand and the sanctity of life on the other will shift, the approach to physician-assisted suicide and active euthanasia may also change. Placing greater moral weight on the sanctity of life, whether a person is suffering or not, may result in an absolute prohibition on active euthanasia and assisted suicide and may even restrict the possibility of passive euthanasia and withdrawal of life support. At the same time, a more liberal attitude that emphasizes individual will, autonomy, dignity, and the person's ability to decide in matters of his life and death may lead to a more lenient approach toward mercy killings.

Profound changes are taking place before our eyes. Liberal states are becoming more conservative and conservative ones more liberal. These social and cultural shifts will have significant implications, including for acts and omissions, especially concerning the number of duties that will be imposed on citizens. I hope this book will serve as a substantial resource for contemplating these implications.

Index

For Product Safety Concerns and Information please contact our
EU representative GPSR@taylorandfrancis.com Taylor & Francis
Verlag GmbH, Kaufingerstraße 24, 80331 München, Germany